South by
      Southwest

South by Southwest

Katherine Anne Porter and the Burden of Texas History

JANIS P. STOUT

THE UNIVERSITY OF ALABAMA PRESS
Tuscaloosa

Typeface: Granjon

∞

The paper on which this book is printed meets the minimum requirements of American National Standard for Information Sciences—Permanence of Paper for Printed Library Materials, ANSI Z39.48-1984.

Library of Congress Cataloging-in-Publication Data

Stout, Janis P.
South by Southwest : Katherine Anne Porter and the burden of Texas history / Janis P. Stout.
p. cm.
Includes bibliographical references and index.
ISBN 978-0-8173-1782-9 (hardcover : alk. paper) — ISBN 978-0-8173-8649-8 (ebook)
1. Porter, Katherine Anne, 1890-1980—Knowledge—Texas. 2. Porter, Katherine Anne, 1890-1980—Knowledge—Mexico. 3. Porter, Katherine Anne, 1890-1980—Political and social views. 4. Texas—In literature. 5. Mexico—In literature. 6. Women in literature. 7. War in literature. 8. Ambivalence in literature. 9. Women and literature. 10. Authors, American—20th century—Biography. I. Title. II. Title: Katherine Anne Porter and the burden of Texas history.
PS3531.O752Z816 2013
813'.52—dc23
2012031750

Cover photograph: Katherine Anne Porter at fifty-four, in the garden of Marcella Comés Winslow's house, 3106 P Street, in Georgetown, Washington, D.C. Photo taken on July 9, 1944, possibly by Sgt. Charles Shannon. Katherine Anne Porter Papers, Special Collections, University of Maryland Libraries, College Park.

Author photograph: Courtesy Loren Lutes

Cover design: Todd Lape/Lape Designs

In memory of two literary women of Texas,

Lou Rodenberger and Nancy Chinn,

and for Beth Alvarez,

Porter scholar and longtime curator of the Porter papers,

and my dear friend

Once you are from somewhere there is not a whole Hell of a lot you can do about it.

—Craig Edward Clifford, *In the Deep Heart's Core*

Contents

List of Illustrations   ix

Preface   xi

Acknowledgments   xvii

Notation   xxi

1. Callie Russell Porter's Texas: History, Geoculture, and the Need to Escape   1

2. Away and Yet Not Away   27

3. The Mexican Dream and Its Realities   34

4. Recalling Childhood: Beauty, Death, and "The Old Order"   54

5. Seizing the Moment: Endless Memory and "Noon Wine"   80

6. Awakening the Southern Belle from Her Dream of a Horse Race   98

7. Racial Nightmares and "The Man in the Tree"   118

8. War's Alarms: Three Texans, Two Wars   141

9. Two Almost-Last Straws   163

10. Sexual Politics and *Ship of Fools*   178

11. Never Reconciled   202

Notes   213

Bibliography   227

Index   235

Illustrations

1. Callie Russell Porter with Catherine Anne Porter (grandmother) and Mary Alice Porter (infant sister), made in Brownwood, Texas, 1893   11

2. Callie Russell Porter, age fourteen, portrait made when a student at the Thomas School in San Antonio, 1904   15

3. Porter, age twenty-three, while she was still married to John Henry Koontz and living in Corpus Christi, Texas   17

4. Katherine Anne Porter, age thirty-three, at Aztec ruins near Cuernevaca, Mexico   43

5. Katherine Anne Porter with Indian children at Xochimilco, Mexico, 1931   49

6. Katherine Anne Porter, age forty-one, aboard the *Werra* bound for Germany   55

7. Katherine Anne Porter, profile snapshot taken at Basel, Switzerland   56

8. Katherine Anne Porter, age forty-five, in garden of her Paris apartment, June 1935   66

9. Katherine Anne Porter, age forty-seven, with her father, Harrison Boone Porter, 1937   84

10. Charred corpse of Jesse Washington, lynched in Waco, Texas, on May 15, 1916, with jubilant crowd members   128

11. Katherine Anne Porter, age fifty-two, made just after she obtained her divorce from Albert Erskine, June 19, 1942, in Reno, Nevada   151

12. Katherine Anne Porter in meadow in front of South Hill, the only house she ever owned, in Ballston Spa, New York, June or July 1941   168

13. Katherine Anne Porter, age fifty-four, in garden of Marcella Comés Winslow's house, 3106 P Street, in Georgetown, Washington, D.C., July 9, 1944   169

14. Katherine Anne Porter during a visit to the University of Texas, October 1958   174

15. Katherine Anne Porter, holding piñata for her eighty-second birthday celebration   205

16. Katherine Anne Porter, age eighty-six, laying roses on her mother's grave at Indian Creek Cemetery during her final visit to Texas, spring 1976   207

Preface

Even today, more than thirty years after her death, Katherine Anne Porter remains a figure of fascination. Probably she is most widely remembered for the award-winning movie made from her one novel, *Ship of Fools.* Readers of a certain age may recall her as a strikingly glamorous public figure whose photographs appeared in upscale magazines. Others may recall reading short stories by her in high school or college anthologies, or the impact of first encountering her stunning volume *Pale Horse, Pale Rider.* Academics will be keenly aware of the high place she occupies in literary modernism—and of her role as one more example of the fragmented minds and lives that characterized so many of her contemporaries among modernist artists.

Callie Russell Porter, as she was originally named, was born in a rural community in central Texas in 1890. Orphaned before her second birthday, she was cared for by a grandmother straight out of the Old South, a woman who had migrated to Texas before the Civil War. Callie, or by then K. R., married far too early and far too unhappily, and escaped both her marriage and her home state when she was twenty-eight. Within five years of that departure she succeeded in remaking herself as an artist and an East Coast sophisticate. She never succeeded in making herself happy.

Throughout her long life (ninety years) Porter remained preoccupied with the twin conundrums of how she felt about being a woman and how she felt about her Texas origins. It is the second of these that I am centrally concerned with here, but the two are in fact inseparable. Also intertwined, both for Porter herself and for her critics and biographers, are the facts of her Texas origins and her Southern roots. She at times sought to distinguish between the two but at other times conflated them. So must we. Her construction of herself as a beautiful but unhappy Southerner, sprung from a plantation aristocracy of reduced

fortunes, required her to construe Texas as a part of the Old South. Such a con-
strual was by no means arbitrary or groundless. Texas *was,* in large part, Southern. It was also in large part Western, with a strong Mexican heritage. That is the
part that has now become the state's dominant image. But the Texas Porter knew
and re-created in her fiction had been settled by Southerners like her grandparents who brought slaves with them. As she wrote of this Texas, the Texas she
knew, she was drawing on fact, but she also enhanced and mythicized the facts.
She exaggerated the beauty, fertility, and gracious ways of the Texas she knew
in childhood fully as much as she exaggerated the disaffection that drove her to
leave. Her feelings toward Texas ran to extremes both ways, and she was never
able to reconcile them.

Porter's lifelong efforts to evade or redefine her Texas origins have been of
persistent interest to biographers and critics. Why, then, another book on the
subject? First, because most writers have largely been content to pronounce her
feelings toward Texas ambivalent while providing little more than gestures toward explaining what that meant. I seek to achieve a clearer definition. Second,
because Porter has sometimes been excluded from the ranks of Texas writers altogether, as if finely wrought writing were inconsistent with Lone Star origins.
I dispute that judgment throughout. And third, because Porter's life and works
have not been sufficiently read against a backdrop of Texas history and culture. I
undertake to fill this omission by reading the author herself as well as her works
within the historical and cultural context from which she emerged. In particular,
I emphasize four main strands in the history of Texas that I believe are of greatest importance in understanding Porter: its geography and border location, its
violence, its racism, and its condescension to women. Let me expand, briefly, on
each of these.

The location of Texas on the border with Mexico and the fact that this vast
territory had been part of Mexico before being wrenched away by means of a
hard-fought rebellion followed by U.S. military invasion are directly related to
Porter's "bordered," or divided, conception of Texas as the South and yet not the
South. Mexico's proximity just on the other side of the Rio Grande gave her a
plausible structure for the fantasies of escape that were a recurrent motif in her
life. Mexico also provided her an opportunity to experience a place at once for-
eign and familiar—the kind of intermediate state that always fueled her imagination. But Texas was and is a "border state" in another sense as well. An unofficial border between East and West Texas, or between the South and the West,
runs north-south through the center of the state. Porter's childhood home in
Kyle lay precisely on that dividing line. Geopolitical and cultural borders have

been seen in recent years as useful metaphors for conditions of indeterminacy of all sorts. I draw on the concept of borders as a way to discuss Porter's emotional and intellectual fissures and ambiguities.

Second, violence. The culture and society Porter grew up in developed out of a history replete with violence both endemic to Texas and brought to Texas from the American South. It remains uncertain whether Porter had much real knowledge of Texas history, but that is essentially beside the point. Culture grew out of history. The violence of one generation—say, the 1830s—authorized, in effect, the violence of the next, producing a social environment so shot through with physical conflict and the implements thereof that it became, in combination with her personal experience of violence in her first marriage, one of the primary "push factors" that set her mind on escape.

Third, the state's long tradition of racism is both reflected and resisted in her writings. In part, this is a tradition of Anglo prejudice toward Mexican Texans, but it is also and more intensely a Texas perpetuation of the ideology of white supremacy that accompanied slavery to Texas. The few but important black characters in Porter's canonical fiction have long been a point of interest. Nannie and Jimbilly, in "The Old Order," are genuinely admirable characters, resiliently independent-minded despite their relegation to "Auntie" and "Uncle" status. Porter's unpublished comments on race, however, are more shifting and problematic. I cite a number of these comments in chapter 6 in connection with her uncompleted, unpublished fragment "The Man in the Tree," which I read against the history of lynching that sullied Texas throughout Porter's life.

Last, gender was an issue in Porter's struggle for self-definition and self-realization all her life. She was brought up within a rigid set of societal expectations for women that sharply differentiated girls' and women's roles from those of boys and men. This was not of course peculiar to Texas, though it may have been accentuated by the muscular lives led by men according to myths of the West. In any event, it was in Texas that Porter first experienced and chafed against restrictive gender roles. The grandmother who raised her expected her to fulfill the roles of Southern belle and later, presumably, Southern lady—expected this, in fact, despite the family's lack of financial means to carry out such a pattern of life and despite the fact that the social era to which such standards belonged was approaching its end. It had not been an era that defined women's lives in terms of careers. When the young Porter expressed artistic ambitions, both her grandmother and her father dismissed them as foolish folderol, if not worse, and she came to early adulthood believing that Texas society more generally cast her as a "freak" because of them. Rightly or wrongly, she remained convinced that she could never have pursued, let alone achieved, her ambitions as a writer if she had stayed in Texas.

The word "burden" in my title carries plural meanings. It refers both to what her Texas origins meant to Porter and to what she made of them in her writing. She perceived that because of her origins she carried burdens of disadvantage in her life. As she attempted to reconstruct herself in ways that would deny her early poverty, the deficiencies she perceived in the culture in which she grew up, and the stigma that the label "Texan" carried in the literary marketplace and the world of letters generally, she felt socially and professionally *burdened* by her origins. At the same time, by providing most of her richest material, Texas served as the *burden* of her tale. Despite her attempts to evade her origins, despite having left at the earliest opportunity in order to become a literary star in the firmament of East Coast modernists, she continued to ponder Texas both from afar and from the perspective afforded by her intermittent visits. Carrying a permanent burden of ambivalence, she lovingly romanticized her home state as often as she decried it.

Throughout, when I use the terms "culture" and "cultural" I do not mean them in the sense of "high culture" (unless that is specified) but in the anthropological sense, as referring to a totality of customs, practices, and ideas that define a particular group of people—the meaning that Richard Millington defines as "the interconnected and particular ways distinct communities construct meanings for the individual lives that unfold within them" (56).

My passion for this subject springs partly from the same qualities in Porter that have fascinated others—her beautifully achieved writing, her contradictions, her combination of glamour with intellect and misery with mastery. It also springs from the fact that I, too, am a daughter of Texas. My mother came to Fort Worth from a poor-dirt East Texas farm as a teenager, and my father lived in Texas for all but the very earliest years of his life. In the late 1930s and early 1940s he in fact contributed to the formation of a distinctive part of Texas popular culture, playing fiddle with a Texas Swing band that still claims a small cult of followers, the Light Crust Doughboys. The two musical westerns the Doughboys made with Hollywood cowboy Gene Autry, with cowboys on horseback wearing boots and big hats, toting guns on their hips, acting out starkly simplified roles of heroes or villains, in no way reflected my parents' lives or my own. Dad was so afraid of horses that when the director of the first movie wanted him to play his fiddle while riding on horseback he flatly refused. They shot the scene with the musicians playing from the back of a covered wagon. Even as a child, I knew that when Dad put on his tight pants, boots, western shirt, hat, and cowhide jacket with fringes, something false was being constructed. If that was Texas, I didn't belong.

What I'm saying is that like Porter, I have always felt more or less like an outsider in my own home state. In elementary school, when teachers referred in sorrowful tones to the South's defeat in the Civil War, I felt secretly glad. It was obvious to me that the right side had won. Certainly that was not how Porter felt about the Civil War, but she did feel like an outsider or a "freak" in Texas, and I think with no clearer understanding of why. We were, both of us, troubled by our history and by our culture. We were both Texas girls whose interests failed to track those that seemed to prevail among those around us. We were both, more specifically, "white" Texas girls, shut off by the rigidities of our culture from any earthly idea of what life was like for brown or black Texas girls. In that way the accident of race that privileged us also limited our social experiences. And no matter how hard we might resist, it pushed us toward racial prejudices that were as pervasive in the Texas of my day as they were in hers.

I have referred to "our culture," but I should say "cultures." Texas was and to some degree still is a collection of dissimilar regional cultures, each with its own geography, customs, patterns of speech, and all the rest that makes up culture. Porter was born very near the geographic center of the state; I was born farther east and north in Fort Worth half a century later. In addition to the central and north-central areas, Texas also has a Gulf Coast region sharing many of the attributes of coastal Louisiana; a small-farm and piney-woods region in East Texas; the desert-like far west, toward El Paso; the high plains of the Panhandle; and deep South Texas, where the influence of Mexico has been the strongest. And Texas has to this day (to disregard for the moment ethnic groups that have come into the state more recently than Porter's time) at least three distinct racial cultures: Mexican, African American, and white, each with its own variations. "White" usually means Anglo, but there were and still are distinct areas of Czech or German culture, as well as others. All of these were and are, of course, intersected by distinctions of social class: the oil-money up-and-comers or the old-money elite; the secure or the scrambling middle class; and those descended from what used to be so rudely called "poor white trash," always trying to climb to a secure place in the next level up and always confident that at any rate the brown and black folks were somehow beneath them. My own family belonged somewhere in this latter group, living according to standards of gentility to which we aspired despite the slimness of our pocketbooks. The social status of Porter's family is more difficult to define except for the clear difference that it harkened back toward an aristocratic past. Mine did not. We were again alike, though, in that we were both brought up according to strict Protestant standards of morality that, even though they might be violated, were not openly defied. The opportunities for irony in such a life were numerous. Porter built out of these a fiction of great subtlety and elusiveness.

Larry McMurtry once wrote that Texas could not take credit for Katherine Anne Porter. He was in effect saying that she didn't belong to Texas; he was calling her a literary alien. I propose to demonstrate that McMurtry was as mistaken in this as he was imperceptive in declaring her work to be lightweight ("there is nothing there"). Pointing out the quality and weight of Porter's writing is easy; many have done so, paying tribute not only to its stylistic artistry but to the fullness of its humanity. My purpose here, however, is not so much critical evaluation as exploration and interpretation of her life and works by way of her perception that being a Texan was a kind of burden to be carried. In doing so, I will be asking two central questions: How pervasive was Texas in shaping both Porter herself and her work? And what, finally, did she make of it in her essays and stories?

Acknowledgments

My gratitude for the help, advice, and good examples on which I have drawn for this book go back so far that I'm reluctant to start mentioning names for fear I will inadvertently omit some. Yet I cannot ignore my many debts.

I particularly want to thank Ann Romines, of The George Washington University, for telling me that she would be eager to see anything more that I might have to say about Porter; Mark Busby, of Texas State University in San Marcos; Walter Buenger and the late Bob Calvert, historians of Texas at Texas A&M University, College Station; Beth Alvarez, Curator of Literary Manuscripts Emerita, the University of Maryland, College Park, for her responses to various questions and especially for her help with illustrations; Aryn Glazier, with the Dolph Briscoe Historical Center at the University of Texas, for assistance with the photograph of Porter made in 1958; Bonnie Shimmin, for assuring me that an early version of the manuscript really was an interesting read; Sylvia Grider, now retired from Texas A&M University, for her perspectives on folklore and material culture; Dan Waterman of the University of Alabama Press; Allison Faust, of the University of Texas Press, Steve Davis, of Texas State University, Ann Close, with Knopf; anonymous readers whose evaluation of earlier versions of the manuscript greatly helped me to improve it; Mary Sifuentes, Carolina de Leon, and other staff members of the Evans Library at Texas A&M University, without whose help I could not have written either this book or several others that preceded it; and of course my dear husband, Loren Lutes, who, though puzzled by my "hurry" to get this book done (before I got too old to write it, I might have told him), was as patient, interested, and supportive as ever. He was, as always, a fount of helpful comments.

For permission to quote from unpublished manuscripts, I am grateful to the University of Maryland Libraries and to the Katherine Anne Porter Foundation. For photographic images of Porter, I am again grateful to the University of Maryland, the Porter Foundation, and the Dolph Briscoe Historical Center, University of Texas. The photographic image of the lynched body of Jesse Washington is from the Library of Congress.

I initially began this book with the goal of pulling together my essays and articles on Katherine Anne Porter scattered among various journals and volumes. As I got into it, though, I found that I was actually reproducing very little from those publications. Even so, for whatever bits I may have used, whether ideas or actual words, I wish to thank the editors and publishers who brought the following before readers in the first place:

"Mr. Hatch's Volubility and Miss Porter's Reserve." *Essays in Literature* 12 (1985): 285–93.

"Miranda's Guarded Speech: Porter and the Problem of Truth-Telling." *Philological Quarterly* 66 (1987): 259–78.

Strategies of Reticence: Silence and Meaning in the Works of Jane Austen, Willa Cather, Katherine Anne Porter, and Joan Didion. Charlottesville: University Press of Virginia, 1990.

"'Something of a Reputation as a Radical': Katherine Anne Porter and the Question of Communism." *South Central Review* 10 (1993): 49–66.

"Katherine Anne Porter's 'Reflections on Willa Cather': A Duplicitous Homage." *American Literature* 66 (1994): 719–35.

Katherine Anne Porter: A Sense of the Times. Charlottesville: University Press of Virginia, 1995.

"Behind 'Reflections on Willa Cather': Katherine Anne Porter's Drafts and Marginalia and the Dilemmas of Literary Sisterhood." *Legacy* 14 (1997): 31–43.

"Katherine Anne Porter." In *Texas Women Writers: A Tradition of Their Own,* ed. Sylvia Ann Grider and Lou Halsell Rodenberger. College Station: Texas A&M University Press, 1997. 124–33.

"Katherine Anne Porter's 'The Old Order': Writing in the Borderlands." *Studies in Short Fiction* 34 (1997): 493–506.

"Katherine Anne Porter and Mark Twain at the Circus." *Southern Quarterly* 36 (1998): 113–23.

"On Stage at the Great House: Cather, Porter, and the Performance of Southernness." *Southern Studies* 9 (1998): 27–43.

"Writing Home: Katherine Anne Porter, Coming and Going." *Southwestern American Literature* 24 (1998): 11–22.

"Katherine Anne Porter." *American National Biography.* New York: Oxford University Press, 1999. 704–6.

"On the Pitfalls of Literary Biography: The Case of Joan Givner and Katherine Anne Porter." *Southern Quarterly* 37 (1999): 129–38.

"'Practically dead with fine rivalry': The Leaning Towers of Katherine Anne Porter and Glenway Wescott." *Studies in the Novel* 33 (2001): 444–58.

"South from the South: The Imperial Eyes of Evelyn Scott and Katherine Anne Porter." In *Evelyn Scott: Recovering a Lost Modernist,* ed. Dorothy Scura and Paul C. Jones. Knoxville: University of Tennessee Press, 2001. 15–36.

"Writing Home: Katherine Anne Porter, Coming and Going." In *From Texas to the World and Back: Essays on the Journeys of Katherine Anne Porter,* ed. Mark Busby and Dick Heaberlin. Fort Worth: TCU Press, 2001. 20–37. Reprinted, with revisions, from journal publication.

"Katherine Anne Porter." In *The History of Southern Women's Literature,* ed. Carolyn Perry and Mary Louise Weaks. Baton Rouge: Louisiana State University Press, 2002.

"Katherine Anne Porter." In *Notable American Women,* ed. Susan Ware. Cambridge, MA: Harvard University Press, 2004.

Notation

The bulk of Katherine Anne Porter's papers are housed at the University of Maryland, College Park. Unless otherwise indicated, all letters quoted or cited here are to be found there. Whenever possible, notes are incorporated into the text with page numbers shown in parentheses. For basic facts of Porter's life I rely primarily on the biographies by Joan Givner and Darlene Unrue, without citation, but I provide citations for information, interpretations, or language distinct to either Givner or Unrue, or any other source used here. Forms used for brief citations are as follows:

CE	Katherine Anne Porter, *Collected Essays and Occasional Writings*
Conv.	Joan Givner, ed., *Katherine Anne Porter: Conversations*
CS	Katherine Anne Porter, *Collected Stories*
Illusion	Thomas F. Walsh, *Katherine Anne Porter and Mexico: The Illusion of Eden*
KAP	Joan Givner, *Katherine Anne Porter: A Life*
Life	Darlene Harbour Unrue, *Katherine Anne Porter: The Life of an Artist*
Refugee	Enrique "Hank" Lopez, *Conversations with Katherine Anne Porter: Refugee from Indian Creek*
SL	Isabel Bayley, ed., *Selected Letters of Katherine Anne Porter*
S/T	Janis P. Stout, *Katherine Anne Porter: A Sense of the Times*
Uncol.	Alvarez and Walsh, ed., *Uncollected Early Prose of Katherine Anne Porter*

I

Callie Russell Porter's Texas
History, Geoculture, and the Need to Escape

The Southerner, and even more the Texan, was always gun-ready.
—William Humphrey, *Farther Off from Heaven*

. . . my America has been a borderland . . .
—Katherine Anne Porter, "Why I Write about Mexico"

Katherine Anne Porter liked to call herself "the first and only serious writer that Texas has produced."[1] By "serious writer," she would have meant a writer of literary fiction or a polished stylist, discounting historical or naturalist writing. In those terms her claim to being the first was well founded, though not, as she very well knew, her claim to being the "only." William Humphrey and William Goyen, for example, were active by the time she asserted it, in 1958, and she was well acquainted with both. Certainly she was a "serious" writer, though, and one "produced" by Texas in more ways than the mere fact of having been born there. She lived in various places around the state until she made a first, short-lived escape at the age of twenty-four, then an escape founded on better prospects four years later, in 1918. She stayed away for most of the rest of her ninety years.

To understand why it matters that one of America's greatest modernist writers was from Texas and did not want to stay there—how her Texas origins did or did not shape her and how she did or did not reconcile the dissonances between her sense of herself and her sense of Texas—we must first establish the outlines of her early life within the cultural context produced by Texas's geography and history.

Biographers often write of Porter in terms of place—where she lived, where she traveled. After she made her break with Texas in 1918 she lived in Denver and then New York, then in 1920 went to Mexico. She was back and forth between Mexico and New York four separate times by 1930, with periods in between spent in Massachusetts, Connecticut, and Bermuda. In 1931 she sailed for Europe and lived variously in Berlin, Paris, and Basel before returning to the United States in 1936. Much later, she made long visits to Belgium and Italy. Yet she was quite clear (as she wrote a novelist friend in 1932) that it was Texas that had made her who she was.[2] Was she seeking to escape *herself*, then, when she escaped Texas, or was she seeking to locate and define a different self that could not emerge there? There is no easy answer. She would certainly have said the latter.

Many of Porter's direct statements indicate that what getting away from Texas meant to her was personal and professional freedom. After 1918 she never again lived in Texas for more than an extended visit. Yet she never stopped yearning for the idealized version of her childhood home that she had constructed in her mind. At the same time, she repeatedly complained about the disadvantages and discomforts she remembered there. Unable simply to set aside the conflicts her bad memories caused her and leave the question alone, she kicked against those pricks as painfully as if they were Texas cactus. After she left, this "little girl from Texas in New York," as she once described herself, never again had a real home (*Conv.* 30). She felt her homelessness all her life. Nearly everywhere she went she entertained fantasies of staying, buying a house, and making a home. She did so one time, in one of those places—then lived in it less than a year.

Katherine Anne Porter liked to say that she was born "right smack dab in the middle of May in Texas" (*Conv.* 34, 32). To be exact, she was born on May 15, 1890, in a log cabin in the central Texas community of Indian Creek, about twelve miles south of Brownwood, the county seat of Brown County. The name given her at birth, which she would report in various versions over the years, was Callie Russell—Callie Russell Porter. At the time she was born, Brown County had been a legal entity for thirty-four years (since 1856), but it had retained its frontier air for quite some time after its legal establishment. The last known Indian attack in the county was in 1863, twenty-two years before Harrison Boone Porter and Mary Alice Jones Porter moved there to live as subsistence farmers in 1885. In the county just to the northeast, Eastland, a settler had been killed by Indians as recently as October 1870, only fifteen years before the Porters moved to Indian Creek, and in Parker County, to the east toward Fort Worth, Indian raids persisted until 1873.[3] Frontier violence, then, was a thing of fairly recent memory, and Harrison Porter may have heard about Indian raids and armed pursuit by settlers from neighbors who arrived earlier.[4] In later years he enjoyed telling his grandsons about such perils and adventures, probably none of which he ever experienced himself.

Brown County, Texas, had also seen other kinds of violence in its brief existence. The notorious John Wesley Hardin gang perpetrated numerous crimes in the area in the 1870s. County citizens hanged a suspected gang member in 1874. The peace was sometimes disturbed, too, by fights and brawls partly attributable to free-flowing liquor, which was mainly but not solely available in Brownwood. Hank Lopez writes of the area, on the basis of what information other than Porter herself he does not say, "There was an ominous hint of violence in that flowery, sweet-smelling country" (13). The sentence appears almost verbatim in Porter's essay "'Noon Wine': The Sources," written by invitation to explain how she came to write what is often considered her finest single work, "Noon Wine." It is perhaps the primary expression of her sense of an "underlying, perpetual ominous presence of violence; violence potential that broke through the smooth surface almost without warning" during her childhood (*CE* 472).

When Porter reminisced to the editor of the *Texas Observer* in 1958 that she was "just a little girl from Texas," then, she could have said a little girl from the rough-and-ready frontier. But that would not have suited her conception of herself. She wished to be regarded as a Southerner. It is not hard to understand why. As Don Graham points out in "A Southern Writer in Texas," the South held a "privileged status" in American literature during the decades when Porter reached her maturity as a writer. Margaret Mitchell's *Gone with the Wind* was the great hit of the 1930s, and William Faulkner was at the top of almost everyone's list of literary greats. There were "distinct advantages," then, quite apart from her equally real feelings of identity, in positioning herself as a Texas Southerner rather than a Texan—or worst of all, a writer of westerns (58–59). She did not want to risk being labeled a regionalist by becoming "associated in any way" with Texas folklorist J. Frank Dobie, naturalist Roy Bedichek, and historian Walter Prescott Webb, often called the Texas Triumvirate (Wade 115). She understood that Texas was a Southwestern state, she told novelist George Sessions Perry in 1943, but her own roots were Southern.[5]

Being born in Indian Creek would not in itself support such a claim. Brown County lay to the west of the geographic division between East Texas (an extension of the South) and West Texas, running roughly along the 97th longitudinal parallel, or in today's practical terms Interstate 35. Texan Craig Clifford defines this geographic division as an "imaginary line that runs somewhere between Dallas and Fort Worth, along I-35 and the Balcones Fault" and concludes that "east of it is East Texas and west of it is West Texas and that East is South and West is West" (58–59). The fine though not prolific Texas novelist R. G. Vliet adds that this "probable dividing line" is not only a geographic but a linguistic one, marking "very nearly a clean division in idiom" between the "soft, drawling pronunciation general to the South" and a "brusque, consonantal harshness understood as 'western'" (19).[6] All this is directly pertinent to an understanding of Porter. The town of Kyle, where she lived with her Porter grandmother from the age of two, is located directly at the break, in Hays County. In Vliet's words, "South and Southwest ran simultaneously through her childhood, right there in Kyle" (21).

That geographic line of meeting or separation means that Texas was, and to some extent still is, a border state twice over. "The border" or "down on the border" usually refers to the Rio Grande River, the Texas portion of the U.S. border with Mexico. We can be sure that, given its context, that is what Porter meant when she called "her" America a "borderland" (*CE* 256). Even so, the unofficial border at the Balcones Escarpment where South butts up against West is equally real. Thinking of Texas and the Southwest as sites of multiple borders and borderlands is not new. Tom Pilkington, in his 1973 book *My Blood's Country,* saw the uniqueness of the topography of the Southwest as its "rims and borders." Nowhere else in the United States, he proposed, are differences of landform "so numerous or so proximate." Pilkington's use of the border idiom here is literal and descriptive; he is speaking specifically of landforms and envisioning the more western stretches of Texas and on into New Mexico and Arizona. But the words "border" and "borderland" also lean toward more figurative meanings. Pilkington, for instance, in writing that the national border with Mexico is "never very far," shifts from a geographic to a legal sense of bordering. He shifts again to a genuinely figurative sense when he points out that the strip along the Balcones Escarpment can also be thought of as a borderland "where cultures clash, where the myth of the South meets the myth of the West" (3–4).

No one knew better than Porter how language could slide between literal and figurative, or symbolic, meanings. Today, accustomed as we are to a public discourse of diversity and cultural pluralism, "border" and "borderland" are useful metaphors referring to all sorts of abutments, breaks, overlappings, ambiguities, and sites of conflict. Such metaphors were not so common, however, when, a decade after Pilkington, cultural critic and poet Gloria Anzaldúa published *Borderlands/La Frontera* (1987). Herself a mestiza from the Texas-Mexico borderlands, Anzaldúa begins her mixed-genre book with the literal, legal border at the Rio Grande but extends the concept to widely encompassing dimensions. Invoking both personal experience and a literary theory of multiple languages or voices within a single space or text,[7] she uses the bilingual borderland along the Rio Grande as a model for thinking about "places" where cultures, races, or classes come together, oppose one another, and overlap. Primarily, though, her concern is with gender—a subject of great importance as we think about Porter. Writers who speak from dual ethnicity or who are torn between old and new ways of gendering, Anzaldúa writes, will tend to see and speak doubly much in the way bilingual writers do.

Both of these critics, Pilkington and Anzaldúa, provide valuable ways of thinking about the importance of place in Porter's early life, conditioned as it was by the presence of not one but two geographic borders. Porter was not bilingual or of mixed ethnicity like more recent Texas writers Sandra Cisneros and Rolando Hinojosa, both of whom write in Spanish as well as English, nor does the act of crossing the Rio Grande into Mexico and back assume as central a position in her work as it does in the fictional world of adoptive Texan Cormac McCarthy.[8] Yet she, too, was a border-crosser. Physically, she crossed the U.S.-Mexican border at least five times. The proximity of Mexico to Texas and the United States plays a major role in her art by providing her at once a congenial refuge and an alternative vision and perspective on her own culture. At the same time, and even more pervasively, her childhood in central Texas provided the awareness of the Old South and of contrasts between South and West that were central to her self-conception and to the work by which she has been best known, the Miranda stories. The ambivalent, or "bordered," quality of her imagination grew from dual roots in dual borderlands.

Growing up in Kyle, Porter was powerfully shaped by tensions and incongruities rooted in the unmarked but quite real border zone between South and West that bisected Hays County—such tensions and incongruities as tradition versus change, allegiance to the past versus an urge toward the future, ladylike demeanor versus free womanhood, dependence and passivity versus self-reliance. She often seemed more concerned with the Southern term in these pairs (tradition, past, being ladylike), but she also had a powerful drive toward values that she and most other Americans associated with the West (change, newness, freedom). The conflict would have major and lasting significance in her life.

In terms of landform and climate, there are enormous differences between the two major divisions of Texas marked by the Balcones Fault. To the east the land is heavily wooded and well watered. To the west, after the initial drop-off, it is higher, drier, and barer. East Texas was farming and lumbering country, "the farthest reach of the Cotton Kingdom"; West Texas was "the home turf of the Cattle Kingdom" (Clifford 60). The distinction has now been blurred by the advent of massive irrigation in the northern panhandle and western plains but was definitely applicable when Porter was growing up. Although Pilkington calls the influence of Spain and Mexico "the one force" that "provides a measure of cultural cohesion" in Texas as a whole (6), in a major part of the state the legacy of the American South was just as unifying. Craig Clifford is closer to the mark when he asserts that "Texas—and I mean all of it—is both Southern and Western" and "Texas, all of Texas, is also Mexican" (68)—a vision more of multilayering than of cohesion.

Texas was indeed from its beginnings as a political entity a space in which Anglo, black, Mexican, and native races overlapped and bumped up against each other. The dominant Anglo group itself became diversified by the mid-1800s with an influx of immigrants from Europe. Primarily these were Germans, who began settling in central Texas in the early 1830s and were joined by a second wave, the "48ers," who left Europe during the tumult of the 1848 revolutions. Several German families lived in and around Kyle, including the family of Porter's best friend, Erna Schlemmer, originally from Prussia. Czechs began arriving in the 1840s, Poles began immigrating around mid-century, and smaller numbers of French settlers established not only Jean Lafitte's "republic" on Galveston Island in 1827 but also a socialist community called La Réunion near Dallas in the 1850s. As Porter said, the America to which she was born—which is to say, late nineteenth-century Texas—was a "borderland of strange languages and commingled races" (*CE* 356).

The most obvious economic differences between East and West Texas were those between farming and ranching. In Hays County the two overlapped. The northeastern quarter or third of the county, where Grandmother Porter owned land, supported or had supported black-land farming; the western part was limestone hill country, better suited to ranching. A young Callie Porter could see both in the environs of Kyle but had a better opportunity to observe the contrast when she accompanied her grandmother to West Texas to visit uncles living in Marfa and El Paso. She then saw firsthand the very different western landscape, a ranching culture, and a far greater preponderance of Mexican workers.

Only a few decades later the entire state would take on something of the image of the West through the purposeful efforts of folklorist J. Frank Dobie. It is in the redoubtable figure of Dobie, who "devoted a lifetime to studying the ranching tradition" (Graham, *Giant Country* 175), that the issue of South versus West comes into focus. Dobie orchestrated a shift in the image of Texas through a reconstruction of its history and culture designed, according to James Lee, to "promote Texas as a far western state untainted by its Confederate background" (*Adventures* 81). That was quite the contrary of Porter's Texas. Dobie's numerous books, beginning with *A Vaquero of the Brush Country* in 1929, were devoted to tales of the ranching past and "men who carried side arms and herded cattle." But as Lee points out, when Dobie launched his campaign in the 1930s most

Texans were in fact—and regarded themselves as—Southerners (*Adventures* 3, 77). According to the 1940 Federal Writers Project guide to Texas, 60 percent of Texans then lived in rural areas where cotton was king. But the "corn, cotton, and mules" Texas (Clifford 46) did not appeal either to Dobie or to Hollywood. Don Graham recalls that even though Collin County, where he grew up, was "entirely southern," the movie houses in nearby McKinney played "countless westerns." What he learned from these and from his reading of westerns was that his own Texas and his own people "did not really count" ("Nine Ball" 47–49). Even Collin County would eventually become "thoroughly westernized" (*Giant Country* 7, 21).

William Humphrey, a novelist from the northeasternmost corner of Texas who once told Porter that he had learned to write by reading her stories, records the same shift in his memoir *Farther Off from Heaven* (1977). Returning to his Clarksville home after some two decades, he found that Red River County had "ceased to be Old South and become Far West. . . . I who for years had had to set my Northern friends straight by pointing out that I was a Southerner, not a Westerner, and that I had never seen a cowboy or for that matter a beefcow any more than they had, found myself now in that Texas of legend and the popular imagination. . . . Gone from the square were the bib overalls of my childhood when the farmers came to town on Saturday. Ranchers now, they came in high-heeled boots and rolled-brim hats" (239–40). Porter's Texas lay over two hundred miles southwest of Graham's Collin County and another hundred or so from Humphrey's Clarksville. Thus the ambiguity that according to Vliet makes it hard to decide which region she was writing about, South or Southwest. If she had been born after the shift in Texas's image propelled by Dobie, she might more easily have thought of herself as western. Because that oversimplifying image had not yet been constructed, she lived in a borderlands Texas that afforded her a body of material inherently complex, conflicted, and therefore rich.

Although the West with its sense of open possibility lay near at hand, the myth in which Porter grew up was not a myth of the West but of the South, or what Nina Baym calls "the myth of the myth of Southern womanhood" ("The Myth" 183). Baym argues cogently that this myth was a postbellum construction, not one held in the prewar Old South. In Porter's Miranda stories, she observes, "the postbellum fictions of Southern womanhood are critiqued even as their suffocating power is acknowledged" (196). Mentally as well as physically, Porter's childhood was passed in the borderland.

The doubts as to whether Porter can be considered a Texas writer at all expressed by both Tom Pilkington and Larry McMurtry, whose opinions on this point are to be valued, have been energetically countered by James Tanner, who insists that she was "always a 'Texas Writer'" and her stories were "preoccupied with Texas settings and Texas characters" (39). Certainly if we take a borderlands consciousness to be at the essence of Texas literature, she is the very epitome of a Texas writer. Whatever label we may pin on her, regionally, she usually chose to face eastward and identify with the South. The transplanted South was the "old order" that formed her even as it inspired her resistance.

In terms of family heritage, Porter's self-definition as a Southerner was entirely accurate. Her father's mother, Catherine Ann Skaggs, was the daughter of a well-to-do slave-owning family in Kentucky, with roots in Virginia, who in 1849 married a second cousin, Asbury Duval Porter, apparently less prosperous but of the same social class. Biographer Joan Givner cites the 1850 slave census as showing that Asbury Porter owned just one slave, a male, besides the female presented to his bride as a wedding gift by her brother Harrison Skaggs, whose New Orleans business included dealing in slaves (*KAP* 30–31). Within a few years of their marriage Asbury sold his holdings in Kentucky and bought 376 acres of virgin farmland in Hays County, central Texas, an area opened for settlement in 1840 by the defeat of a local band of Comanches. After a long trek, they arrived at their new home in 1857. Harrison Boone Porter, their fourth baby out of an eventual nine, was born that same year, possibly along the way in Louisiana. In a community history of Hays County compiled by Mary Barkley, Porters are listed among the "pioneering settlers" of Mountain City, located in the northeastern part of the county near the community of Buda. The records of a doctor who practiced in Mountain City in the 1870s list five Porters, including one A. D., surely Asbury Duval. It was an area of good black farmland at the time, until it began to "gully and wash" in the early 1900s (Barkley 139).

Less is known about the family of Porter's mother, Mary Alice Jones. Her parents, John and Caroline Jones, also came to Texas before the Civil War. They had a farm in Guadalupe County, south of Hays County, near the town of Seguin (named for Juan Seguín, one of the Tejanos, or Mexican Texans, who supported Texas independence in the 1830s). Mary Alice was educated at the Coronal Institute in San Marcos, which Givner calls "the most popular Protestant school" in that part of Texas (*KAP* 35). One wonders how many there were to compete for popularity. At any rate, the school's strong religious tone suited her inclinations. She excelled and went on to teach school, give organ lessons, and write discreet though rather flowery letters to Harrison Porter during their courtship. He, too, was educated—at a military school—and his letters are quite readable. In 1882, having decided he was a drinker, Mary Alice broke off their engagement, but they were reconciled the next year—partly, perhaps, because her family situation had been drastically altered and she needed to establish herself. Her mother, Caroline Jones, had been declared insane and placed in a home for the mentally ill, and her father had sold his land in Guadalupe County and moved 145 miles northwest to a 640-acre farm in Brown County, along with his two sons. Learning about her Grandmother Jones's illness and isolation from the family would cast one of the many dark shadows on Katherine Anne Porter's life.

Harrison Porter and Mary Alice Jones were married in the summer of 1883. For two years they lived on his mother's farm in Hays County—or what was left of it, since she had parceled it out a few acres at a time to her children when they married (*CE* 163) and had sold a few acres to a relative who never paid her a cent beyond his small down payment (*KAP* 45). What she had left was apparently not enough to provide much of a living. Harrison had not wanted to be a farmer anyway; he had worked in railroad construction in Mexico as well as Texas before his marriage, and he wanted to go back to the railroad business. But in 1885, when their first child was born, Mary Alice's father offered them free tenancy on his land in Brown County, and Harrison surrendered to his fate. The young family moved to Indian Creek, settling near the rocky-bottomed creek for which the community was named.

This is all a little hard to understand. Catherine Porter's land in Hays County must have been still fairly good, even if deteriorating, farmland. The land in Brown County was probably not. Life must have been hard. Callie Russell (she would have her name legally changed when she was twenty-five) was the fourth of her parents' five children born in seven years. The third, a baby boy, had died in 1889, and Mary Alice was frail, her health overstrained by her pregnancies and grief, when Callie was born the following year. Less than two years later Mary Alice bore her fifth baby, then died within a few weeks, possibly of tuberculosis though Porter would later say it was pneumonia or bronchitis (*KAP* 39). Fortunately, Harrison's doughty mother had come to help out, and she took the family back with her to Kyle.

Orphaned at twenty-two months old, Porter carried the sorrow of her mother's death for the rest of her life. Her father was too devastated by his bereavement to function properly and would remain so. Many years later (October 21, 1952) when Porter wrote to Mary Alice's friend Cora Posey, thanking her for sending copies of some of her father's letters written soon after her mother's death, she said they reminded her of the pall his gloomy presence cast over her childhood.

Although Catherine Ann Porter is not mentioned by name in Barkley's community history of Hays County, she is elsewhere said to have been well regarded and to have been often called Cat Porter or Aunt Cat. Her willingness to take on the care of four small children at the age of sixty-five demonstrates that she was a woman of determination and a strong sense of duty. The eldest of the four, Gay, was only seven at the time; Harry Ray, who later had his name changed to Harrison Paul and was called Paul, was five; Callie was not yet two; and the baby, named Mary Alice after their mother but always called Baby, was just two months old. Grandmother Porter undertook the challenge of providing for them and giving them a religious, moral, and civilized rearing, plus the thankless task of managing her languishing son. She was a staunch churchgoer with rigid standards of propriety.

Grandmother Porter had built her home in Kyle in 1879, after Asbury's death, when a number of the settlers of the Mountain City area moved to the new town as a group (Barkley 142). The house would have been quite suitable for just herself but was clearly inadequate for the group she brought in to live with her. Even after being built onto and approximately doubled after her death, it is still a small house. When Porter recalled it as a six-room house in her late essay "Notes on the Texas I Remember," she was enhancing it considerably. There were two bedrooms (one of them now a bathroom), a smallish front room, and a dining room. The kitchen may have been outside, joined to the house by an enclosed passage, since the present kitchen appears to be part of the added space. Perhaps Porter was counting as rooms the "front and back galleries" that in summer, when they were screened by shutters and thick honeysuckle, "add[ed] two delightful long rooms to the house." If so, that is a great stretch. Don Graham, who has also visited the house, as I have, insists that "what she calls a gallery on the front" of the house is "a front porch, nothing more," and equally so the back ("Katherine Anne Porter's Journey" 5). Two adults, three children under ten, and an infant lived there crowded together, sharing beds or sleeping on pallets on the floor (*KAP* 46–47). Harrison sometimes retired to the even smaller house or shack on his mother's farm.

Many Southerners had lost resources and abruptly descended into poverty after the Civil War, but Cat Porter's problem did not fit the usual pattern. For one thing, she and her husband seem to have weathered the economic storm of Civil War and Reconstruction rather well; they made advantageous land deals and consolidated their acreage. For another, she was not "land poor" in the way of many formerly prosperous families in the South who now had nothing left *but* land, without the unpaid labor of slaves and without cash for hiring labor or pur-

1. Callie Russell Porter with Catherine Ann Porter (her grandmother) and Mary Alice Porter (her infant sister, always called Baby). Portrait made in Brownwood, Texas, in 1893. The face of the grandmother, who appears to be wearing mourning clothes for her daughter-in-law, also displays her sternness. Katherine Anne Porter Papers, Special Collections, University of Maryland Libraries.

chasing animals and tools to replace what they'd had. If they were able to hold onto their land, such people at least still had a major asset to build on. But having gradually let go of hers without having built up a supply of funds, Catherine Porter had little hope of recovery. In later comments, Porter never disguised the fact that her family shared in the South's general loss of resources, but she did give the impression that she had spent her childhood in a far more capacious home, with more lavish amenities, than her grandmother's house in Kyle actually was. It is little wonder, though, that she developed a habit of stretching the truth; she came by it honestly, as Texans used to say. Her grandmother regaled her with "myths and legends" of antebellum Kentucky throughout her childhood (*Life* 36).

During the Kyle years, according to Givner, the family led "a hand-to-mouth existence" in "grinding poverty," the children having to wear cast-off clothes given to them by neighbors (*KAP* 45–46). By contrast, Darlene Unrue's avowedly revisionist biography reports that the records of Asbury Porter's estate show him to have been "a careful investor and competent provider." Unrue attributes Porter's lifelong love of fashionable clothes not to any humiliation at having to wear hand-me-downs but to the combination of Aunt Cat's stories of lost affluence and her "adherence" to old-fashioned styles the children considered "dowdy" (*Life* 15, 20–21). When Unrue also accepts as fact Porter's statements that Aunt Cat hired a succession of "tutors or governesses who lived in the house with the family" (21), one wonders where they would have put themselves. The disparity between the two biographers' accounts of Porter's childhood illustrates their widely differing views and assumptions—Givner ever ready to accept negative or debunking interpretations, Unrue reaching for evidence to support a more positive view; Givner perhaps too skeptical of Porter's own words, Unrue perhaps too easily believing them.

Porter retained no memory either of her mother or of Indian Creek. Her writings about a fertile, flowery place with a beautiful, clear stream were mostly idealized versions of what she heard from her older sister, Gay, reinforced by a return visit in 1936. She did, however, remember life with her grandmother in Kyle. Her accounts of the house, the farm in summer, and the "old order" there, complete with attentive servants and leather-bound editions of the major English authors, were greatly embroidered versions of the truth, perhaps compensatory efforts to offset the relative poverty of her childhood and the fact of being orphaned early. She claimed to have had an early ambition to be a writer and to have produced a "nobbel," or novel, at the age of six, writing it with crayons and sewing it together "like a book" (*Conv.* 142–43). She also said that her grandmother gave her a hard whipping when she announced an ambition to be an actress. She spoke of her grandmother's drinking toddies with old gentlemen who came to call. It is hard to know the precise truth of such stories; she habitually mingled fact with fiction in complicated ways. Her tales of a prosperous past were largely based on the already-embroidered stories told by her grandmother. Touched-up versions of family stories about old times went into both her fiction and her supposed nonfiction.

In a very real sense, Porter's longest fictional work was her reconstruction of her own life. One of her misrepresentations was the basic matter of her age. She often claimed to have been born in 1894 rather than 1890. This was not simply a mistake on someone else's part that got picked up by others but her own revision of fact. In a 1958 interview published in the *Texas Observer* she explicitly said she was born in 1894 and was impressively able to maintain the four-year differential, telling Winston Bode she was twenty nine in 1923 when her first major story, "María Concepción," was published, rather than her actual thirty-three (*Conv.* 32, 30). It is a small matter but an indicative one. The greater puzzle is what drove her to make such claims. Her sensitivity about her age seems to have sprung partly from vanity and a wish to retain a youthful, glamorous image but more from embarrassment about her late start as a writer. A different person might have taken pride in having persevered and become a writer of consummate artistry in spite of the many adversities that delayed her. The wonder is she had a career at all.

If she shaved off a few years from her age, Porter also understated her ties to Texas. Her frank acknowledgment of her Texan-ness in the *Texas Observer* interview was an exception; she was in Texas at the time, being interviewed for a Texas publication, and expecting to be greatly honored by the University of Texas. More often she preferred to transplant her early life eastward, claiming Louisiana and a latter-day plantation aristocracy as its primary settings as well as a convent school in New Orleans like Miranda's in "Old Mortality." A 1962 interviewer, believing all this, reported that she had "gone to small convent schools in Texas and Louisiana" (*Conv.* 70); another in 1973 quoted without question Porter's statements that she spent her childhood in San Antonio and "went to school at Our Lady of the Lake convent" and that when she was thirteen "the family moved to New Orleans" (*Conv.* 158–60). None of this was true. Harrison Porter may have taken his children to San Antonio to visit his sister, and Callie and her grandmother would doubtless have changed trains there when they went to visit her two uncles in West Texas, but these trips would have ended when

Callie was eleven and was in effect orphaned a second time by the death of her grandmother. The Porter family did move to San Antonio at some time after that, but they did not move to New Orleans.

In a moment of greater candor Porter told an interviewer in 1965 that after her grandmother died "everything was scattered . . . the family life and all" (*Conv.* 100). The years of her early adolescence are the cloudiest of any period in her life. The family seems to have lived from pillar to post—on the farm of a cousin of Harrison Porter's named Thompson (the original of the farm in "Noon Wine"), in San Antonio, in Victoria, and by the time Porter was approaching sixteen, in piney-woods Lufkin, near the Louisiana border. She sometimes told people they lived in Mexico for a while. (In Hank Lopez's book this becomes a "short visit to Mexico City" when she was ten.) It is possible that they did, but no evidence of it has been found.[9]

At any rate, the Porters were in San Antonio for the 1904–5 school year. Harry Ray, or Harrison Paul—it was about this time that he changed his name—was sent to the Peacock Military Academy until he enlisted in the navy in April. Gay and Callie were enrolled as day students at the Thomas School, founded and run by a graduate of the Coronal Academy who had known their mother. It was the only year of good schooling either of them ever had.

Callie (soon to be calling herself K. R.) concentrated on what she liked—literature, social skills, music, performing arts—and ignored uncongenial subjects like mathematics. She and Gay developed some acting ability and took roles in local theater during the summer of 1905. When the season ended, Harrison and his three daughters moved to Victoria, where Gay and Callie opened a little studio teaching music, dancing, and elocution, or interpretive reading. Their father may have found occasional work, but it appears that the two girls essentially supported the family—contrary to Porter's later statement that her family believed a woman's talents "should be cultivated for the decoration of life, but never professionally" (*Conv.* xv, 9). If Harrison really held such views, he managed to reconcile himself to the situation.

At a Christmas party that year she met a young man of twenty named John Henry Koontz, who had taken time off from his railroad job in Lafayette, Louisiana, to spend the holidays with his well-off ranching family. Both, it seems, were smitten. In the spring of 1906 the Porters moved to Lufkin, where they stayed with cousins. Koontz had maintained contact, and on June 20, 1906, ignoring Callie's age (barely sixteen) and the difference of religion (he was Catholic), they were married in a double ceremony along with Gay and one T. H. Holloway.

2. Callie Russell Porter: a portrait made in 1904 when she was a student at the Thomas School in San Antonio. Already, at age fourteen, she shows the beauty that would be both one of her most notable assets and the source of major problems. Katherine Anne Porter Papers, Special Collections, University of Maryland Libraries.

This was one of the worst decisions of Porter's life. She must have thought she was getting herself into a safe harbor financially, but Koontz proved to be both abusive and, in her eyes at least, stingy. Givner questions whether there was physical abuse, but Unrue records that in 1908, soon after they moved from Lafayette to Houston, Porter sustained a broken ankle when Koontz threw her down a flight of stairs and in 1909 he beat her unconscious with a hairbrush (*Life* 43–44). One wonders if the title "No Safe Harbour," which Porter at first planned to give the novel that became *Ship of Fools,* drew on her sense of having missed out on safety during this violent first marriage. Nevertheless, she remained with Koontz for seven years. In April 1910, after not quite four of these years, she converted to Catholicism, but if she hoped this would appease him and gain his parents' acceptance, she failed. He had previously, it seems, threatened to kill her if she tried to leave him, but she became more and more determined to do so.

In 1912 the Koontzes moved to Corpus Christi, where Porter found her childhood friend Erna Schlemmer, now Johns. Erna again became her confidante but strongly disapproved when Porter told her she was planning to leave her husband.

Nevertheless, in February 1914, having saved up small bits of money to buy a ticket, Porter took a train to Chicago. She later told both Hank Lopez and Archer Winsten (a 1937 interviewer) that she "had to leave Texas" because "they all" (meaning everyone in Texas or only her family?) thought "women who wanted to write" were freaks (*Refugee* 39; *Conv.* 10). It is clear, however, that the perils of being married to an abusive husband were a more immediate reason.

During her stay in Chicago, Porter worked as an extra for a movie studio but earned so little she sometimes couldn't afford to eat. She also suffered from the cold on mornings when she had to report early, then stand and wait. When she heard that her sister Baby had been widowed while pregnant, she bought a train ticket to Beaumont, Texas, and then went on to Gibsland, Louisiana, to take care of Gay, whose husband had deserted her in advanced pregnancy. Gay already had a two-year-old named Mary Alice, a great favorite of her Aunt Callie's since infancy. Soon Gay went into a labor so difficult it was appalling. The baby was born with a broken arm. While caring for all three, Porter thought of a way to bring in a little money by drawing on her singing lessons and slight theatrical experience. She made herself a costume and devised an act for the rural lyceum circuit. Upon the return of Gay's straying husband Porter left for Dallas, where she tried to support herself in low-paying jobs until she could get a divorce, which was granted on April 21, 1915, after Koontz signed an admission of unfaithfulness and abuse. Her change of name to Katherine was granted at the same time. She added the Anne later without legal action.

Less than five months later, on September 7, 1915, she married again. This marriage, not documented until Unrue's 2005 biography, was to a man from England named H. Otto Taskett. Whether because she immediately learned that he intended to go back to England and she did not want to or because she refused to have sex and the marriage was never consummated (Unrue offers both possibilities; *Life* 54), Taskett left the country without her. It is not clear whether there was ever a formal divorce.

That fall Porter fell ill and was diagnosed with tuberculosis. Now a public health menace with nowhere else to go, she was sent to the Dallas County Detention Home, which provided virtually no care. But she hung on until spring and was then moved to a "rather pleasant" private sanitarium in Carlsbad, Texas,

3. Portrait of Porter made in Corpus Christi, Texas, in 1913, while she was still married to John Henry Koontz; dated in her own hand. This picture shows her great beauty as a young woman in her early twenties. Katherine Anne Porter Papers, Special Collections, University of Maryland Libraries.

near San Angelo, paid for by her brother (*Refugee* 44). Among the patients there she met Kitty Barry Crawford, a newspaperwoman from Fort Worth, who would become both a faithful friend and a model of female achievement. By the end of 1916, though still not entirely well, Porter returned to Dallas, this time to the Woodlawn Hospital, where she made a little money looking after the children who were patients. She organized a school for them, and when the *Dallas Morning News* printed a story about it she received donations adding up to $67.50 to buy them Christmas gifts, plus a shower of gifts for herself, some of them sent by an otherwise unidentified man she referred to in family letters as Himself.

In early 1917, the year in which the United States entered World War I, she was married a third time. This marriage, to one Carl von Pless, was not known to Givner when she wrote her biography nor to Hank Lopez when he wrote his lively but unreliable *Refugee from Indian Creek*. It was Unrue who discovered the registration of the marriage to von Pless in Baton Rouge, Louisiana. There must also have been a divorce, since Porter would otherwise have been at risk of a bigamy charge when she had to swear to her marriages in order to buy land in Louisiana some years later, after entering into another marriage there. Unrue's summary of how she conflated her first three marriages merits quoting for the insight it affords into her way of fictionalizing her life: "In the last decade of her life she identified her first husband as John Pleskett, a conflation of *John* Koontz, Otto Tas*kett,* and Carl von *Pless.* . . . 'I don't like to talk about it, and I never mention it,' she said, 'but it was twenty-six years before I married again.' It was twenty-six years between her first and her fourth weddings. In Cat Porter's style, she had revised the first and wiped out the second and the third" (*Life* 57).

Back in Fort Worth in the fall of 1917, Porter went to work for a small newspaper, the *Critic,* taking over duties such as theater reviews, society columns, and miscellaneous that Kitty Crawford was still unable to resume. For a while she was also publicity chair for the Red Cross, ramping up its work because of the war. Characteristically, she overstrained her energies, fell ill, and had to give it all up. But this proved to be an opportunity when in the spring of 1918, she and Kitty Crawford left together for Denver to enter another sanitarium. It was one of the defining moments of her life.

It has sometimes been said that Porter left Texas early in life. The only time she is so much as mentioned in Tom Pilkington's book about southwestern literature is as a comparator for Jean Stafford's also leaving "her native region very early" (192). In fact, Porter did not leave early at all. She was twenty-four when she made her abortive getaway to Chicago and almost twenty-eight when she made her real break. After this she returned to Texas only six times over the course of the rest of her life. (In "Notes on the Texas I Remember," written when she was in her eighties, she says only once.)

If we ask why Porter was so intent on getting away from Texas, as we must, the reasons are numerous but far from clear. Certainly her early years had been unhappy. Not only had her childhood been scarred by the deaths of her mother and grandmother, she had also been deeply scarred by what she felt to be her father's indifference to her welfare. Her marriage at sixteen had been abusive, a disaster in every way. It is entirely understandable that she would want to get away from the scenes of such unhappiness. Another reason was that she felt thwarted in her desire to write by both her own family and the social atmosphere of Texas generally. She had also been immersed in the post–Civil War myth of the Old South, with its emphasis on loss. She must have had, from as far back as she could remember, an awareness of the Civil War and what it had entailed, both in terms of maiming and killing and in terms of economic hardship and loss of a way of life. And it is unmistakable in her later writings that she had come to associate Texas with a repellant level of social violence.

How much she knew of the specifics of Texas history is up for debate. She had little formal schooling, and history was not taught then, as a school subject, as much as it is now.[10] Still, it is hard to believe she was unaware of at least some of the hero stories that have often made up "Texas history" as passed down to the young. Obviously she picked up a sense of culture, both generally and in specific indicative details, as readily as a sponge absorbs water. A culture grows out of its history. And as the following summary will emphasize, the history of Texas was undeniably violent. She would later write of the culture in which she came to maturity that potential violence was an "underlying, perpetual ominous presence" that "broke through the smooth surface almost without warning" (*CE* 472).

Like the idealized history of the South, the very different but overlapping history of Texas was, until very recent years, written from an almost solely white perspective and was conceived as a succession of key events in which white males took all the major roles. Often it was idealized and aggrandized in a way that airbrushed blemishes out of the picture. In this story, with Texans (or Texians) cast as heroes and Mexicans as villains, the central chapter was the sequence of battles fought in the 1830s that led to Texas independence. Centering on the Alamo, it is presented as a kind of morality play pitting "freedom-loving" Anglos against a Mexican army led by the sinister Santa Anna (Zamora, Orozco, and Rocha 5). Many Texans still speak earnestly about not only the uniqueness and splendor of the state's landscape but also the gloriousness of its past: the nobility of the heroes of the Alamo, the staunch integrity of Sam Houston (often vilified during his lifetime), and the brave self-reliance of Jane Long, Mother of Texas.[11] Publisher Frances Brannen Vick, for example, writes proudly, "Texas is so big and has such a colorful history that it is nigh impossible to know it all intimately. It is an incredibly rich field to mine" (235, 243). It is indeed a rich field, but the mining of it has traditionally followed a certain seam. Historians who mine that field today are energetically challenging the Anglocentric myth, while Texas novelists Elizabeth Crook and Stephen Harrigan are also more engaged in debunking grandiose ideas than in perpetuating them. Craig Clifford declared in the 1980s that "the greatest bugaboo" for Texas writers was not anti-Texas sentiment but "the Texas mystique" (4). It was a mystique Porter never accepted, though she did at times adopt the related mystique of the South.

Whether elevated to mythic status or not, the condition of Texas's birth, both as a republic in 1836 and as a state in 1846, was violence. The republic was established by means of a war for independence, and the annexation of Texas to the United States precipitated a war with the then twenty-five-year-old Republic of Mexico.

～

Conflict in the space we call Texas had of course begun long before—at least with the coming of the Spanish in the late seventeenth century, whatever the tribal conflicts that went on in precontact times. Spain began establishing missions and guard posts—not colonies—in the 1680s. When Spanish authorities in Mexico City learned that a French group led by René-Robert de la Salle had landed at Matagorda Bay in 1684, they sent out a succession of expeditions to locate it. When they finally succeeded, in 1689, they found only ruins; except for a few taken captive, the colonists had been exterminated by Karankawa Indians.[12] All this activity—the establishment of missions and forts, the 1684 French settlement, the Spanish expeditions trying to locate it—naturally led to increased contact with natives, provoking attempts to repel the intruders, which led to more incursions, which provoked more conflict as the tribes attempted to drive them out: an upward spiral. Spanish colonists suffered killing and mutilation; natives suffered not only response in kind but also death by disease pathogens against which they had no resistance. It is thought that by as early as 1690 the native population had been reduced to half or less of its pre-contact levels (Foster 261–64). Some of the South Texas native groups observed by Cabeza de Vaca in the 1530s virtually ceased to exist (J. Thompson 13). Texas, then, was a dark and bloody ground long before its first Anglos arrived.

By the mid-1700s ranches were being established under Spanish land grants along the San Antonio River and the Nueces, farther north. These *rancheros* were the beginnings of the Texas cattle industry. But the possibility of a French takeover of territory in Texas would trouble Spain for many years. It was this anxiety that eventually led to the admission of colonists from the United States as a buffer against both Native Americans and the French.

As all Texas schoolchildren know, the first organized colony of Anglo settlers to enter Texas was Stephen F. Austin's "Old Three Hundred," who began to arrive in 1821, the year Mexico achieved independence from Spain.[13] These settlers brought a very different social and economic system. Not ranchers but farmers, they came from the American South, many of them bringing slaves to work the rich bottomlands they took up along rivers in eastern Texas. Along with slavery they brought an ideology of white supremacy. Both would have ramifications far into the future (Nevels 15). It was this social migration initiated by Austin and his colonists that eventually, in 1857, brought Porter's paternal grandparents, Asbury and Catherine Skaggs Porter, to central Texas. They, too, brought a slave.

Any society that accords almost unlimited power to one ethnic group over another is characterized by systemic violence, and the pre–Civil War South was no exception. Added to the violence endemic to the slave system was a class-based Southern culture of white-on-white mayhem characterized by, among the elite, dueling and a code of male honor embracing revenge, and among the plain folk, feuds, brawls, and fights, often including eye-gouging.

In every respect, this imported bent toward violence was compounded by conditions peculiar to Texas. Although the Austin colonists of the 1820s settled hundreds of miles from the Mexicans of South Texas, their coming not only provoked increased resistance on the part of native tribes but also soon led to Anglo-Mexican conflicts. It might seem that the reverse would be true, but the new settlers' distance from Mexican settlements in South Texas meant that the two groups had little opportunity to become acquainted free from the adverse filters of rumor and stereotype. Hardly any of the Southerners spoke any Spanish. As early as 1837 a Mexican government official noted that six Mexican settlers had been "assassinated" by Anglo Texans out of "hatred for the Mexican nation" (Carrigan 17). The Southerners' predominantly white supremacist and exclusionary politics meant that when the movement for Texas independence began, even Tejanos who fought for independence were regarded as "other" or "the enemy" (Montejano 27; Zamora, Orozco, and Rocha 3).[14] Prejudices on the part of Anglos against blacks, Native Americans, and Mexicans "remained entrenched in Texas politics for the entire century" despite a rapid series of governmental changes (Stewart and De León 8). Violence between brown and white in the early years carried forward into the late nineteenth century and well into the twentieth in the form of protracted armed conflicts and summary "justice," while from the Civil War on, the existing pattern of white-on-black violence endemic to slavery grew inexorably into a culture of lynching.

The war of 1836 in which Texas became an independent republic arose largely out of two issues: Texians' realization that their degree of de facto autonomy within the Republic of Mexico was not growing, as they wished, but was decreasing as President Antonio López de Santa Anna centralized the political power structure. Texas had been a separate province, Nuevo Santander, when Anglo settlers began to arrive, but in 1823 the province was absorbed into the State of Temaulipas (J. Thompson 40), reducing the Texians' degree of autonomy. The second issue was slavery. The two became joined.

Under Mexico's constitution, slavery was illegal. There had been 443 slaves in Texas as early as 1825, four years after Austin began bringing in colonists, but the population of both whites and slaves quickly burgeoned until by 1836 the two together greatly outnumbered the Spanish-speaking population. Slave owners feared forced emancipation and looked toward independence in order to legalize their "peculiar institution." Certainly there were some among the Anglo Southerners in Texas who did not favor slavery, just as there were Tejanos who disliked the policy of centralization, but their dissent would not affect the course of events, only add to the social conflicts of both the Texas War for Independence and the Civil War. West Texas, settled by whites later than the eastern region, was never slave country. Following the dictates of the land, it developed a farther-flung ranching economy where slaves would not have been assets. The conflict over slavery, then, also swept up conflicts over region and economy.

Fighting began in October 1835 with the Battle of Gonzales. From then until the Battle of San Jacinto on April 21, 1836, when a greatly outnumbered army led by Sam Houston used a surprise attack to rout a large Mexican force led by Santa Anna in person, atrocities were committed on both sides. The Texians suffered many casualties in the earlier engagements and massacres of the war, but at San Jacinto they sustained only nine fatalities compared to 630 Mexican dead. These numbers were long seen as evidence of the glory of the victory, but that glory is somewhat dimmed when one reads that they are not entirely explained by the cleverness of the surprise attack. An unknown number of Mexican soldiers were killed while trying to surrender or were burned to death in a deliberately set fire of marsh grass where the wounded lay trapped. Certainly, as a Texas child myself, I was never taught that in the public schools of Fort Worth in the 1940s. I was, however, made aware of the massacre of heroic Texans at the Alamo and at Goliad.

The fighting of 1835–36 that culminated at San Jacinto, traditionally called the Texas Revolution or the War for Independence, is now often designated in less elevated terms. Elizabeth Crook, in her gripping novel *Promised Lands* (1994), calls it "the Texas rebellion"; others call it the "Texas insurgency."[15] Call it what we will, the achievement of Texas independence in 1836 did little to tone down the cultural bent toward violence. Fighting over the Nueces Strip—the strip of land between the Rio Grande, where the truce at San Jacinto had placed the border, and the Nueces River, the Mexicans' customary idea of where Texas began and the boundary ratified by the Mexican Congress—increased the polarization between whites and browns. Santa Anna was determined to regain his lost land, and raids and armed clashes continued for years, with Laredo and San Antonio taken and retaken multiple times (J. Thompson 41–49). When Texas became part of the United States in 1846 the border dispute continued. Mexico still regarded the legal border as the Nueces River, and the United States claimed the entire area to the Rio Grande. American troops were stationed along the northern bank, and the U.S.-Mexican War erupted. It ended in 1848 with the Treaty of Guadalupe Hidalgo under which the United States took over about two-thirds of the territory of Mexico. Even then, the Nueces Strip remained a place of resentment, hostility, and sporadic ethnic violence.

The nature of political power in the new state of Texas remained much as it had been during the days of the republic, with slaveholders continuing to comprise the majority of state legislators (Carver 227; Carrigan 50). As the Civil War approached, they increasingly feared both the loss of their labor force and the possibility of uprisings, especially in areas where the slave population was most numerous.[16] In an entry titled "Slave Insurrections" in the valuable online *Handbook of Texas,* James Smallwood offers this bit of irony: "Although a committee of the [lower chamber of the Texas legislature] concluded in 1857, 'Our slaves are the happiest . . . of human beings on whom the sun shines,' in 1858 the legislature passed a measure to repress insurrection and punish its participants." Even before independence Mexican Texans had exhibited widespread sympathy with the slaves, and slave owners had realized and resented it. Thus the one racial hostility fed the other. There had been an outbreak of violence in South Texas in 1857 in which hostility between Anglos and Mexicans flared into months of beatings and killings centering on the freight operations of Mexican carters, seventy-five of whom were killed by masked Anglos (Carrigan 29). But Mexicans were killed by white mobs for all sorts of other offenses as well.

Hostility between pro-slavery and anti-slavery Anglos also sharpened in the years leading up to the Civil War as it became compounded with the issue of secession or nonsecession. Historian Ralph Wooster points out that most Texans were Unionists and three out of four did not own slaves, but even they did not want to see slavery eliminated because they saw it as an economic engine. They, too, therefore leaned toward secession.[17] As governor, Sam Houston tried to keep Texas in the Union, but a convention was called in January 1861 at which the overwhelming majority voted in favor of joining the Confederacy. When that decision was upheld by popular plebiscite the following month, Houston refused to take an oath of loyalty to the Confederacy and retired to his home in Huntsville, which now boasts a snowy-white giant statue of the once-blackened hero. Persons of lesser stature who dissented from secession faced suppression of a rougher sort. Unionists caught attempting to leave the state were sometimes hanged, and those who remained might also find themselves jailed or hanged after summary court hearings. In Gainesville, near the Red River (the border between Texas and present-day Oklahoma), in October 1862, 150 Union sympathizers were rounded up and tried by a "citizens' jury" stacked with slave owners. At least two were shot, and forty were summarily hanged, some without even the pretense of a trial.[18]

During the war about ninety thousand Texans served in the Confederate Army, Porter's grandfather Asbury Porter among them. About a third of these remained in Texas as home guards against both invasion and Indian attacks. Comparatively speaking, the war was fairly easy on Texas. There were clashes between the two armies but nothing to equal the mammoth battles farther east. With the Union navy maintaining a blockade of the Texas coast for most of the war, civilians experienced shortages of household commodities (coffee, flour, cloth) such as Porter reports in her essay "Portrait: Old South," about her grandmother, but again, the shortages were not so severe in Texas as elsewhere in the South. After Lee's surrender at Appomattox, however, fighting between Confederates and Union soldiers or irregulars continued for a month in the Nueces Strip. Supposed Union sympathizers were killed by vigilante mobs even after that (Carrigan 90; J. Thompson 115–17).

After the Civil War racial violence between blacks and whites flared. Although lynching of blacks by white vigilantes would wax and wane, there was an overall increase in the heinous practice for decades. The first ten years of Porter's life, the 1890s, were an "especially deadly" decade for African Americans in central Texas, with twenty lynchings in that section of the state alone (at least ninety-four in the state as a whole). The practice continued well into the twentieth century, with ever more horrific methods employed—such as burning alive. A long history of racism with roots in the South but twists of its own in Texas had produced a lynching culture. During the period 1882–1968, Texas was exceeded in numbers of lynchings (493) only by Mississippi (581) and Georgia (531).[19] We will explore the culture of lynching in greater detail later in connection with Porter's uncompleted and unpublished "The Man in the Tree."

The role of the Texas Rangers in this long panorama has been much disputed. Walter Prescott Webb, in his book *The Story of the Texas Rangers*, presents them as heroes, writing that they were "quiet, deliberate, gentle" men. Examples of Ranger actions call these descriptive terms into question. Clearly the organization served Texans' interest in security in the mid-nineteenth century and served it well, but oppression of Mexicans is a recurrent theme in its history. Larry McMurtry, with accustomed irreverence, terms the Rangers "ruthless." He writes that in one instance when the Rangers entered Mexico City with the U.S. Army in 1847, a Mexican was shot merely for stealing a Ranger's handkerchief, and when a Ranger who had entered a dangerous part of the city was killed, eighty Mexicans were shot in retaliation. In 1875, he continues, when the Rangers were sent into the Nueces Strip primarily to solve a problem of cattle stealing, "any Mexican unlucky enough to be caught was tortured until he coughed up information, then summarily hung" ("Southwestern Literature" 40–41).

To Mexican Texans, the "Rinches" were by no means heroes but a cohort of violent Anglos who inflicted beatings and killings on people with brown skin. Folklorist Americo Paredes's *With His Pistol in His Hand* (1958) provides a polished narrative of one such case, the story of Gregorio Cortez. His story is based on numerous *corridos* (folk ballads) chronicling the South Texas border conflict, typically featuring a "hard-working, peace-loving Mexicano . . . goaded by Anglo outrages into violence, causing him to defend his rights and those of others in his community against the *rinches*" (Saldívar 176). The most notorious period of conflict was the Tejano Revolt during the second decade of the twentieth century, the period during which Katherine Anne Porter twice made her escape from Texas. During 1915 and 1916 the Rangers killed an estimated one hundred to three hundred Mexicans on South Texas ranches and farms, imposing a "virtual reign of terror" that included "summary field executions" (Rocha 107; J. Thompson 140–41).

Whatever the truth of the sometimes heroized, sometimes vilified Texas Rangers, Porter seems to have been aware of their persistent reputation for racial oppression. In a letter to her father on March 30, 1935, she wrote that she did not at all approve of her nephew Breck's being in the Rangers and killing innocent Mexicans. My assumption is that in making such a comment she was drawing on hearsay, nothing more. I have found, however, one indication in her voluminous correspondence that she at least thought she was fairly conversant with the subject of Texas history. In a letter of July 30, 1940, to her then husband Albert Erskine, she reported that she had told a publisher she would accept an advance of $2,500 to write a history of Texas. Although the book never materialized, one assumes she must have thought she had at least some basis of knowledge to draw on.

∾

This, then, was Callie Russell Porter's Texas—the place and culture in which Katherine Anne Porter grew up. Whether she knew even as much about its history as this abbreviated outline has provided is not clear. On the other hand, her father was a habitual reader, and both he and Grandmother Porter were opinionated and talkative. We know that they impressed on her an awareness of her Southern heritage and what they regarded as the tragic injustice of the Civil War. Porter herself was also, of course, a habitual reader, and the readiness with which she picked up newspaper work in her early adult years indicates both an attentiveness to what was going on and a degree of knowledge of how newspapers worked. All of these factors indicate a likely awareness of the world around her and something of its history.

History flows into and shapes culture, and culture is a shaping context for every life. Experience teaches us that the ramifications of prolonged enmities radiate through society in far-reaching ways. And indeed we come across frequent indications in Porter's works and in her letters that she was aware of racial tensions in the Texas of her early years and that she perceived violence as a constant presence in the background of her life. Many critics have noted that violence is ever-present *beneath* the surface of her fiction, though violence, whether historical or contemporaneous, is rarely her overt subject. We might contrast, for clarification, Elizabeth Crook's *Promised Lands*. Crook's novel is *about* history. By means of keen novelistic imagination, *Promised Lands* explores the relatively brief conflict usually called the Texas Revolution and makes it vividly present to the reader's eye. Crook could well say of her work what popular West Texas novelist Elmer Kelton once said of his: "One of my main uses of fiction has been to dramatize history" (13). For Porter the terms must be reversed. One of her main uses of history was to lend depth and meaning to fiction. She drew on her ingrained sense of history in developing the consciousness through which her fiction emerged. Thus we never find her commenting directly on Texas's past but rather on the consequences of the past. In "Noon Wine," for example, she writes of how violence suddenly, almost automatically, erupts on a sleepy Texas farm, and in the nonfiction or quasi-nonfiction piece "'Noon Wine': The Sources" she singles out the implements of potential violence as cultural indicators.

In the Texas of her childhood, she writes, the "perpetual" potential for violence took on visual reality in the "loaded pistols" men carried "inside their shirts next to their ribs" and the "cold eyes of shotguns and rifles" into which one stared, she wrote, with the opening of a closet door. She recalls living among "loaded guns and dangerous cutting edges" every summer—that is, when she went to her grandmother's farm (*CE* 472–73). However routine these implements may have seemed to rural people accustomed to hunting or killing coyotes and snakes, the omnipresence of such tools of violence left Porter remembering an atmosphere of peril.

2

Away and Yet Not Away

I am doing more, and meeting cleverer people, than ever I did in all
my days.
          —Katherine Anne Porter to "Baby" (sister), 1919, from Denver

Lord, how we do go back to the soil we sprang from as we grow up . . .
[but] here is where I can work, and where I can work, there I live.
                    —Katherine Anne Porter to "Dad" and "Sis,"
                         April 1, 1920, from New York

Katherine Anne Porter's departure from Texas in the spring of 1918 was one of
the defining moments of her life. When she finally, at the age of twenty-eight,
managed to get away more or less permanently, she found opportunities for career advancement and maturation as an artist that she had not been able to put
together in her home state. At first this meant newspaper work (though she later
denied she was ever a newspaperwoman). She quickly, however, moved on to literary writing.

Soon after arriving in Denver with Kitty Barry Crawford, she met Jane Anderson, a college roommate of Kitty's, who had also only recently arrived. A
journalist and short story writer just back from feats of war correspondence in
Europe, Jane quickly persuaded Kitty to go in with her in renting a mountain-
side house near Colorado Springs. She then brought in her current lover, Gilbert
Seldes. When Kitty found the threesome awkward, Jane persuaded Katherine
Anne to come into the rent sharing arrangement (Seldes apparently having a
free ride). Soon the situation became intolerable, and first Kitty, then Katherine
Anne went back to Denver. There Porter found a job on the *Rocky Mountain
News* doing local reporting and routine columns. This was the very fall when
the notorious flu epidemic hit Denver.[1] When the second death was recorded, on
October 2, the city was essentially shut down, but by then the virus was rampant.
Hospitals quickly filled up, and city streetcars were used to ferry the dead. When
Porter fell ill, no place could be found for her until Kitty's doctor at the tubercu-
lar facility intervened and she was put on a cot in a hospital corridor.

Her sister Gay rushed to Denver and found her near death. The newspaper
actually set her obituary in type. When news of the armistice (ending fighting

in World War I) arrived on November 11, she was still so ill she could scarcely grasp what was happening. She was pulled back from the brink by an experimental injection of strychnine but not before experiencing what Givner calls "death and rebirth" (*KAP* 124). Porter would later tell a *Paris Review* interviewer, Barbara Thompson, the experience "just simply divided my life, cut across it like that" and left her "in some strange way altered" (*Conv.* 85). It served, almost two decades later, as the genesis of "Pale Horse, Pale Rider," where the deadly flu is imaged as a poisoned well in Texas—a detail that illustrates how Porter's imagination fused widely separated aspects of her life in making her art.

One minor puzzle relating to her near-death experience is her hair color afterward. She said it turned white, and both Hank Lopez and Darlene Unrue accept this as fact, yet Joan Givner quotes a coworker at the newspaper to the effect that her hair was still dark. It is dark in her passport photograph of 1920. She may have dyed it, of course, but a 1931 snapshot made onboard the *Werra* on her way to Germany shows her with dark but graying hair. The claim that her hair suddenly turned white appears to be another instance of self-staging, possibly as a way to beg the bothersome question of age. White hair at twenty-eight is far more dramatic than graying hair at forty-one.

After a brief respite in Texas to complete her recovery, Porter resumed her newspaper work in Denver in January 1919 but in a different way. Her close call with death had moved her goals to a new level of seriousness. Her writing style became more concise and disciplined, and as drama critic, she began to write reviews criticizing both the level of stagecraft on display in Denver and the level of seriousness in contemporary theater generally. That is, she began to formulate artistic standards. Old habits do persist, however. She now became secretly engaged to the manager of a local theater company where she had done some acting. Then, in July, another shock came—a telegram informing her that her six-year-old niece, Gay's Mary Alice, the child Katherine Anne had so loved, had died. She fell into a period of intense grieving that apparently, by the end of the summer, her fiancé began to think excessive. Partly to escape his disapproval but also because she now felt she was ready, she left for New York.

This second departure meant another dramatic unfolding in Porter's life. She took a room in Greenwich Village, got a job writing publicity material for a movie company, and soon produced what were, until recently, thought to have been her first three published stories. She told her family in a letter of January 3, 1920, that she was doing a group of twelve children's stories that were to appear in consecutive issues of *Everyland* and then as a book. The volume never materialized. But the first three stories, all retellings of folktales, were published in the January, February, and March 1920 issues. Her career as a writer of fiction was—modestly enough—begun.

The surprising aspect of this is that a newcomer with no record in children's literature was so readily able to get such a contract. Porter's only previous publications (or so it was believed until recently) were an anecdote in the *Chicago Tribune* in 1914 and a poem celebrating Texas, with no hint of the conflicted state of her actual feelings, in an undated issue of the *Citrus Fruit Grower*.[2] The first of the six stanzas goes:

Ye shivering ones of the frozen North, list to my happy song
   Of the seventh heaven nestled here below,
In our rich, fertile valleys, midst sunkissed fruits and flowers
In Texas, by the Gulf of Mexico.

This unimpressive and essentially ungenuine poem, plus the trivial anecdote, were not in fact, after all, her only freelance publications up until the three *Everyland* stories. Darlene Unrue reported in 2009 the discovery of a children's story published in the *Dallas Morning News* even before Porter left Texas and conjectures that there were others as well. If so, the credentials Porter had to offer to New York publishers were "children's stories," plural.[3]

At first glance the three stories published in *Everyland* seem to have no connection either to Porter's personal history or to her later work. They do reflect her long concern with gender and gender roles, but their main importance is in showing that she could use existing skills to produce salable work—skills rooted in Texas, during her confinement to a sanitarium and during bouts of storytelling, entertaining both Gay's and Kitty Crawford's little girls (and also, one assumes, the children at Woodlawn). But a fourth story published later in the year in the magazine *Asia*, "The Adventures of Hadji: A Tale of a Turkish Coffee-House," is of more obvious significance. It, too, is a retelling of a folktale, but this time for adults, and it is more compellingly focused on gender. "The Adventures of Hadji" expresses a vision consistent with the strong convictions about women's rights that Porter had held for some years.

As a direct result of this publication in *Asia*, Porter now received a contract to ghostwrite the autobiography of an American woman married to a Chinese husband. Her life was becoming crowded with new endeavors—and also with new acquaintances, most of them literary and politically leftist: Kenneth Durant, Mike Gold, Floyd Dell, Malcolm and Peggy Cowley, Rose Wilder Lane, Edmund Wilson, Edna St. Vincent Millay, Ernestine Evans, Genevieve Taggard, and others, including a group of Mexican expatriates. When one of these latter, art theorist Adolfo Best Maugard, told her about the revolution in Mexico and the profound effects on art that it was having, and urged her to go and see for herself, her friend Ernestine Evans, an editor with the *Christian Science Monitor*, arranged for her to send back freelance pieces. In addition, improbable as it seems, a group of American businessmen commissioned her to establish a publication to be called *The Magazine of Mexico*. How she expected to maintain her distinctly leftist politics while writing for a business audience remains a mystery. She would describe the backers in a letter to her family dated December 31, 1920, as a group of rich bankers who "love oil and silver and coal and gold—love the very sound of those unctuous words, and can think of nothing else by day or by night, drunk or sober." In the same letter she told her father, "I can not tell you how far I have come." She did not mean it in a solely geographical sense.

Between 1920 and 1936 Porter lived, for the most part, in New York, Mexico, and Paris. She was back and forth between Mexico and New York four times between 1920 and 1930, and in between spent time in Massachusetts, Connecticut, and Bermuda. Success was slow in coming, and her life remained restless and disorderly. Yet in the eighteen-year period between leaving Texas and returning to the United States after five years in Europe she transformed herself from a low-level newspaperwoman into an accomplished writer with a following among literary peers. She also became a person who reflected seriously on her own past and her historic moment. And always among her reflections was the dilemma of what Texas meant to her.

It is ironic that Porter's report to her family on how far she had come would be associated geographically, with Mexico, because in order to reach Mexico to witness its revolution and its new spirit in the arts she had to go through Texas—in more ways than one. Literally, her train crossed the international border at El Paso. But her approach to Mexico was by way of Texas in a larger sense as well. In crossing the legal border, she also crossed a border of consciousness. To the extent that she was able, she stopped regarding Mexico and Mexicans from a northern, Anglo perspective (as the song lyrics "south of the border, down Mexico way" implicitly do) and adopted a perspective anchored in Mexico itself. This enabled her, at least intermittently, to identify with Mexico's people and view gringos satirically, as intruders. Very few Texan—or American—writers have done so.

Both as a Spanish colony and as a republic Mexico had played a major role in the political and cultural development of Texas. Certainly it had left its traces, though not such as to support Porter's calling Mexico, as she did, a "familiar country" before 1920.[4] She justified this claim by saying that she had been "born near San Antonio" and her father had "lived part of his youth" in Mexico and told her "enchanting stories" about it. These clearly inadequate justifications were bolstered with references to sojourns in Mexico during which she had learned the country firsthand. So far as I have been able to discover, except for the statements about her father, these claims are spurious. San Antonio was not a Mexican town, even if Porter did call it that (*Conv.* 113); it was an American town with a large Mexican community. Moreover, there was a sharp divide between the city's Anglos and Latinos, with a long history of white hostility and abusive treatment toward Mexicans.[5] A scant year in San Antonio, possibly reinforced by what she had heard from her sister Gay, who did live in Mexico for a time after her marriage, could hardly have made Porter familiar with the country. It seems inescapable that her familiarity with Mexico—and even a degree of expertise, despite her very limited Spanish—was gained during her four life-transforming stays between 1920 and 1931.

It was during the first of these that she experienced wide-scale public violence for the first time. Yet that experience does not seem to have repelled her in the way that she was repelled by the violence endemic in the culture of Texas. Perhaps her awareness that she was going into a society undergoing revolution prepared her to expect violence, at least as an idea, and even to hope that it would serve a useful larger purpose. Or perhaps, contrary to her claims that Mexico was her "familiar country," she had no such personal feelings for it as she did for Texas and therefore did not react so intensely when discordant elements disrupted her idyllic fantasies. Certainly she supported the goals of Mexico's revolution. She was concerned with the country's future, primarily with ideas of social justice in that future. As to Texas, she was more concerned with the past and its heritage, which she badly wanted to conceive of as a nourishing and gracious one.

~

Like her departures from Texas in 1914 and 1918 and her decision to move on from Denver to New York in 1919, Porter's impulsive trip to Mexico City in 1920 was part of a lifelong pattern. Whenever she fell into periods of depression or felt herself overwhelmed by commitments or problems, she preferred to leave wherever she was and go somewhere else. Four separate times during the 1920s and into the early 1930s, Mexico provided an accommodation for this urge to escape. She might not have been so amenable to the suggestion that she go see the Mexican Revolution for herself if it had not already been one of those times when she felt an imperative to go somewhere. Her "wild dash" for Mexico, as Darlene Unrue terms it, was as much an escape from commitments as it was a response to the beckoning of new experiences (*Life* 70).

Traveling by rail in 1920, she had plenty of opportunity to observe contrasts and continuities from her train car window. Years later she described the trip as a bold and adventurous one, telling Hank Lopez that after she crossed the international border armed soldiers and their families rode on top of the train cars. Lopez, who tended to accept what she told him as fact, reports that when she stepped off the train during a stop in Chihuahua she "casually glanced at the roof of her own coach" and saw a virtual "militarized mobile kitchen, with bayoneted rifles silhouetted against the darkening sky" and smoke ascending from braziers where men, women, and children were cooking (*Refugee* 58). Thomas F. Walsh, the leading researcher on Porter's time in Mexico, scotches this account completely: "The fact was that not even armed guards had accompanied trains from the border for months" (*Illusion* 6).

Besides Best Maugard's suggestion, the readiness with which Porter decided to go to Mexico drew on a fantasy her father had communicated to her long before. There is abundant evidence that Harrison Porter was a big talker who exaggerated his stories, and the idea of Mexico that he planted in Porter's mind, from his days in railroad construction there, would without doubt have been a romanticized one. In a letter to his future wife dated January 15, 1882, he sketched just such a version of a Mexico populated by pretty girls who were good dancers and who came from a higher social class than the Mexicans "as seen in our country." Ever the melancholic, he added a plaintive wish that he could stay and become a different person altogether: "Were it possible I would blot from my memory the knowledge of my mother tongue, and link my name, my future" to Mexico's "rising star."

The Mexico of the early 1920s was a "rising star" for Katherine Anne as well. Escape was by no means its only significance for her, however. This was her period of greatest radicalism in politics. She hoped to see Mexico's revolution succeed in establishing a just society in which the poor and the dark-skinned could have a fair opportunity to improve their lives and the rich would no longer wield disproportionate power. In pursuing these dreams, she also reaped great benefits as a writer. Mexico's revolutionary art provided an example of creative work rooted in the dailiness of its own time and place. By providing this model of art as well as needed distance from Texas, Mexico gave her an opportunity to balance her emotional ties to her native material with a degree of detachment. Moreover, she learned in Mexico the art of caricature that would prove important in much of her work, lending sharp edges to her descriptions and characterizations.

It was while she was away in Mexico, New York, Paris, and various other places of shorter duration that Porter began to reach back into her family past to revise both her own memories and various stories she had heard from her family. This was her bedrock material. In building on it, though, she did not so much relate as reconstruct her personal history. The Texas origins that had shaped her would be recaptured and reshaped in both fiction and (supposed) nonfiction. But she was able to access it only when she was away—and *because* she was away. For years she struggled to produce out of this material a novel or even multivolume family saga, a project in which she never succeeded. Only when she drew on her unsuccessful drafts for encapsulated stories in the shorter forms best suited to her was she able to produce the art of which she was capable. In the meantime, she drew on her time and experience in Mexico for an entirely separate body of work based not on memory but on observation, empathy, and dashed dreams.

Throughout her years away, Porter's thoughts kept turning back nostalgically to what she called the land of her heart. Yet she could reverse herself on a dime. In a 1920 letter to her father and sister, for example, she said that she found herself "think[ing] all the time of a house in the country, a riot of old fashioned growing things all mixed up together." These were the terms in which she reminisced about Texas in "'Noon Wine': The Sources" and "The Old Order." Two sentences later in her 1920 letter, however, she wrote, "On the other hand, I hate like the devil to think of the south again for a residence." This time, when she said "the south," she meant Texas. That was not always so.

3

The Mexican Dream and Its Realities

I am perfectly certain that my time in Mexico was one of the very important times of my life. I think it influenced everything I did afterward.
—Katherine Anne Porter, "The Mexico I Knew"

Mexico is a disturbing country.
—Katherine Anne Porter, review of *Idols behind Altars,* by Anita Brenner

During her four stays in Mexico during the 1920s, Porter completed her emergence as an artist. Some of her most celebrated short fiction appeared during this decade. The fact that these two events—her experience of Mexico and her emergence as a serious writer—coincided was not mere happenstance. Mexico provided what she needed in order to bring to fruition her long preparation as a writer not only in terms of material—though it provided that as well—but also in terms of perspective. She gained a needed distance from which to see the life of her own place more clearly. She gained, too, from her immersion in Mexican visual art as it was unfolding during the 1920s, and in particular from her acquaintance with the art of caricature as practiced in Mexico, a new honed-down technique along with a willingness to draw on the everyday and the familiar as the material for art. At the same time, the social turmoil she witnessed and participated in while in Mexico propelled Porter toward a more active commitment to the leftist politics she had already, to a degree, embraced. All the worse, then, was her disillusionment when she came to believe that the social revolution she witnessed there, from which she had hoped so much, had failed and that the powerful were continuing and would continue to exploit the powerless.

Porter's arrival in Mexico City on November 8, 1920, was just in time for the inauguration of the revolutionary general Alvaro Obregón as president. She immediately made contact with the leftist editor of the English-language page of *El Heraldo de México,* Thorberg Haberman, who introduced her to Luis Morones, the head of the radical labor union CROM (Regional Confederation of Mexican Workers) and one of the most powerful figures in the Obregón government. That is, she quickly immersed herself in Mexican politics. Her contact with Thorberg Haberman also meant that Porter quickly gained an outlet for her writing. First a biting review of *Mexico in Revolution* by Blasco Ibañez, then, on December 13, the essay "The Fiesta of Guadalupe" appeared in *El Heraldo*. These two important pieces, published in little more than a month after her arrival, were the first drops in a spate of work she would produce during this initial nine-month stay.[1] During the same period she would also place pieces in the *Christian Science Monitor*, the Socialist *New York Call*, and the business-oriented *Magazine of Mexico*; she would complete *My Chinese Marriage* (1921); and she would begin some fiction. At the same time, she was also working "informally," as Beth Alvarez puts it, for Morones.[2] That is, she was moving in Communist Party circles in more than a casual way.

"The Fiesta of Guadalupe," her second publication in *El Heraldo*, is especially remarkable in that Porter had witnessed the Feast of the Virgin of Guadalupe only the day before the essay appeared; her account was apparently written overnight.[3] What is most stunning about the essay itself is its keenness of observation and its compelling rendering of traces of the Indian celebrants' unrelenting hardships. Watching them "dancing in religious ecstasy . . . fantastically dressed," she seems to have been struck by a discordance between their garish get-ups and their innate dignity. The cheap, gaudy costumes they wear represent, as she writes of them, the trappings of a religion imposed "with fire and sword." She deplores even as she in a sense honors their "terrible reasonless faith," writing, "I see the awful hands of faith, the credulous and worn hands of believers; the humble and beseeching hands of the millions and millions who have only the anodyne of credulity." With the word "anodyne" she echoes Marx's labeling of religion as the opiate of the people. Good revolutionary as she was at the time, she wished that, instead of clinging to a fantasy of help from a "vast and empty sky," they would put their energy into demanding a reality of less work and more food (*CE* 394–98).

The anticlericalism evident here and in much of Porter's other early writing in Mexico was one of the principles of Mexico's revolution. The constitution of 1917 limited the church's ability to own property or operate religious schools, and two of her friends in Mexico City—Roberto Haberman, Thorberg's journalist husband, and Manuel Gamio, founder of Mexican social anthropology—encouraged Porter to see religion as an enslaving power Mexico had "freed itself from" (*Illusion* 7, 49–50). If so, it is a freedom not evident in "The Fiesta of Guadalupe." Tom Walsh seems to find her acceptance of Gamio's (and other Marxists') views surprising and finds her reference to Christ as a "magnificent Egoist" particularly incredible.[4] His reason for this surprise is that she had been raised a

Methodist and converted to Catholicism. Yet that can equally well be seen as the explanation. Her Catholicism was a vestige of a marriage she would have preferred to forget, and the Methodists of her childhood would have regarded Catholicism as anathema. Her rejection of the Church as she saw it in Mexico, then, is another act in the drama of her conflicted Texas past.

Porter would avow an anticlerical position explicitly in "The Mexican Trinity," published in August 1921, where she points precisely and correctly to three destructive forces contending for dominance in Mexico: an invading horde of capitalists, mainly oil interests; the Catholic Church, plotting with any and all for a return to power; and Spanish hereditary landowners, whom she pronounces a "scourge." Caught among these enemies of reformed Mexico she sees a native bourgeoisie confident in big business, the practical middle-leftists of the Obregón government trying to address present needs, a few idealistic radicals, and, trapped without a voice, the "inert and slow-breathing mass" for whose sake futile efforts at land redistribution have been made. Although Porter sometimes overestimated her own political acumen, her analysis in "The Mexican Trinity" is impressive, especially considering she had been close to the subject for only eight months.

Her position on the Church in Mexico was asserted even more forcefully in a set of notes she made while visiting the village of Teotihuacán, where Gamio was conducting excavations of Aztec ruins. (These same excavations, interestingly enough, appear in Barbara Kingsolver's 2009 novel *Lacuna*.) Although her notes on the visit to the excavations were never polished and published in their own right, Porter used excerpts from them in "Where Presidents Have No Friends" (1922) and her magnificent story "Flowering Judas" (1930). Focusing especially on the ornaments of an old church in the village, which included a figure of the dying Christ with "supporating [*sic*] wounds," she views the church as having been "wrung from the blood of the poor." The "accentuated insistence" on "physical torment" in such "awful, pallid blood streaked" figures strikes her as evidence of the Spanish Church's need to "compete" with the bloody rituals of the Aztecs by transforming the "so-called cannibalism" of their sacramental human sacrifices into the "subjective," or ritual, "cannibalism of . . . the body and blood eaten under a symbol of bread and wine" (*Uncol.* 102). Despite its efforts, Catholicism remained in her view "an alien faith" planted on top of the old. Like invaders everywhere, the Spanish "killed many of the people and enslaved the rest, and destroyed their temples. . . . And afterward they taught the Indians that statues could work charms, and relics could make magic; that Virgins painted on cloth" (a reference to the tilma magically painted with flowers in the miracle of

Guadalupe) "could speak, and little figures of wood could cure their sicknesses, and a man in a black dress could free their souls from sin" (105).

There is little record of Porter's political views before she went to New York in 1919 except for evidence that she supported woman suffrage, but her leftist principles far exceeded that support by the time she reached Mexico. Her early years there, when she believed she saw in Mexico the coming fulfillment of her hopes for a leftward turn in American political life, coincided with the period in her life when she was most sharply skeptical of religion and most closely associated with communism. Many years later she told Josephine Herbst that she had first wanted to go to Russia to get training in Marxist principles in 1917—that is, before she left Texas.[5] So early a date scarcely seems plausible. But in a letter to her father of June 26, 1931, she said that her sympathetic interest in Russia dated back twelve years. That would place its origins at 1919 or thereabouts, a dating that agrees well with a statement Porter made to Peggy Cowley in 1932 that she had been a communist by 1920. Even later, in 1935, she told Caroline Gordon that when she went to New York in 1919 she ran with a crowd who had been to Russia and proclaimed over and over that a communist revolution would soon come to America. Clearly her friends in New York during those days, both American and Mexican, held socialist and revolutionary sympathies.[6]

Yet the taproot of Porter's leftist politics may have gone deeper than the influence of her New York acquaintances, into Texas soil. During her childhood and almost until the time she made her definitive departure, in 1918, central Texas was (surprisingly enough, from today's perspective) the ground of a lively radical ferment, especially among the German communities. In the 1890s the impetus for this radicalism came from the populist movement, stronger in Oklahoma than in Texas but appealing to small-scale Texas farmers such as her father. Some 40 to 45 percent of all votes cast in Indian Creek precinct throughout the 1890s were for the Populist Party.[7]

After the turn of the century, populism joined with labor unrest to form a socialist drive lasting well into the 1910s. Two socialist-oriented newspapers—*The New Era*, beginning about 1904, and *The Rebel*, beginning in 1911—were published in Hallettsville, seventy miles southeast of Kyle. *The Rebel* maintained a circulation of around eighteen thousand until 1917, when the Post Office suppressed socialist publications throughout the country. It is impossible to know whether Porter ever saw these papers, but having turned ten in 1900 she was of an age to be at least somewhat politically aware during the full span of Socialist Party activity in Texas. According to James R. Green in *Grass-Roots Socialism*, in the years leading up to World War I the American Socialist Party had its "strongest grass-roots support" (xi) in Oklahoma, Texas, Arkansas, and Louisiana. Porter once told Kenneth Durant, director of the ROSTA (later TASS) bureau in New York, that her father took her to hear Eugene V. Debs, perennial Socialist Party presidential candidate, when she was fourteen. Debs did make speaking tours through Texas in 1902, 1904 (the year she was fourteen), and in 1908, fourteen years after the birthdate she usually claimed. It seems unlikely that she was referring to the 1908 tour, however, since she was married by then. There was also agitation by the Socialist Party and the Industrial Workers of the World (IWW; "Wobblies") around Lufkin when Porter and her family were living there at the time of her marriage, as well as in western Louisiana, where she and John Koontz lived until 1908. It is worth noting, too, that Texas socialists supported the "class-conscious revolutionaries" Emiliano Zapata and Pancho Villa in Mexico and that *The Rebel* compared exploitation of the rural poor in Texas to exploitation of "peons" in Mexico. None of this shows conclusively that Porter's leftist politics were formed in Texas, before her 1918 departure, but it is clear that sufficient shaping factors were in place.

Her sympathies were strongly with the revolution and with Obregón from the time she arrived in Mexico in 1920. The first issue of the business magazine she had been hired to launch, *The Magazine of Mexico* (dated December 1920 but not actually published until March 1921), featured a picture of Obregón on the cover and an article by Porter praising his practical leadership qualities, peaceful principles, and "passion for setting disorder to rights" (*Uncol.* 53). Even after she began to take a more disillusioned tone, by 1923 she still praised the "noble simplicity" of Obregón's vision for Mexico. She may have overidealized him; he was a pragmatic leader who courted American business and official U.S. recognition even while bringing radical pro-labor leaders like Morones into his government. In "Why I Write about Mexico" (*Century* 1923) she characteristically asserted things she did not know, such as that Obregón supported land redistribution; he was in fact holding the redistribution mandated by the 1917 constitution to a slow pace. Her praise merits quoting, however, for what it shows of the idealism of her politics and her aspirations for Mexico:

> They all are convinced, quite simply, that twelve millions of their fifteen millions of peoples cannot live in poverty, illiteracy, a most complete spiritual and mental darkness, without constituting a disgraceful menace to the state. They have a civilized conviction that the laborer is worthy of his hire, a practical perception of the waste entailed in millions of acres of un-

tilled lands while the working people go hungry. And with this belief goes an esthetic appreciation of the necessity of beauty in the national life, the cultivation of racial forms of art, and the creation of substantial and lasting unity in national politics.

As a nation, we love phrases. How do you like this one? "Land and liberty for all, forever!" If we needed a fine ringing phrase to fight a war on, could we possibly improve on that one? (*CE* 415)

Her endorsement of Mexico's prospects not only for its own people but as a potential model for the United States stands in striking contrast to her contemporary Walter Prescott Webb's placement of Mexicans "on the fringes" of society.[8] Porter's first stay in Mexico ended in episodes that sound almost like comic melodrama, though they involved real danger. On her thirty-first birthday, May 15, 1921, Obregón decreed that Bolsheviks and foreigners who interfered in the government would be expelled. Roberto and Thorberg Haberman went into hiding, and Porter realized she was at risk (*Illusion* 41). What caused her the most anxiety was her role in exposing a convoluted bit of intrigue against the Obregón government sometimes called the "Oaxaca conspiracy." She had seen and secretly copied some letters addressed to anthropologist William Niven and had then revealed what they contained to Paul Hanna, a writer for the *Nation,* and possibly also to Joseph Retinger, a political adventurer from Poland with whom she had had a desultory affair. The letters implicated General Sidronio Méndez in the conspiracy. Retinger had connections with Luis Morones, so telling him was virtually telling the regime. Porter's belief in Obregón would have sufficiently motivated her to betray the plotters, but she may not have anticipated what would happen to them: Méndez and several other officers were executed. Tracing the episode in exhaustive detail, Walsh provides compelling evidence that she suffered from guilt for years afterward (*Illusion* 22–24, 44–46).

Only a month after the deportation edict the minister of education, José Vasconcelos, offered her a job as dance teacher at several girls' schools. Still nervous about staying, however, she appealed to Kitty and Garfield Crawford for train fare to Fort Worth. The Crawfords invited her into their home on Lipscomb Street, on the city's South Side, and Garfield hired her to work for the *National Oil Journal* and the *Fort Worth Record,* where she wrote a shopping column. After Kitty introduced her to members of the Vagabond Players, a little theater troupe that performed only a block or so from the Crawfords' house, she acted in two productions.[9] As a result, she fell into such an active social life that she wore herself down and was unable to complete any of the writing she had begun—a pattern that was to become familiar. At the end of the year the Crawfords provided her a train ticket to New York.

Porter stayed in New York only three months before leaving again for Mexico. Retinger had gotten her appointed to a team preparing an exhibition of Mexican popular arts; her particular charge was writing the English-language catalog. Diego Rivera was also working on the project, and in the introduction to her *Outline of Mexican Popular Arts and Crafts* she credits him, along with Adolfo Best Maugard and painter Xavier Guerrero, with having helped her develop her artistic sympathies.[10] Despite border delays, a major portion of the exhibit was shown in Los Angeles that fall. But the great value to Porter was the developing aesthetic sense she gained through immersion in a culture-specific art. She would soon produce several stories rooted in this aesthetic, set both in Mexico and in Texas.[11]

The first of these was "María Concepción," published in the respected magazine *Century* in December 1922. Invoking mysteries of race within the context of revolution, it portrays an indigenous culture being studied and inevitably corrupted by representatives of modernism. The primary intention of the story is not entirely clear. This may be because, though very fine, it is an early work and not fully controlled, or may be only an instance of Porter's characteristic art of ambivalence, leaving readers uncertain. It is not surprising, then, that critics differ in their readings of it. Unrue sees "María Concepción" as a story about the "difficulty" of "educating" or "civilizing" the Indian (*Truth* 107, 113). I see it very differently, as primarily a tribute to the strength and resistance of indigenous life in a Mexican culture centered on maternal power.

The title character is a devout Catholic who, unlike other women in her village, has been married by the priest. Yet she has failed to hold her husband, and her only child died four days after birth. By then the husband, Juan, had already gone off to the fighting with a young woman named María Rosa. When the two return María Rosa is pregnant, and Juan goes back to his previous job with an anthropologist named Givens (after William Niven, whose excavations Porter visited and whose letters she copied). Like many Anglos, Givens "liked his Indians best when he could feel a fatherly indulgence for their primitive childish ways." He enjoys telling "comic stories of Juan's escapades" (*CS* 7). Porter's narrative voice distances itself from such condescension.

When Juan and María Rosa's baby is born, María Concepción—whose powerful physique and Guadalajara origins are modeled on Diego Rivera's Indian wife, Lupe Marín—shows that she, at any rate, is not a woman to be condescended to. With her ever-present knife for slaughtering chickens for market, she kills her rival, then takes the baby as her own. Juan, having come home drunk while she was away, helps her hide the evidence of her guilt before the police arrive, and the other women of the village, even María Rosa's godmother, draw together and vouch for her. At the end of the starkly pictorial story we see María Concepción seated on the dirt floor of her house, the baby sleeping in the hollow of her crossed legs. Breathing slowly and deeply, hearing the sleeping Juan's slow breathing and the baby's faint breaths like "a mere shadowy moth of sound in the silver air," she is at one with her village and with life itself. The very earth beneath her seems to "swell and recede . . . with a limitless, unhurried, benign breathing" (CS 32).

~

Along with her great hopes for Mexico and her emergence as a writer, a third theme that characterized Porter's life in the 1920s was sexual profligacy. She was known to have had many affairs in Mexico with men involved in the arts and politics, including the powerful Morones and the puzzling Retinger.[12] Another was Nicaraguan poet Salomón de la Selva, the model for the sexually exploitative Carlos in "Virgin Violeta" (1924). According to Porter's friend Mary Doherty, this affair led to an abortion. The painter David Siqueiros reported that she had an affair with Diego Rivera, and she had romantic involvements of some sort with socialist politician Felipe Carillo Puerto and radical painter Xavier Guerrero, who seems to have proposed marriage.[13]

During the winter of 1922–23, in New York, Porter became engaged to an apparently quite eligible man named Sumner Williams but kept postponing the date. When she was invited back to Mexico in June to edit a special issue of the art magazine Survey Graphic, she went. This time, as she sporadically had been before, she was followed by U.S. Military Intelligence and written up in a file report stating, "While it is not known whether Miss Porter is a radical or not, it is believed she is more or less of a socialist" (Illusion 58)—an illustration of the fuzziness of political distinctions at the time. It was during this brief third visit that she developed her command of the art of caricature as practiced by José Clemente Orozco and the young Miguel Covarrubias. She drew on her newly heightened satiric techniques for "The Martyr" (1923), based primarily on Rivera, even while coauthoring a piece with him for the special issue.

Upon returning to New York in September, she broke off her engagement with Williams, only to become involved with a Chilean poet and graduate student eleven years her junior, Francisco Aguilera. Like de la Selva in Mexico, Aguilera wrote romantic poems to her. Once they became sexually intimate, however, he distanced himself, letting weeks pass in silence; then there was another rendezvous, another silence, and finally an end to it. Soon followed a single "night of happiness" with Aguilera's friend Alvaro Hinojosa (*Life* 100). One of these two involvements may—or then again may not—have left her pregnant. She told friends she was and that if the baby was a girl she would name her Miranda, the name by which Aguilera had called her; yet friends who saw her during the ensuing months said they saw no evidence of pregnancy. She spent the summer of 1924 in a farmhouse in Connecticut with friends Liza and John Dallett, but they were often away and she became lonely and depressed even though she was working well, writing book reviews and finishing "Virgin Violeta," which Carl Van Doren accepted for *Century*. She began to believe, not for the first time, that she was being visited by the spirit of her dead niece, Mary Alice. In December she wrote Genevieve Taggard that her baby had been born dead.

With these many sexual liaisons in mind, it is surprising to read Porter's statement that "you're brought up with the notion of feminine chastity and inaccessibility, yet with the curious idea of feminine availability in all spiritual ways, and in giving service to anyone who demands it" (*Conv.* 95). The evidence is overwhelming that she was never either chaste or inaccessible but rather was quite available in ways that were only remotely if at all spiritual.

In 1925, again trying to plot a course after returning to New York, she became increasingly friendly with Malcolm and Peggy Cowley, sisters Dorothy (founder of the Catholic worker movement) and Delafield Day, writer and political radical Josephine Herbst, Josie's soon-to-be husband novelist John Herrmann, and poet Allen Tate and his wife, novelist Caroline Gordon, devotees of the Old South. By the spring of 1926 she had met Ernest Stock, a twenty-five-year-old Englishman, former Royal Air Force pilot, and sometime painter knocking about Greenwich Village, and the two joined Herbst and Herrmann in rural Connecticut for the summer. Givner numbers Stock among Porter's marriages; Unrue does not. Either way, Porter soon became tired of "Deadly Ernest" and went back to New York but with a souvenir: gonorrhea. Treatment required removing her ovaries. She knew then that she would never have children but for years continued to pretend she had menstrual periods.

During the next few years, until she returned to Mexico in 1930 for her fourth and final period of residence there, Porter lived from one crisis to the next. She was now reviewing for high-quality outlets, the *New York Herald Tribune* and the *New Republic,* and writing thoughtful nonfiction pieces, often related to Mexico. Under a pseudonym she compiled a volume of published comments titled *What Price Marriage*—an ironic commission indeed. She also, in spite of her tie to

4. Katherine Anne Porter, age thirty-three, at Aztec ruins near Cuernevaca, Mexico, in 1923. Her fascination with Mexico and its artifacts would remain with her throughout her life. Katherine Anne Porter Papers, Special Collections, University of Maryland Libraries.

art rooted in its native soil, entered into a contract with Boni and Liveright toward the end of 1927 for a book that would take her far into unfamiliar territory, a biography of Puritan divine and witch hunter Cotton Mather. While in Massachusetts to do research for the biography, she participated in communist-organized protests of the execution of Nicola Sacco and Bartolomeo Vanzetti, proud anarchists whose conviction of murder on thin evidence had become a cause célèbre. Her notes on the experience would be excavated from her miscellaneous papers and published as *The Never-Ending Wrong* (1977) near the end of her life.

During this period Porter produced some of her finest stories: "Rope," "Magic," "The Jilting of Granny Weatherall," and "He," one of the stories that she told Texas novelist George Sessions Perry, in a 1943 letter, were set between San Marcos and Austin. "Granny Weatherall" is more difficult to place geographically, "Magic" is clearly set in New Orleans, though unnamed, and "Rope" draws on her summer in Connecticut with Ernest Stock.

After "Rope" was selected for a volume published by Macaulay, Porter signed on as a copyeditor with the publishing house and there met Matthew Josephson—staff editor, aesthete, and author of a biography of Emile Zola. She was thirty-eight, Josephson twenty-nine, married, and a father. An affair under such circumstances violated her nominal principles, but she shoved principles aside for three months before breaking it off.

∼

Ill and depressed, she was once again rescued by friends. Writer friends John and Becky Crawford solicited funds to provide her a year away in the hope that she would recover her health and return to writing. In March 1929 she gratefully sailed for Bermuda, where she swam, fished, bicycled, and rested while getting back onto the Cotton Mather project, for which she had accepted an additional $250 advance. But the work again stalled, and after six months she returned to New York and asked Liveright to stop announcing the book. She then turned to Harcourt, Brace, which gave her a contract for a volume of stories. That winter she wrote "Flowering Judas," one of her masterworks and the title story of the small volume that appeared in 1930.

For all the symbolism of its technique, "Flowering Judas" is a far more direct rendering of Porter's own experiences in Mexico than "María Concepción."[14] A particularly compelling treatment of covert violence threatening to boil over, it centers on the anxieties of an American woman named Laura caught in the political turmoil of Mexico City. Probably Porter's most celebrated single work, the beautifully crafted story is a superlative example of her pictorial method. At the same time, it draws indirectly on the Texas she would later write about autobiographically in her essay explaining, or purporting to explain, the genesis of "Noon Wine."

In "Flowering Judas," like "'Noon Wine': The Sources," latent violence is made visual and concrete in the real but also symbolic form of a gun. In neither work do we witness actual mayhem committed through the use of these weapons, but they give us, as the narrative voice in "Flowering Judas" says they give Laura, "uneasy premonitions of the future" (*CS* 91). Even before her quasi-suitor Braggioni, a dangerous man powerful in the Mexican revolutionary government, asks her (in effect, tells her) to clean his firearms, Laura feels "a slow chill, a purely physical sense of danger, a warning in her blood that violence, mutilation, a shocking death, wait for her with lessening patience" (*CS* 93).

Braggioni's attentions are a sinister and disturbingly ambiguous mix of desire and menace. "You think you are so cold, *gringita!*" he tells her. "Wait and see"

(*CS* 97). Sitting fatly spread on a straight chair, he serenades her, "O girl with the green eyes, you have stolen my heart away!" Although he "seems harmless" while singing, he readily owns that "a thousand women have paid" for the fact that a girl he was in love with once as a teenager had laughed at him (*CS* 99). At first as he sings to Laura he is wearing his pistols and ammunition belt, but then he spreads the "laden" belt across her knees for her to oil and load the pistols. As she wipes the shells with a cloth dipped in oil, he taunts her for claiming a devotion to the revolution despite having no lover caught up in the fighting. At that point Laura enacts a moment Porter would recall in "'Noon Wine': The Sources," where upon opening a closet one finds oneself "star[ing] down into the cold eyes of shotguns and rifles": she "peers down the pistol barrel" (*CS* 100). The echo is slight, easy to miss. Yet it makes the connection. In these few words Porter's imagination drew on memory to link Texas with Mexico, an actual experience with a fictional action.

When Laura "peers" into the barrel of the gun—which means, obviously, pointing it at herself—she is positioning herself as the classic female victim. A "long, slow faintness rises and subsides in her" while Braggioni goes on singing, "curv[ing] his swollen fingers around the throat of the guitar" in a quasi-murderous posture and "smother[ing] the music out of it." Then, speaking to her of the future of the revolution, he shares his repellent vision of what is to come: a time when "this world, now seemingly so composed and eternal, to the edges of every sea shall be merely a tangle of gaping trenches, of crashing walls and broken bodies."[15] Nothing in the text indicates that Braggioni is disturbed or horrified by the vision, but he abruptly becomes "restless" and stands up for Laura to give him the ammunition belt. Emboldened by "the presence of death in the room," she tells him, "Put that on, and go kill somebody in Morelia, and you will be happier" (*CS* 100).

After Braggioni leaves, Laura is aware that she has displeased him—a dangerous thing to do. Telling herself to "run while there is time" (*CS* 101), she nevertheless stays where she is, immobilized by conflicting impulses. That night, caught between the innocence of her victimhood and the knowledge that a prisoner to whom she earlier brought sleeping pills used them to kill himself, she dreams that, in an ambiguous, tightening circle of guilt, aggression, and death, the suicide twice calls her "Murderer" (102).

In both "Flowering Judas" and the later essay on the sources of "Noon Wine," violence is at once societal and domestic, deeply rooted in culture. According to Porter herself, "Flowering Judas" was written around the "central idea" of "self-delusion."[16] Perhaps she meant by this not only the delusive belief that she could absolve herself of Texas and her life there by escaping but also the futility of trying to escape violence itself.

∾

When Porter departed for Mexico again in the spring of 1930 it was without her usual zest for a getaway. She had had a difficult winter, including broken ribs suffered during a night of carousing, and she was feeling pressured to complete work for which she had accepted advances—$500 from Harcourt, Brace for a novel and another $180 from Liveright to resurrect the Cotton Mather project. At first she moved into a small house in Xochimilco with Dorothy Day but quickly changed her mind and rented a house in Mexico City. There she met twenty-six-year-old Eugene Pressly, who became her lover and eventually her fourth (if our count is correct) husband.

Earlier in the decade she had seen Mexico as the locus of a dreamed-of new political order actually coming into existence. She was troubled by the persistence of the Indians' consignment to an inferior status despite the vision of an equality in *mestizaje* espoused by artists and intellectuals, and she aggressively deplored the clinging to power and wealth on the part of the Spanish elite who were resistant to that vision, but she supported the aims of the revolution. As late as 1926 she expressed her support in a *New York Herald Tribune* review of a volume of letters written from Mexico by Rosalie Caden Evans, a Texas woman who had married a British owner of several haciendas acquired during the Díaz regime. The haciendas were confiscated for redistribution under Carranza, and Evans spent her life subsequent to her husband's death trying to get his property back. She was shot from ambush in 1924.

Porter sarcastically conjectured in her review that the reason for publishing the volume must have been to "present" Evans as a "martyr to the sacred principles of private ownership of property." Actually, she asserted, the woman was driven by "avarice," was "ruled by a single-minded love of money and power," and her mind was never touched by a "single glimmer of understanding of the causes of revolution or the rights of the people involved." By dying in an attempt to regain private property, Porter wrote, Evans gave her life for "a grotesque cause" (*CE* 416–26). The intensity of these pronouncements conveys her commitment to the cause of Mexico's revolutionary plan of redistributing large landholdings but may also have been driven in part by the fact that this troglodyte was a sister Texan. In excoriating the "avaricious" Mrs. Evans, Porter showed that she could still justly claim the title socialist or communist, small-c, as well as advocate for "the wronged, the disinherited, the endlessly exploited."[17]

By 1930 all that had faded. The revolution now seemed to her to have degenerated into a cynical sellout. Back in Mexico for her fourth stay, she launched into heavy socializing to distract herself from both the disappointment of her political hopes and the work she had obligated herself to produce. Frustrated and unhappy, lashing out at everyone she knew, she began to fantasize about making a life in the Old South—to the point that she wrote to Caroline Gordon and Allen Tate to begin landscaping a spot on their property in Tennessee where she might build a cabin. This plan evaporated when in March 1931 she received news that she was being awarded a Guggenheim Fellowship of $2,000 for a year in Europe. She was especially heartened because she was now making some progress on her family-history novel. With the arrival of poet Hart Crane, however, the project again sputtered and died. Crane generated disorder all around him.[18] When he seduced her houseboy, her existing dislike of homosexuals took on a new intensity.

Porter's last significant act before leaving Mexico at the end of the summer was a three-day visit to a pulque plantation where the Russian director Sergei Eisenstein was filming material for *Que Viva México!* Her experience there would yield the novella "Hacienda," a work permeated by disillusionment.

"Hacienda" was first published in 1932 as a nonfiction piece, then in 1934 as a limited edition short novel, and finally in *Flowering Judas and Other Stories* in 1935. In a sense, these are two entirely different works with a common title. According to Porter, the first, considerably the shorter, was an article, not a piece of fiction at all. As reprinted in *Uncollected Early Prose,* edited by Alvarez and Walsh, it is a mere twelve pages long. The second version, clearly a work of fiction though extrapolated from fact, takes up thirty-five pages in the *Collected Stories.* The version published as a freestanding volume by Harrison of Paris was this expanded and fictionalized version of the material. It is obvious that Porter greatly reworked the material after the first version was published in *Virginia Quarterly Review,* though both grew from the same source, her visit to the mescal hacienda Tetlapayec in July 1931 to see Sergei Eisenstein filming material that came out as *Thunder over Mexico.*

Both versions of "Hacienda" open with the narrator, Porter herself, on a train to Tetlapayec. By happenstance, Hunter Kimbrough, the business manager of Eisenstein's film project and the brother of Upton Sinclair, who was investing in the film, is also on the train. In the first version he is called K——; in the second, Kennerly. Both K—— and Kennerly are accurate portraits of the real Hunter Kimbrough, who was hypochrondiacal and constantly feared catching some disease in Mexico. The opening sentence of the fictional version captures his distaste: "It was worth the price of a ticket to see Kennerly take possession of the railway train among a dark inferior people" (*CS* 135). In both versions, as in fact, he is just returning from a trip back to California ("God's country," he says) and is bringing packaged foods and drinks that he can believe are clean. Conspicuously nervous, he attributes his state of mind to the people he has to deal with: "'It's these Mexicans,' he said as if it were an outrage to find them in Mexico. 'They would drive any man crazy in no time'" (*CS* 139). Porter's detached narrative style in reporting this, like her detached narrative voice in "That Tree" and other satiric stories she wrote about Mexico, is a distancing technique that reveals her own views as being quite different.

When the train reaches the next-to-last stop before the hacienda, a Mexican youth playing the main character in the segment Eisenstein is now filming gets aboard to alert Kennerly and Andreyev, an assistant to Eisenstein, that there is a problem. One of the peons being featured in the film killed his sister during the noon break that very day and ran away through the fields but was chased down and arrested. Such a killing did in fact occur during Eisenstein's filming at Tetlapayec. Whether it happened the day Porter arrived, as she seems to claim, or she heard about it after the fact, she uses it as a central driving action in both versions. Kennerly's reaction when told about the killing makes her point about the exploitative Anglos' attitudes toward the peons: "My God, we're ruined! His family will have a damage suit against us!" (*CS* 147).

They arrive at Tetlapayec to find the hacendado, Don Genaro, away trying to get the killer released so filming can continue. We can guess that he would probably have found a reason to be out in his car anyway, running others off the road, because "speed and lightness at great expense was his ideal." Soon, however, he returns, "in a fury" because the judge has refused to release the boy until an inquest can be held unless Don Genaro gives him a bribe, which he refused to do because then there would be no end of it. "I told him," he says, "Justino is *my* peon, his family have lived for three hundred years on our hacienda, this is MY business . . . and all you have to do with this is to let me *have* Justino back at once" (emphases added; *CS* 155). This is postrevolutionary Mexico and yet, as Andreyev remarked back on the train, "Nothing has changed, nothing at all!" The same point is made at the end when an Indian driver taking the narrator back to the train station tells her wistfully that she should come back in about ten days because "then the green corn will be ready, and ah, there will be enough to eat again!" (*CS* 170).

Porter wrote Dorothy Day in 1930 that during her first days in Mexico she had felt like Eve in a kind of Eden—a new being in a newly made world. In

5. Katherine Anne Porter with Indian children at Xochimilco, Mexico, in 1931. Despite her disillusionment with Mexico's social revolution, she fantasized about living in an idyllic adobe house in Amecameca, perhaps much like this one. "This, no matter what end is prepared for me in the stead [*sic*], is my dream" (*Illusion* 47). Katherine Anne Porter Papers, Special Collections, University of Maryland Libraries.

1931 she wrote Dorothy's sister Delafield that Mexico had become an awful place.[19] She had come to regard it as, in Unrue's words, "a land of death and corruption and vanished promises" (*Life* 131). The peons in "Hacienda" are still landless and hungry, the hacendado still regards them as property, and his wife, Doña Julia, calls them "animals" (*CS* 169).

Porter's dream of an egalitarian socialist society was not unusual among certain classes of Americans in the 1920s. Such a dream would become even more common in the 1930s as artists and intellectuals in great numbers came to identify themselves with a politics of the left in general and communism specifically. The precise depth of Porter's commitment to communism during these decades is hard to estimate, but until as late as 1938 (*Illusion* 195) she referred to herself in letters as a fellow traveler.

In accordance with requirements of the Mexican Constitution (later rescinded),

Obregón's presidency had ended in 1924 after a single term. Distracted by the need to balance factions, his effort to gain U.S. recognition for the revolutionary government, and having to lead the military suppression of a rebellion toward the end of his term, he left office without advancing very far toward his goals beyond providing a degree of stability after years of turmoil. Elected president a second time in 1928, he was assassinated before he could take office. Porter saw all this as the betrayal of the revolution. Land reforms, nationalization of both the oil industry and the electrical power industry, and increased support for public education would in fact be achieved under the presidency of Lázaro Cárdenas beginning in 1934. By then she was in Europe and taking little heed of Mexico.

～

Porter's writing about Mexico constitutes a sizable body of her work: six published stories beginning with "María Concepción" in 1922 and including the long story "Hacienda," various scraps of uncompleted fiction, newspaper reports and columns, book reviews, the introduction to the folk art exhibit, and several literary essays, including "The Fiesta of Guadalupe" and a late, important piece that defies classification, "St. Augustine and the Bullfight." Virtually all of these bear the marks not only of her conflicted feelings about the Mexican Revolution but often her conflicted feelings about Texas as well.

Alongside her sense of the Mexican Indian as an eternal victim, this major body of work reveals her hope for the success of the revolution linked to her fear of its failure, her respect for the greatness of some of its leaders and artists alongside her dismay at what she saw as a prevailing veniality and foolishness, and always the tense coexistence of beauty with violence. This tension, which would wind its way through her memories of Texas as recorded in "'Noon Wine': The Sources," darkens her sharply pictorial "Notes on Teotihuacán," where rosebushes bloom in a "desperate fecundity" alongside a boy "leaning on a double-barrelled shot gun," and "Flowering Judas," with its lush flowers juxtaposed with Laura's "peer[ing] down the pistol barrel."

One aspect of Porter's experience in Mexico that we might expect to be entirely unalloyed by disillusion was her involvement with the art community there. As Walsh points out, though, she had reservations about the feasibility of plans formulated by Diego Rivera, David Siqueiros, and Xavier Guerrero for a proletarian art to be pursued as a collective effort. In this and in other ways her communist sympathies came into conflict with her commitment to an individualistic fine art. Nevertheless, she greatly admired the public art fostered by the government-sanctioned mural movement, most notably Rivera's but also murals by Siqueiros and the "caustic" Orozco (*Illusion* 66). "Wall art" was a genuinely indigenous form. Pulque shops in Mexico City and elsewhere in Mexico often had walls covered with painted caricatures. At the popular Los Monotes these had been done by Orozco and the clever teenager Miguel Covarrubias, still only eighteen when his caricatures began appearing in *Vanity Fair* in 1923. She was also acquainted with Jean Charlot, who like Rivera had trained in France before returning to Mexico; José Vasconcelos, who as minister of education and fine arts commissioned numerous public murals celebrating the prehistoric past of the Indian population; and American photographers Edward Weston and Tina Modotti. (Modotti gave Porter one of her cameras when she left Mexico for Russia.) In short, it would seem that Porter was at the center of an exceedingly creative period in western hemispheric art. Yet she was probably, in fact, more at the fringe. In Rivera's autobiography *My Art, My Life* she barely appears.

Rivera had returned to Mexico in 1921 after years of apprenticeship in France shortly before a nervous Porter fled to Fort Worth. When she came back in 1922 to work on the traveling exhibition of folk art, J. H. Retinger took her to Rivera's studio to watch him work on figures for his Creation mural, for which his noted model, lover, and second wife, Guadalupe Marín, was posing. Soon Porter was mixing paint for him—as did many female admirers; the term was sometimes used as a euphemism. Strangely, so far as I know Porter never mentioned Frida Kahlo except in a letter of February 18, 1931, to Peggy Cowley where she reported Kahlo's marriage to Rivera. Her relative silence may have indicated another of the many awkwardnesses caused by Rivera's amorous life, since Porter had greatly admired Lupe Marín and had at least once, along with her romantic interest at the time, Salomón de la Selva, spent a night of drinking and dancing with Marín and Rivera.

Her admiration for Rivera's work entered several of her early nonfiction pieces. In a letter incorporated into a short article published in the *Christian Science Monitor* in 1922 she called him "one of the great artists of the world" and said that when she stood and looked at his fresco at the National University she was certain that she was "in the presence of an immortal thing" (*Uncol.* 133). She declared that it was he who initiated the revolution in Mexican art. Nevertheless, even while she was working with Rivera and praising him, she used him as a target for satire, drawing on techniques of caricature that she had learned in Mexico.

Rivera is transparently caricatured in her short story "The Martyr" in the figure of a grossly overweight artist named Rubén, a story of tumultuous love drawing on what Porter had observed of Rivera's relationship with Lupe Marín. The story opens with Rubén, the "most illustrious painter in Mexico," delightedly in love with a woman named Isabel and making drawings of her for his mural, as Rivera did of Marín. As Rivera seems to have been even at that early date, Rubén seems jovially impervious to the fact that he is "getting fat" (CS 33). When a rival sells a painting for a large sum, Isabel leaves a note and goes off with him. Rivera seems to have lost a great deal of weight at the time Marín left him, but Rubén, quite the opposite, continually weeps and eats—plateful after plateful, sweet after sweet, until "layers of fat piled insidiously upon him" and he "bulged until he became strange even to himself." But still he ate and drank wine until after some weeks of this, at the Little Monkeys, Porter's name for Los Monotes, he stands up from a dish of tamales and pepper gravy, makes "rather an impressive gesture," and dies. The friend who comes to interview the owner of the Little Monkeys for Rubén's obituary says that the café will be "a shrine for artists"—and promises to mention the tamales. Since Los Monotes (sometimes translated "the big monkeys" or sometimes "the cartoons") was decorated in part by Orozco, who was not a friendly admirer of Rivera, and since the place was already known as a "shrine" famous for its tamales with chili gravy, the comic satire spins in many directions.

Porter wrote two other satiric stories of Mexico: "That Tree," caricaturing American writers and journalists who came to Mexico to live the easy primitive life but could not escape inevitable complications, and "Virgin Violeta," using details from her own romance with de la Selva to paint a repulsive example of male privilege. Like almost everything Porter wrote, both stories have autobiographical significance. "Virgin Violeta" incorporates, probably without intention, her anxiety about sex in her early life. "That Tree" not only sketches real people she met in Mexico but reveals her mixed feelings toward her father in the figure of the poet's father-in-law who "threatened constantly to come for a visit, in spite of Miriam's desperate letters warning him that the country was appalling, and the climate would most certainly ruin his health" (CS 74). But "That Tree" (published in 1934) also sadly and ironically anticipates Porter's later change in attitude toward Mexicans in the American wife's refusal to "have an Indian servant near her" because they were "dirty." When she wrote these words, Porter clearly intended them as a barb against the woman's unenlightened views. She had written with affectionate amusement about her own Indian housemaid's upward mobility in "Leaving the Petate," published in 1931. But on September 20, 1957, in another letter not included by Bayley, Porter expressed very much the same view as the wife in "That Tree." She wrote publisher Donald Elder (an editor and later vice president at Doubleday) that she might consider going to live in some "backward" country like Puerto Rico if it weren't for the natives; she couldn't bear the thought of having a native servant pick her bones clean, though at least Indians were better than Negroes.

At that moment she had returned to her Texas acculturation in race relations.

4
Recalling Childhood
Beauty, Death, and "The Old Order"

I am the grandchild of a lost War.
—Katherine Anne Porter, "Portrait: Old South"

Porter and Eugene Pressly sailed for Europe from Veracruz on August 22, 1931, aboard the German ship *Werra.* During the crossing she kept a journal-letter to Caroline Gordon, dotted with barbed descriptions of fellow passengers. This would become the germ of her novel *Ship of Fools,* where the *Werra* reappears as the *Vera.* Otherwise, she did not work during the voyage. Frustrated by her inability to complete her family-history novel, she must have found it irritating that Pressly was able to make progress on a manuscript of his own. He was translating José Fernández de Lizardi's 1816 picaresque novel *El Periquillo Sarniento,* sometimes rendered "The Mangy Parrot." His translation, touched up by Porter, would appear in 1942 over her name as *The Itching Parrot.*

When they bought their tickets on the *Werra,* the two had hoped to debark in France, but this proved impossible because of lack of visas. So they continued to Bremen as their booking indicated, then went on to Berlin. The following year, in October 1932, Porter would write Mary Doherty, back in Mexico, that they were "instantly bowed down" by the "tonnage of the German spirit," but her journal-letter to Gordon indicates that she at first "loved" the city and felt "at ease" there.[1] It is hard to know how much of her recoil into antipathy toward Germany and Germans reflected immediate impressions, how much arose from the depression she quickly fell into, or how much was a retroactive reconstruction.

Pressly helped Porter find lodgings, then left to look for work in Madrid, where his fluency in Spanish would be advantageous. She was left alone in a stuffy room in the house of a fussy older woman of reduced means. Although she made contact with the German Communist Party and developed a few acquaintances, she felt lonely and depressed by the postwar economic problems and resentments she saw around her. Her winter in Berlin was cold and gloomy

6. Katherine Anne Porter, age forty-one, aboard the *Werra* bound for Germany. Snapshot probably taken by Eugene Pressly. Inscription on the back reads, "On board ship, mid-Atlantic, sunset, September 1931." Katherine Anne Porter Papers, Special Collections, University of Maryland Libraries.

but relieved by some shopping and occasional nights out. One of these evenings out included a more or less date with Hermann Göhring, then a prominent member of the Reichstag, later commander of the Luftwaffe and Hitler's designated successor.[2] Her time in Berlin would go toward the making of "The Leaning Tower" but did not much advance the work she already had in hand.

After four months she left for Madrid to join Pressly, but stopped off in Paris on the way. After a few days of being shown the sights by a group including Ford Madox Ford, she went on to Madrid but at once decided that nowhere but Paris would be acceptable. On the strength of an offer of two weeks' work, Gene accompanied her back, but at the end of this short job he had to return to Madrid. On commission from Monroe Wheeler and Barbara Harrison, owners of the fine art press Harrison of Paris, she turned to the pleasant task of assembling a volume of old French songs translated into English to fit their original melodies. Her French not being very strong, the translations were probably provided by friends for her to touch up, just as "her" translation of *The Itching Parrot* was provided by Pressly. The songs made a fine volume that folksinger Pete Seeger, for one, used in performance for many years.

Porter finished the French song book during a stay in Basel, Switzerland, from June to December 1932. There she also gathered ideas that would ultimately shape *Ship of Fools* and resumed work on her family-history novel but

7. Snapshot of Porter at age forty-two taken by Eugene Pressly in Basel, Switzerland. The photo shows, once again, the extraordinary beauty of her profile. She would wear the same striking dress in one of the most familiar of the glamorous portraits of her made by George Platt Lynes in Paris. Katherine Anne Porter Papers, Special Collections, University of Maryland Libraries.

soon concluded that she would never be able to finish it. This conclusion proved, however, to be a positive one. She was able to identify six well-polished segments from the manuscript to pull out as short stories. These, plus an earlier-written seventh that was located among her papers many years later, made up the sequence of linked stories she titled, as a group, "The Old Order." Long undervalued because they were labeled "sketches," a less prestigious genre than stories, the seven look back at her childhood within a keenly sensed though unnamed Texas environment. When Porter wrote her introduction to Pressly's translation of *The Itching Parrot* in 1942, she called attention to the "extraordinary vividness" of Lizardi's writing even though it had "very little actual description." That assessment is precisely applicable to her own work at its best—and some of the "Old Order" stories are indeed among her best. Together with her later novella "Old Mortality," the sequence represents her deepest thinking about childhood in the narrow strip of central Texas where the outermost border of the South meets the Southwest.

Of fundamental importance in shaping Porter's sense of self, the borderland between East and West Texas also contributed to her ambivalence toward the state. Her own family had participated in a small way in bringing slavery to Texas, with consequences she could plainly see. In "'Noon Wine': The Sources" she states that from her earliest years she felt an anxiety springing from the pervasive taint of violence around her. Winston Bode recalled in the *Texas Observer* that when Porter addressed an Austin audience in 1958 she "remembered her people" as having a potential for violence that "broke through without warning" (*Conv.* 37). She also had to cope with an early and very personal awareness of death—her mother's death even before her first memories, the death of her grandmother that plunged her into insecurity, and if we are to believe "'Noon Wine': The Sources," a nearby murder. All this was added to an early awareness of Civil War deaths. Certainly her father and grandmother, and probably everyone she knew, mourned the "Lost Cause." Harrison was a member of the Travis Rifles, a group with traditional ties to the Confederacy, nominally committed to defending Southern values in Texas, and he once recalled in an undated letter that *his* father, Asbury Porter, was a Klansman during Reconstruction. South, race, violence, and death intertwine in Porter's life story.

If she recalled being frightened and repulsed by the "dreary" violence lurking just under the surface in central Texas, she was also quite conscious of the Old South's heritage of violence. Gary Ciuba observes that in chronicling the way her society replicated (though in shifting forms) its Southern past, Porter regularly reveals latent conflicts that threaten to lead to bloodshed. Overt violence is rarely enacted in her stories, but it is pervasively "covert" in them, just as it usually lay "below the surface of southern society" (60). Ciuba adds that the South "cultivated the Lost Cause" after the Civil War "through a recommitment" to its "bedrock" values (123)—an observation Porter confirms when writing, in "Portrait: Old South," that she was "the grandchild of a lost War" and her elders remained "nobly unreconstructed to their last moments" (*CE* 161). She is playing here on the word "Reconstruction," but the values from which they may have remained unreconstructed included standards of male honor that often led to vengeance and dueling. The violence inherent in the culture in which she grew up, then, was a factor of both frontier Texas and Southern tradition and pride.

Just as her world was divided geographically by the imaginary line between South and West, so was Porter herself divided between the South's traditionalism and an urge toward freedom. In her essay about "Noon Wine," even while revealing the violence and fear that could shatter a child's summer day or a woman's marriage, she directly praises "my own place, my South, . . . the native land of my heart" and in true Southern fashion refers to the Civil War as the "War Between the States" (*CE* 470). Yet the pattern of her life was a rebellion against the South's prescriptive ways and an affinity for ideas of freedom usually associated with the West—a rare but significant presence in her work.

In "The Journey," the grandmother's prospective daughter-in-law is characterized as a woman of the West, a tall, handsome, firm-looking young woman, with a direct way of speaking, walking, talking . . . self-possessed . . . [taking charge of] the wedding arrangements down to the last detail. . . . She had even suggested at the wedding dinner that her idea of a honeymoon would be to follow the chuck-wagon on the round-up, and help in the cattle-branding on her father's ranch. Of course she may have been joking. But she was altogether too Western, too modern, something like the "new" woman who was beginning to run wild, asking for the vote, leaving her home and going out in the world to earn her own living. (*CS* 333)

The negative terms in this passage—"altogether," "too," "run wild"—reflect the perspective of the grandmother, who finds this "modern" woman the antithesis of what she believes right and proper. The positive adjectives—"direct," "self-possessed," "modern"—reflect instead the controlling authorial perspective, Porter's own. The two clusters of thought exist together in a fine ironic balance, very much as Southern (traditional) and Western (modern, assertive) coexisted in Porter herself. At the dramatic end of the story the Southern grandmother enters her decidedly Western daughter-in-law's house elated by the clear, dry air and by her start toward reshaping things to suit herself and falls dead across the threshold. Emblematically, the old order yields to the new.

Catherine Skaggs Porter, the central female figure in Porter's early life, was the embodiment of that old order. A traditional Southern lady who had maintained her genteel class standards despite the post–Civil War economic collapse that forced her to scrimp and save, she both modeled and enforced propriety and "decency." The trip to the daughter-in-law's house in "The Journey" was based on an actual trip to Marfa and El Paso that Porter made with her grandmother. While there, Grandmother Porter died—but in bed, not over the threshold. The essay in which Porter wrote about the actual trip, "Notes on the Texas I Remember," is not nearly so subtle and perceptive as "The Journey," published some forty years before. It is most interesting, perhaps, precisely because it is so rambling and unreliable. She recalls that she and her grandmother traveled by train and, on the way, crossed the Pecos High Bridge. With characteristic inaccuracy she calls it the highest railway bridge in the world. It was in fact the third highest at the time. She also states incorrectly that it had been condemned for some years when she and Grandmother Porter crossed it. But it had been built only in 1892, nine years at most before she saw it, and it remained in use until World War II created a greatly increased need for transcontinental rail transport of heavy freight. In addition, Porter claims in her "Notes" that passengers had to get off and walk across the bridge. I have found no evidence of such a practice, but it was indeed customary, as she recalled, for the train to pause and then proceed slowly across—not for fear the bridge would collapse, as she implies, but to allow passengers to look down into the canyon to the river 321 feet below.

Porter's sketch of her grandmother in the essay "Portrait: Old South" shows her as wielding "matriarchal authority" in the household, dressing in an old-fashioned way, having a quick hand for punishment, and passing on a conviction that there was a right (and of course a wrong) way to do everything, from setting tables to sitting properly to imagining one's life course. One of the "right" principles of her grandmother's value system was that women should maintain at least an appearance of submissiveness to men. Not that she was a retiring blossom herself; however strongly she might insist on feminine meekness, she was a strong-willed, controlling presence who ran every aspect of family life, including business matters. She apparently accorded herself such unconventional liberties as smoking and taking nightly toddies. Moreover, Porter represents her as being deeply envious of "the delicious, the free, the wonderful, the mysterious and terrible life of men!" (CS 335). By her very existence, she authorized Porter to find her own way, even while punishing her for doing so. Aunt Cat's importance as a role model and Porter's wish to emulate her, at least in some ways, are evident in her habit of referring to herself in letters to her niece Ann as Aunt Kat.

Porter also had other models of Southern womanhood in childhood. Her aunt Annie Porter Gay, a sister of her father's whom she knew only in family legend, was reputed to have been a great beauty and was apparently held up as a standard for younger girls in the family to emulate. Annie impulsively married a "dashing young man who owned a string of racehorses" (KAP 55) and died of mysterious causes only four months later, thus fulfilling the height of pathos as defined by the South's favorite poet, Edgar Allan Poe. The Aunt Amy of "Old Mortality" is clearly a fictional version of this beautiful aunt. She, too, marries unwisely, though not so much impulsively as willfully, and dies in mysterious circumstances soon after the wedding, prompting this bit of graveyard poetry written by her grieving husband:

She lives again who suffered life,
Then suffered death, and now set free
A singing angel, she forgets
The griefs of old mortality. (CS 181)

These lines were in fact written by Porter's father for his sister Annie's, or Anna's, headstone. Unrue notes that Porter avoided admitting that both her parents were given to writing graveyard verse. The fact that they did so demonstrates the pervasiveness of their culture's sentimentalizing of death and of women, as well as the closeness of its impression on Porter.[3]

Another role model was cousin Anna Laredo Bunton, named for the border town where she was born but called "Lady" Bunton. She was the daughter of Aunt Cat's daughter Belle, who had married into a prosperous West Texas family presumably connected to some Buntons who settled at Mountain City, Hays County, about the same time as the Porters. Belle died not long before Callie's mother (Barkley 139). Despite living far away in West Texas, Lady Bunton attended the Coronal Institute in San Marcos, Mary Alice's school, and came to Kyle for weekend visits. She, too, appears in "Old Mortality," both individually— as Cousin Isabel, with her fine black hair, creamy white skin, and grace as a horsewoman—and generalized to a group of unnamed "dashing young ladies" who "came visiting from school for the holidays, boasting of their eighteen-inch waists" (CS 174). Miranda, eight years old at the opening of "Old Mortality," hopes to be exactly like Cousin Isabel when she grows up, even though her short stature, coloration, freckles, and volatile disposition mean that it would take a miracle for her to "grow into a tall, cream-colored brunette, like cousin Isabel." In case she does, she means "always to wear a trailing white satin gown" (CS 175–76).

Yet another model of feminine elegance in Porter's extended family was Ione Porter, the young wife of Porter's considerably older uncle Newell, a gambler whose luck was usually good and who liked to buy her presents. Tante Ione, as she liked to be called, had lived at a New Orleans convent prior to becoming Newell's bride. She served as a source for Maria's and Miranda's attendance at a convent school in Part Two of "Old Mortality." Combined with Aunt Annie Gay in the character of Aunt Amy, Ione enjoyed showing her elaborate wardrobe and jewelry to her young nieces, who wished they could have a similar life.

These four women—Grandmother Porter, Aunt Annie Gay, Lady Bunton, and Ione Porter—provided the young Callie Porter her ideas of the woman she hoped to be, just as the characters based on them in Katherine Anne's stories serve Miranda (KAP 55–58). They were also appropriated by Porter in supposedly factual autobiographical statements that greatly misrepresented her early life.

Grandmother Porter's conflicting facets were not the only directly contradictory models of womanhood held up to Porter in childhood. Another, very important model was Grandmother Porter's sister Eliza, apparently depicted with

close fidelity in the Great Aunt Eliza of "The Fig Tree." Like her fictional portrait, Porter's great-aunt does seem to have taken an interest in scientific learning
and to have cared not at all for propriety. A woman of inquiring mind—and, it
has been reported, sticky fingers for the belongings of others—might not have
been an acceptable role model in Porter's eyes had it not been for her father's
sometimes aggressive freethinking, which made such attributes interesting. In
disregard of societal norms, Harrison Porter allowed Callie to dress in sturdy
boys' clothes in the summertime and ramble freely, barefoot.

Even then, however, enjoying her quasi-boyish freedom when school was
out, Porter wished to grow up to be beautiful and ladylike. This was not surprising, given that her beautiful aunts and cousin provided a strong contrast to
the women she usually saw in rural central Texas—dowdy drudges like the old
women in "The Grave" who smoke corncob pipes (CS 365) and class-conscious,
studiously proper women like Grandmother Porter, who never left the house
without her black dress and gloves. Beauty was an unquestioned priority of the
higher social class Grandmother had enjoyed before the war and struggled to
maintain, at least to some degree. Her traditionalism is reflected in the Miranda
stories in the requirement, for example, that the little girls wear sunbonnets to
keep from getting tanned or freckled during their summer visits to the farm.
The Miranda of "The Grave," with her "gray eyes" like those of Pallas Athene
representing wisdom or a bent toward thinking, is of two minds about her prospective womanhood. She likes rambling around in overalls and straw hat, shoot-
ing rabbits, but at times feels an unaccountable urge to bathe, dress up in her
"most becoming" dress with a sash tied around her waist, and "sit in a wicker
chair under the trees," acting out a more ladylike role (CS 365).

Porter's wish for feminine beauty was driven not only by her awareness of social class and her grandmother's strictures about ladylike behavior but also by her
wish to be admired and loved by men. At its origin, this was specifically a wish
to believe that her father loved her. The extremity of Harrison Porter's withdrawal into grief after his wife's death was irresponsible in that it led him to ignore his children, but beyond that, his outbursts that they were to blame for their
mother's death and he wished they had never been born were cruel. And the ar-
bitrariness with which he occasionally provided some semblance of love made
it worse than none at all. This is precisely how the father figure is seen in "Old
Mortality" and "The Old Order." Miranda and her older sister Maria yearn for
fatherly attention, but their "pleasant, everyday" father "held his daughters on
his knee if they were prettily dressed and well behaved, and pushed them away
if they had not freshly combed hair and nicely scrubbed fingernails. 'Go away,

you're disgusting,' he would say, in a matter-of-fact voice" (*CS* 184). Accordingly, in "Old Mortality" we see Miranda and Maria sitting dressed up and behatted, waiting for a fatherly visit that may or may not come. Porter's experience of an unreliable father-love dispensed, if it was at all, on the basis of whichever of his little girls looked prettiest at the time was almost surely one reason for her disordered relations with men. For the rest of her life she was burdened by "an insatiable hunger for masculine admiration" (*KAP* 51) that led to emotional instability and promiscuousness.

Despite her conflicting notions as to who she should be and who she wanted to be, and despite her ingrained desire to emulate the family beauties who populated her grandmother's stories and occasionally popped in on her childhood, Callie Porter displayed an independent mind early on. If we can trust her various reminiscences, she not only wrote and stitched together little books and once announced that she wanted to be that socially unacceptable professional woman, an actress, she and her friends played Joan of Arc complete with a stake and rode pigs for bucking broncos. This does not mean that she entirely rejected Grandmother Porter's standards of propriety—though as Jane DeMouy argues she *had* to resist, if not reject, them if she was to gain "independence for the sake of her art" (7). It means that she preferred emulating the more liberated aspects of her grandmother's behavior. As she wrote in "Portrait: Old South," her grandmother was "an individual being if ever I knew one" (*CE* 164). She, too, would be an individual being.

Complicating this tension over gender roles was the transitional ambiguity of "having been bred to the manners of the South" at a time when "that culture was already receding before a new, faster, and cruder century" (DeMouy 7). The West had quite other implications to offer a child growing up female in Texas—implications alluded to in "The Journey" in the figure of the West Texas daughter-in-law with her own ideas. Just as Porter's early childhood was positioned on the geographical border between South and West, so was her sense of self positioned on the gender border between elegant femininity and vigorous independence. The duality remained with her into her maturity. Only after long reflection was she able to explore, by way of Miranda, her own conflicted process of female identity formation within a male-dominated and sometimes violent culture.

Her stretching of the truth when she did so has been a thorny issue. When Larry McMurtry called her "genteel to the core" in the *Texas Observer* in 1981, he did not mean it as a compliment. His phrasing hints at such qualities as effeteness, insecurity and envy about class, and perhaps attempted social climbing. Don Graham calls the statement "hopelessly off base" yet also concedes that she "ratchet[ed] up the social level" of her family by several notches (*Giant Country* 88–89). Porter's embroidering of her social status can be overstated; she never actually claimed her immediate family had wealth. She did, however, let people believe she was raised in the "decayed splendor of an earlier age" that *had* been affluent. In her 1963 *Paris Review* interview, she famously said that she belonged to "the guilt-ridden white-pillar crowd" (*Conv.* 83). Even to her close friend Josephine Herbst she reminisced about life "at the plantation" with bath water brought to her bedroom by servants and stately dinners served in a beautifully paneled room (Porter to Herbst, April 16, 1930). Herbst's reply puzzled over whether New Orleans was really a part of the Old South in the first place and how it was that Porter claimed such a background when she had spent most of her early years in Texas, which certainly, in her view, did not count as part of the Old South. When Robert Penn Warren was preparing to write a tribute after Porter's death, he was dismayed (having accepted her statements at face value) to find no records supporting various of her claims, including a Catholic schooling in New Orleans.[4] He was not the only friend to be led astray by such invented or highly revised memories. Yet her construction of a personal myth did usually have at least some basis in fact, even if only slight. For example, Unrue has found records supporting the claim of Catholic schooling in New Orleans but for only a couple of months at most (*Life* 31–32). The misrepresentation was not so much an invention out of whole cloth as a great exaggeration.

Clearly social class was a matter of deeply rooted anxiety for Porter. She greatly wished that she had been brought up in social circumstances appropriate for a true lady. Since she was not, she compensated by blurring the line between memory and imagination. She "remembered" going to concerts and plays as a child—a claim that knowledge of her location and the family's financial condition can only lead one to doubt. This matter of "high culture" is conjoined with the issue of social class in complicated ways. It is to high culture that James Tanner is referring when he identifies the "central tension" in Porter's work as "the conflict between the Texas Porter and the urbane-sophisticate Porter" (2), as if the two were mutually exclusive. Actually she was both at once—Texan *and* an "urbane sophisticate."

Similarly, Porter's noted ambivalence toward Texas has made it difficult to define her feelings toward home. Attempting to resolve the difference between her idealizations and her disaffection by invoking concepts of irony and satire, Graham writes that in "The Old Order" she "viciously caricatures Southern manners, Southern character, Southern narratives, the whole Southern mystique"

(*Texas* 66–67). Although Porter was indeed a master ironist and caricaturist, I doubt that many readers of the "Old Order" stories would agree. Graham himself—not alone among Porter's critics in finding himself of at least two minds about her—writes elsewhere that she rendered her grandmother's house and style of living in Kyle "*straight* out of southern plantation mythology" (*Giant Country* 88–89, emphasis added). If "straight," then not satiric. Her stories are sufficiently distanced in their perspective to see things clearly but not so distanced as to throw off the bonds of love.

We might better begin to think about Porter's ambivalence by noting that it was rooted both within herself and in the culture. The clash she perceived between the natural bounties of Texas and its pervasively violent tone is part of the explanation but not all of it. She felt very keenly the inconsistencies and conflicts of the geographic and cultural borderland she inhabited. She felt pulled back and forth between, on the one hand, a grandmother who expected her to adhere to standards of young womanhood carried forward from a more genteel society in the South and, on the other, a father who undermined those strictures by letting her run barefoot and free in the summer, who insisted that women should not have careers yet was pleased for her to support him during her mid-teens, who allowed her and Gay to perform in plays even though their grandmother had whipped Callie for expressing a desire to become an actress.[5] Tensions and ambiguities relating to racial difference pressed on her from every side as she was growing up. It is scarcely surprising that as an adult she was torn between yearnings for her home place and a pronounced disaffection from that same place.

∽

Pondering childhood and the culture in which she grew up in her essay "'Noon Wine': The Sources," Porter made a statement that is perhaps the primary key to her writerly method: "Endless remembering . . . must be the main occupation of the writer" (*CE* 468). The essay opens with a companion statement: "By the time a writer has reached the end of a story, he has lived it at least three times over—first in the series of actual events that, directly or indirectly, have combined to set up that commotion in his mind and senses that causes him to write the story; second, in memory; and third, in re-creation of this chaotic stuff" (*CE* 467). The process of memory is formulated somewhat differently in her narrative essay "St. Augustine and the Bullfight," where the terms "adventure" and "experience" lead to a similar conclusion, that adventure is what happens or what one does, often for no discernible reason, while experience is adventure recalled, reflected on, and interpreted. Its kernel of meaning is identified through a process of struggle and thought. In whichever formulation, the result is what we see in the "Old Order" stories, where her musings on childhood first bore artistic fruit.

The seven stories or sketches that comprise "The Old Order" give us Porter's clearest view of what it meant to her to grow up female on the cultural border between the South and the Southwest at a three-way intersection in time: a present always preoccupied with the past but awkwardly bumping up against it, questioning it, and a future beginning to make itself felt when women would be empowered in new ways. The sequence of linked stories is complex (in Porter's distinctive way of being complex, which was by seeming simple) both in substance and in its composition and publication history. After journal publication beginning in 1935, the initial six were first published together under their collective title in 1955 in the volume *The Old Order: Stories of the South from Flowering Judas; Pale Horse, Pale Rider; and The Leaning Tower.* Only with the award-winning *Collected Stories of Katherine Anne Porter* in 1965 did the sequence reach completion, when "The Fig Tree," published in *Harper's* in 1960, was slotted into place.

The form of "The Old Order" can be thought of as resembling a patchwork quilt, or perhaps a crazy quilt, in that it is made up of separate pieces dissimilar in size and texture, stitched together into an idiosyncratic whole. Popular during the late nineteenth century, the crazy quilt was a handcraft usually associated with female creativity and thus is a form well suited to this collection exploring the development of precisely that. And indeed in "The Journey," placed second in the final order, we see the grandmother and Aunt Nannie, her former slave, piecing crazy quilts, carefully lining them with silk, and laying them away for purposes they cannot clearly define. As they do, they piece together their memories.

The final ordering of the stories, with "The Fig Tree" added and Porter's vision of the sequence as a whole clarified, reflects neither their order of composition (to the extent that we know it) nor the order of first publication. Nor does it follow the chronology of the characters' lives. If the stories appeared in order of composition, "The Fig Tree" would probably be first; Porter's papers show that she submitted the story to the little magazine *Gyroscope* (edited during its brief life by the respected critic and teacher Yvor Winters and his wife, Janet Lewis) in late 1929, only to have it rejected. But in the final order it is next to last. If they were arranged in order of first publication, "The Grave" would be first rather than last; it appeared in April 1935, followed by "The Circus" in July of that year, and then "The Journey" (initially called "The Old Order," by itself),

8. Porter at age forty-five, stylishly dressed, in the garden of her Paris apartment, June 1935. Katherine Anne Porter Papers, Special Collections, University of Maryland Libraries.

"The Source," "The Witness," and "The Last Leaf," with "The Fig Tree" last. If the sequence were chronological according to the characters' lives, the order would be entirely different but impossible to determine. Not only are their ages less than entirely clear, but we would have to debate whether to go by the time at which they remember things or the time remembered. Both are fully integral to the stories. Unrue remarks that Porter's way of looking at the past was "nonlinear"—a term that nicely describes the handling of chronology in the sequence (*Life* 26). Its parts move back and forth in time in an order that teases out narrative relationships so that they comment on each other and make the past a real presence in the present.

In chronology of *remembered* time, the earliest event in any of the stories is Sophia Jane's wedding back in Kentucky, long before Miranda's birth. It is recalled as she and Nannie sit quilting in "The Journey," talking about "the past, really—always about the past" (*CS* 327). In the present-time of "The Journey," however, when the two old women sit talking and remembering, Miranda is about ten or eleven, considerably older than in some of the other stories. Both Sophia Jane and Aunt Nannie are also older here than in some of the others.

According to a chronology of fictional time-present, "The Journey" would appear somewhere after "The Fig Tree," where both old ladies are quite active, but before "The Last Leaf," where Aunt Nannie is seen still hanging on after the grandmother's death, still piecing quilts, though now in plainer patchwork.

In the order Porter finally settled on, the sequence opens with "The Source," whose title refers to the grandmother figure. She is both the family's biological source and its source of good order or authority. Following the grandmother's seasonal journeys between town and farm, the sketch establishes her as almost a principle of nature. Her yearly cycle is seen as a kind of ritual, a way of binding life together as if with back-and-forth stitches. "Once a year"—that is, every year—"in early summer, after school was closed and the children were to be sent to the farm"—as Porter and her siblings in fact were—"the Grandmother began to long for the country." A series of conditional verb forms then draws out the idea of recurrence: "she *would* ask," "she *would* remark," the children *"would* begin to feel the faint sure stirrings of departure," their father *"would* assume" an air of patience, the grandmother *"would* pack," and so forth. The regularity of this annual occurrence provides the children, Miranda and her brother and sister, a point of certainty in an uncertain world, their "only reality . . . in a world that seemed otherwise without fixed authority or refuge" (*CS* 324).

The same ritual journey structures "The Fig Tree," but Miranda is younger here, the youngest we see her at any point in the sequence, and it is she rather than Grandmother who is the story's center. "The Fig Tree" is a story of maturation in her awareness of the world around her and also a story of female emancipation. The first sentence tells us she is very young by the way she is being held between Aunt Nannie's knees, being dressed and groomed for the family's departure to the farm: "Old Aunt Nannie had a habit of gripping with her knees to hold Miranda while she brushed her hair or buttoned her dress down the back. When Miranda wriggled, Aunt Nannie squeezed still harder, and . . . gathered up Miranda's scalp lock firmly, snapped a rubber band around it, jammed a freshly starched white chambray bonnet over her ears and forehead, fastened the crown to the lock with a large safety pin, and said: 'Got to hold you still someways'" (*CS* 352). The gently humorous passage emphasizes containment; Miranda is as helpless in the grip of her elders as dough being kneaded. Throughout the "Old Order" sequence and the first two sections of "Old Mortality," where Miranda is shown as a school-age child, she will continue to "wriggle" in resistance to outside powers that try to pen, or pin, her in.

When released from Nannie's grip, Miranda "[gives] a little skip and [runs] away" while her elders finish collecting their gear. At this point, though the narrative is still from a slightly distanced third person, we stop seeing her from the outside and start seeing the adult world and the natural world around her as if through her eyes. The story enters her mind. An adult voice privileged to share the perceptions and thoughts of this small child reports them simply and directly through the filter of her non-understanding, so that we both share and observe her puzzlement. As Miranda goes "hopping zigzag" down a flagstone walk after she leaves Aunt Nannie, she finds a chick that doesn't run after its mother hen like the other chicks but lies "spread out on his side with his eyes shut and his mouth open" (CS 355). Recognizing death when she sees it, because the chick does not rouse even to the poke of a toe, she runs into the house for a shoebox, wraps the dead chick in the paper that had been around the shoes, and buries it, as is her custom with all dead things.

The adults are now ready to go, and using the old ploy of thoughtless adults everywhere when they try to hurry children, they tell her to come on *now* or she's going to be left behind. Not yet old enough to understand that grownups just talk that way, she takes them at their word. But at that very moment, still standing under the fig tree where she has buried the chick, she hears a "tiny sad voice" crying "weep, weep." Confused, not recognizing the sound but not wanting them to go without her, she runs to join her impatient elders, trying even as she does to reason it through: "Things didn't make sounds if they were dead. They couldn't. That was one of the signs. Oh, but she had heard it." She concludes that it must have been the chick she buried; it may not have been dead after all; she needs to rescue it. "She had to go back and let him out. He'd never get out by himself, all tangled up in tissue paper and that shoebox. He'd never get out without her" (CS 357). Crying hysterically, she demands that they stop and let her go back for something, but she is unable to give a coherent reason and the adults refuse. They try to distract her with promises of kittens to play with at the farm, but she is not to be consoled. She is carried off down the road, still crying, weighed down by what she believes to be her guilt.

At the farm, holding herself aloof in her guilt and resentment, she begins to notice gaps between what her elders say and what they do. She knows that old women exercise authority over children, telling them "all day long to come here, go there, do this, do not do that, and they were always right," yet she sees Grandmother and Great-Aunt Eliza "bickering like two little girls at school" (CS 359). She observes how different they are, her grandmother slim and graceful and pleasantly scented, as ladies ought to be—she "had always been the pretty one" and "was pretty still"—while Aunt Eliza "was not pretty now and never had been." So obese she nearly fills a door going into a room and chairs "disappear" under her when she sits down, Eliza constantly smells of the snuff that she dips not quite surreptitiously, and she violates good manners by bringing her microscope to the dinner table to examine the raisins in her pudding. The children would never be allowed to do such a thing. Nevertheless, with her newfound modicum of independent judgment, Miranda finds Great-Aunt Eliza interesting and begins to haunt her steps, curious about this unconventional great-aunt. The point is that though she needs information in order to puzzle out things like the "weep weep" sound, Miranda is beginning to think for herself. It is a point also made in the first part of "Old Mortality" when as a child of eight she again notices inconsistencies in what her elders say, the first step toward an ability to judge them.

In the end it is unmannerly, un-genteel, unfeminine Great-Aunt Eliza, a woman of scientific curiosity and an active mind along with a rebellious spirit, who releases Miranda from her mistaken guilt to a life of rationality and intellectual wonder. (The root meaning of Miranda is "to wonder," from the Latin *miror*, also the root of our word "miraculous.") When the family first drove up, Eliza had been up on a ladder overseeing the setting up of her telescope on top of a henhouse, and Grandmother had scolded her for failing to appreciate "appropriate behavior" at her age (*CS* 358). Hearing Eliza's pointed retort, Miranda had withheld judgment. But on the last night of the visit, when Eliza invites her to come up and look through the telescope, she eagerly goes up the ladder with her great-aunt to look at the moon and stars, and cries out in "pure rapture," "Oh, it's like another world!" Great-Aunt Eliza, in her "growling voice," answers, "Why, of course child, other worlds, a million other worlds." "Like this one?" Miranda asks. "Nobody knows, child" (*CS* 361). As they walk back to the house, Miranda sings it in her mind: "Nobody knows, nobody knows"—a liberating message that allows her to work out for herself what she believes rather than accept things on authority.

Yet even this gift of wonder is not all that the unconventional, snuff-dipping Eliza has to give. She also offers the gift of freedom through knowledge. Hearing the "weep weep" sound again as they are walking back from the henhouse, Miranda cries, "Oh, there's something saying 'weep weep' out of the ground!" Realizing she is too far from the house in town to be hearing the buried chick, she knows it has to be something else, though still the sound seems to come from "the smothering earth, the grave" (*CS* 361). But Eliza informs her "in her most scientific voice" that the "weep weep" is the sound made by tree frogs, which it seems are as much a part of the wonder of the natural world as the heavens above.[6] Receiving this information that frees her from her guilt, Miranda is "so dazzled with joy" that she falls back a moment before remembering, through her "fog of bliss," to thank her aunt (361).

Both in Miranda's determined activity in "The Fig Tree" and in her preference for withdrawing to herself to savor her delight, we see early indications of the independent mind and unwillingness to accept her society's expectations of passivity in girls and women that she will exhibit in other works. When she finds the dead chick, she makes a judgment based on experience of other dead things and at once sets out sturdily to do what is needed. No need to go find her brother or father to take care of things!

> Mama was dead. Dead meant gone away forever. Dying was something that happened all the time, to people and everything else. Somebody died, and there was a long string of carriages going at a slow walk over the rocky ridge of the hill towards the river while the bell tolled and tolled, and that person was never seen again by anybody. Kittens and chickens and specially little turkeys died much oftener, and sometimes calves, but hardly ever cows or horses. Lizards on rocks turned into shells, with no lizard inside at all. If caterpillars all curled up and furry didn't move when you poked them with a stick, that meant they were dead—it was a sure sign.
>
> When Miranda found any creature that didn't move or make a noise, or looked somehow different from the live ones, she always buried it in a little grave with flowers on top and a smooth stone at the head. Even grasshoppers. (*CS* 354)

These hints of her ability to make up her own mind would be fulfilled in the longer Miranda stories that Porter completed in 1936 and 1937, "Old Mortality" and "Pale Horse, Pale Rider."

If the portrait of Miranda as a young child in the "Old Order" stories, especially "The Fig Tree," reflects the author herself with anything approaching accuracy—and I believe it does—the young Callie Russell Porter growing up in Texas was also drawn into the South's Poe-esque obsession with death. In addition to "The Fig Tree," we see this fixation on death in "The Witness," "The Circus," and the last story in the group, "The Grave."

In "The Witness," where Miranda is explicitly identified as being six years old, she and her older sister and brother (representing Gay and Paul; Baby was never included in her fictional family) are seen pestering old Uncle Jimbilly, a relic of slavery, to carve small tombstones for their burials of dead things. These tombstones, sometimes complete with names and dates, "were often needed" by the children, "for some small beast or bird was always dying and having to be buried with proper ceremonies" (*CS* 341). While he carves, Uncle Jimbilly reinforces their fixation on death by telling them stories about the torturing of slaves who "died by de thousands and tens upon thousands" in the old times. (We will return to Uncle Jimbilly's witness in chapter 7.)

In the frequently lauded and richly resonant "The Circus," a work that critics have often identified as both a sexual initiation and an encounter with images of death, Miranda's grandmother reluctantly allows her to attend a traveling circus. Though she insists the child is too young for such a spectacle, she gives in because the outing has been organized as part of a family reunion—as if family trumps all else and the familial continuation of the past into the present will protect her from any ill effects. It doesn't. Small and inexperienced, Miranda is overwhelmed by sights and sounds that strike her with exaggerated impact because she has no frame of reference within which to understand them. She is far too young to be able to interpret these from an adult perspective. But as the story makes clear, an adult perspective is not necessarily a true perspective. It may only be a perspective hardened against direct perceptions—such as perceptions of cruelty.

The Miranda of "The Circus" is undoubtedly naïve and therefore mistaken in her interpretations. As Robert Brinkmeyer has written, she "understands little of what is going on" because she lacks a knowledge of the "conventions" operative in the circus (157). But that is scarcely the point. Her naïveté is shown to be not so much a limitation as a guarantee of authentic response. Because she does not bring preconceptions with her to the circus, her impressions can be free and direct, much as Huckleberry Finn's are when he also goes to the circus and sees it as a spectacle of cruelty and deceit. It is because she is naïve that Miranda can, as Walsh puts it, see "what others do not" (*Illusion* 176).

Her visit to the circus brings her three frightening encounters. First, she notices a group of boys standing underneath the tiers of board seats and looking up in a "bold grinning stare without any kind of friendliness in it" (*CS* 344). When she asks Dicey, the black teenager charged with looking after her, what the boys are doing, Dicey draws her knees together "and her skirts around her" and tells Miranda to stop throwing her legs around. As adults, we understand at once, especially if we are women old enough to have grown up wearing skirts—just as Porter's narrative voice clearly understands, though the child does not.

Her second frightening encounter, announced by a startling fanfare from the circus band, is with a clown in a ghostly costume that hints of campy cross-dressing, who does a tightrope act in which he pretends to be about to fall to certain death:

> A creature in a blousy white overall with ruffles at the neck and ankles, with bone-white skull and chalk-white face, with tufted eyebrows far apart in the middle of his forehead, the lids in a black sharp angle, a long scarlet mouth stretching back into sunken cheeks, turned up at the corners in a perpetual bitter grimace of pain, astonishment, not smiling, pranced along a wire. . . . He paused, slipped, the flapping white leg waved in space; he staggered, wobbled, slipped sidewise, plunged, and caught the wire with frantic knee, hanging there upside down, the other leg waving like a feeler above his head; slipped once more, caught by one frenzied heel, and swung back and forth like a scarf. (*CS* 344–45)

Blessed with an abundant willingness to believe, Miranda does not at first fear for his life because she assumes the wheeled pole he is carrying somehow allows him to fly or to walk on air. It is only when she sees the wire and realizes that he is as dependent on it as she would be that she panics, fearing that he will fall to his death right in front of her. Even then her horror is not so much caused by the clown's simulation of danger as by the reactions of those around her, who, instead of showing concern, "roared with savage delight, shrieks of dreadful laughter like devils in delicious torment." The clown replies with "sneering kisses from his cruel mouth" (*CS* 345). Not realizing that the shrieking spectators—including her own family, the adults who provide her entire sense of security—are complicit in a mutually understood joke, she sees them as participants in a perversely cruel spectacle. The scene has become one of "barely suppressed sadism" (Ciuba 71). Screaming and crying with terror, Miranda is sent home.

The last encounter comes at the exit as she and an exasperated Dicey leave. She bumps into an uncanny dwarf, the same height as herself, who makes the clown's implicit mirroring of the crowd explicit and direct, eye to eye:

> A dwarf was standing in the entrance, wearing a little woolly beard, a pointed cap, tight red breeches, long shoes with turned-up toes. He carried a thin white wand. Miranda almost touched him before she saw him, her distorted face with its open mouth and glistening tears almost level with his. He leaned forward and peered at her with kind, not-human golden eyes, like a near-sighted dog; then made a horrid grimace at her,

imitating her own face. Miranda struck at him in sheer ill temper, scream-ing. Dicey drew her away quickly, but not before Miranda had seen in his face, suddenly, a look of haughty, remote displeasure, a true grown-up look. She knew it well. It chilled her with a new kind of fear: she had not believed he was really human. (*CS* 345)

The dwarf's phallic wand and beard hint at sexual dimensions of adult life, and his mimicry of her own facial expression implies Miranda's implication in that life as well. All this is beyond her conscious understanding. But she recognizes herself in the dwarf and the scarcely humanlike dwarf in herself.

In her initiatory experience at the circus, categories are frighteningly jumbled into a grotesque mix: male with female, human with nonhuman, child with adult, crying with laughter, cruelty with amusement, sexuality with death. And as Tom Walsh points out, the mirroring extends to the author as well. Miran-da's reactions to the circus "reflect Porter's own terror of sex and death" (*Illu-sion* 176).

Sex and death are again compounded in the final story of the sequence, "The Grave." It is an astonishingly fine work. At the opening, a nine-year-old Miranda and her twelve-year-old brother are rambling around the countryside with twenty-two-gauge rifles, meaning to shoot rabbits or else just targets, when they come across what used to be the family cemetery. The graves now lie open because the coffins buried there were taken up and moved when that part of the family land was sold. The children prop their rifles against the fence and go in to explore. Symbolically scaling her tie to the past, taking onto herself its death and (when she jumps out) its birthing of the present, Miranda drops into "the pit that had held her grandfather's bones" (*CS* 363). There, idly picking up and shattering clumps of earth, she finds a silver coffin nut or screw head in the shape of a dove with spread wings. Down in another grave, Paul also finds a treasure: a gold ring carved with leaves and flowers. They swap, then continue their hunt for "rabbits and doves or whatever small game might happen along." But now, under the spell of the gold ring on her grubby thumb, remembering past encoun-ters with "old women of the kind who smoked corn-cob pipes" who reproached her for wearing overalls (*CS* 365), Miranda begins to want to go home, have a bath, dust herself with Maria's lilac-scented talcum, and put on frilly clothes. She wants to look pretty. Just then her brother kills a rabbit.

Death, already present in the story in multiple forms—the graves, the cof-fin screw (paradoxically shaped like the life-giving spirit), the guns, the actual kill—now enters in yet another and more startling form. After skinning the rabbit, Paul points out its "oddly bloated belly" and tells her it "was going to have young ones."

> Very carefully he slit the thin flesh from the center ribs to the flanks, and a scarlet bag appeared. He slit again and pulled the bag open, and there lay a bundle of tiny rabbits, each wrapped in a thin scarlet veil. The brother pulled these off and there they were, dark gray, their sleek wet down lying in minute even ripples, like a baby's head just washed, their unbelievably small delicate ears folded close, their little blind faces almost featureless.
>
> Miranda said, "Oh, I want to *see,*" under her breath. (*CS* 366)

Miranda, of course, always wants to see and, as her name indicates, to marvel. This time, through seeing, she discovers that most basic fact of all, how animal life comes into the world: from inside a mother. But instead of representing incipient life, the baby rabbits have become another visual evidence of death. The mother's death has become their own. It is a bold authorial riff on the old, usually stale echo of "womb/tomb" already evoked in "The Fig Tree" and now made new by Porter's boldness and visual precision. Moreover, the knowledge Miranda gains, which she now realizes her brother already possessed, is a forbidden one. He tells her she must not tell anyone, especially their father. Their beautiful discovery takes on the taint of sexual guilt. Complicit in her brother's revelation of forbidden secrets, the Miranda of the story never tells.[7]

In the final paragraph of "The Grave" we see Miranda "nearly twenty years later" in an open-air market surely in Mexico (though not named as such) on a hot day. All around her are "piles of raw flesh and wilting flowers" reeking of "mingled sweetness and corruption" (*CS* 367). Suddenly, just in front of her, she sees a tray of little sweets in the shapes of small animals, including baby chicks (like those in "The Fig Tree") and baby rabbits. The day of hunting with her brother immediately leaps up from its "burial place" in her memory, just as she and Paul had leaped out of the graves, just as life emerges from its buried source within the body. Instead of thinking about it as a time of killing and of forbidden knowledge, she now recalls it as "the time she and her brother had found treasure in the opened graves." In memory, she sees his "childhood face" with "a pleased sober smile in his eyes, turning the silver dove over and over in his hands" (*CS* 368). Memory, including the emblematic dove, proves to be just possibly redemptive and restorative. With her usual fine sense of restraint, Porter does not press the point but leaves us with the memory of past and kin and the place where she grew up, a memory that we can guess will help Miranda begin to make sense of her life as a whole.

In "The Grave," as she would later in "'Noon Wine': The Sources," Porter renders her memories of childhood in terms of death and violence but also of possible redemption. From the grave of the past and from her own child self, to whom she reaches back, she draws a structure of restored selfhood. Her memories of childhood in Texas were by no means entirely negative but genuinely ambivalent. At times she burst out with resentful intensity, as she did to her sister: "I know now it was nobody's fault, but that does not change my remembrance of life in childhood as being just about damned near unbearable from one day to the next. . . . In fact, my life until I got out of Texas was unbearable altogether" (Porter to Gay Porter Holloway, January 18, 1959). At times she remembered her Texas childhood as a time surrounded by beauty and vitality. And always it was a touchstone for directness and honesty of vision. But as Walsh argues with single-minded insistence, it was always a death-haunted vision.

The recurrent reminders of death in the "Old Order" stories are an accurate replication of Porter's early awareness of death. She said that she clearly understood her mother was dead before she was three. Joined with this awareness of a specific death was an early initiation into the cult of the Lost Cause, the death-dealing Civil War. Both her grandmother and her father were given to lamenting the South's defeat in long backward-looking diatribes. Indeed, she told Hank Lopez that her father somehow managed to link Mary Alice's death to the (white) South's larger tragedy, "indirectly" blaming her mother's death on the aftermath of the War (*Refugee* 8). Perhaps he believed her health had been undermined by wartime privations.

In a psychologically lethal mix that would have far-reaching consequences, this childhood consciousness of death was intertwined with an awareness that her mother had been beautiful. Among her early memories was her father's practice of gathering his children about him for periodic rituals of mourning over Mary Alice's feminine trinkets—an exhibition transferred to the teary grandmother mourning her daughter Amy in "Old Mortality." In her set of rough autobiographical notes captioned "Pull Dick—Pull Devil" she wrote that he "made a cult" of her mother's memory, speaking of it in "beautiful and romantic" terms and exhibiting these pitiful relics to the children. All the relics she mentions are items related to appearance: dresses, gloves, locks of hair, "bits of jewelry." This compounding of beauty with death produced the deadly pathos in which the South's own poet, Edgar Allan Poe, luxuriated.

Poe and his eulogizing of beautiful dead women were part of the Southern culture in which Porter was brought up—among devotees of the Confederacy in a staunchly Southern family, in the part of Texas settled by Southerners, and with such social standards of the South as feminine propriety, the cult of beauty, and the Poe-esque tie between female beauty and death. The father in "Old Mortality" tells his daughters that Poe was "'our greatest poet,'" and they know that "'our' meant he was Southern" (*CS* 178). Porter's active sharing in this culture, or cult, of death is evident in all the Miranda stories. She had a death-haunted childhood, and it was impossible for her to remember one without confronting the other.

She in fact used the word "confronted" when describing the process of reflecting on her childhood that went into her essay on "Noon Wine." Given the many parallels between the story and her actual life, it is not surprising that she would say the effort to reach behind it when writing the essay was like looking at her actual past (*CE* 468). Even so, the word "confronted" is surprisingly strong. It implies an undisguised, unexpected, or perhaps unwelcome encounter, perhaps one that requires courage, perhaps an encounter with something previously hidden from oneself. Certainly it is understandable that she would prefer not to confront a childhood that could be described as "damned near unbearable," and she often hid the realities of her childhood from others by recourse to evasions and misrepresentations. Yet she again and again recalled it in her fiction. Long after she left Texas in 1918, she kept turning back to memories of childhood, trying to search out or construct their meaning.

Psychologists tell us that children often feel a personal guilt for disruptions of their families by death or divorce yet generally get over it. Porter did not get over it. Lopez reports that she told him explicitly her mother died "less than six weeks after I was born, and it was my birth that caused her death."[8] This would have made her also responsible for her father's anguish. He "prayed desperately for her survival," Lopez reports her as saying; it was the "saddest experience of his life" (*Refugee* 3). But a week later, when she listened to her own taped voice saying these words, "she expressed complete surprise": "But it simply isn't true. My mother died two years after I was born, and my birth had no bearing on her death—none whatever." Whether this sequence of conversations is reported accurately and in correct order or represents only Lopez's interpretive conjectures thrown into the form of dialogue, it does appear to reveal the traces of a long-standing, deeply troubling guilt that darkened Porter's childhood from her earliest years.

One consequence of her mother's death was that for the most part, she faced the dilemmas of being female alone. She could scarcely expect her stern grandmother to understand the anxieties of a girl-child so dissimilar to herself, and when she married at barely sixteen she lost immediate access to whatever council her older sister might have given her. As we have seen, she did have other female role models in her childhood, but we might well view those as destructive ones in that they focused her attention on physical beauty. In any event, they did not include a close or supportive relationship. For this reason among others, she did not handle problems of her sex and gender roles very well. Torn between adherence to a traditional pattern and an urge to assert her freedom, she found it difficult to develop a consistent or healthy way of being a woman or performing female gender roles. The beauty trap set for her in childhood by her father and others meant that no matter how significant her achievements, she could never get over a need to define and value herself by her physical appearance and her sexual appeal to men. She was never able to let go of her grief for her mother, who, she must have felt, might have helped steer her through these difficulties.

The "Old Order" stories show us Miranda at her youngest (in "The Fig Tree") and at her oldest (at the end of "The Grave"). As Mary Titus observes, they also show us two of Porter's most genuinely "heroic" female characters: the Grandmother and Aunt Nannie. I would expand that number to three, to include Great-Aunt Eliza. All three are in some ways unlikely heroes. Grandmother Sophia Jane is subjected to gentle humor because of her lack of self-criticism, Aunt Nannie is black in a white-dominated culture, and Great-Aunt Eliza in no way fits the pattern of the Southern lady. Nevertheless, all three exhibit memorable strengths exceeding the demands of their typecast roles.

Great-Aunt Eliza's countercultural heroism derives from her independent spirit and keen, freethinking mind. Possessed of a degree of self-assurance that allows her to remain impervious to what others may think of her, she pursues her interests as a naturalist without regard to elegance of appearance or of manners. By doing so—by demonstrating that she finds science more interesting than, say, parties—she implicitly pronounces the customary preoccupations of the belle or the lady trivial in comparison to learning.

Given her time and place, Aunt Nannie is an even more unexpected hero. She is seen at her youngest in Kentucky in 1832 when newly bought for a mere twenty dollars, "a scrawny, half-naked black child" of five "with a round nubbly head and fixed bright monkey eyes." Five-year-old Sophia Jane claims her with an impulsive "I want the little monkey" (CS 330). At her oldest, no longer a slave but still limited by conditioning and by Southern racial attitudes, she is seen in Texas probably about 1901 to 1903. She has lived a life of hard work and devotion, and in the later years before Sophia Jane's death the two had been friends in a way that makes them close though never social equals. Nannie is unafraid to speak her mind and bold in making demands on the family. All this prepares us for "The Last Leaf," where, after Sophia Jane's death, Aunt Nannie is revealed in her full heroic identity. Declaring her independence by moving into a vacant cabin away from the main house to end her days in solitary aloofness, wearing and eating and smoking what she chooses, she rejects an imposed identity by reclaiming her authentic self—"an aged Bantu woman of independent means" (*CS* 349).

In some ways Grandmother Sophia Jane, for all her conventionalism, is the most complex of the three. Appearing both in "The Old Order" and in "Old Mortality," she is the center and primary shaping influence of Miranda's life. Yet she is also an impediment in that she holds up to Miranda the ideal of the Southern belle, which Miranda must find her way past as she matures. The Grandmother expects her to take various family beauties as her models, but these role models are shown to be counterconstructive. Moreover, it is through Miranda's far-from-overawed voice that the narrator at times regards Grandmother with a distinctly unheroizing tone of amusement. Nevertheless, she remains a monumental presence. While having amply fulfilled the conventional roles of Southern belle and lady, she is also a woman unafraid to assert her opinions. This in itself makes her heroic in a society where a lady is expected to be submissive.

There is more. Having unquestioningly accepted the institution of slavery and having benefited from the work of slaves all her life, the Grandmother nevertheless defies racist conventions in taking her former slave as her primary friend and companion and looking forward to another life with Nannie in heaven. And though there is no indication that Miranda is aware of it, the reader is told that long years earlier Sophia Jane had defied conventions of both race and white upper-class femininity by electing to nurse her own babies. She and Nannie had engaged in a "grim and terrible race of procreation," each having a baby about every year and a half. "Thirteen of 'em," Nannie marvels, "yas, my Lawd and my Redeemah, thirteen!" At first Sophia Jane painfully bound her breasts every time to suppress her milk while Nannie served as wet nurse to both babies. But when Nannie is struck with puerperal fever after one of the births, Sophia Jane not only insists on nursing her own rather than getting another wet nurse, she takes the black baby to her own breast as well, impervious to family protests. She feeds them "justly turn about, not favoring the white over the black" as Nannie had felt "obliged to do." For a white plantation lady to breastfeed a black child would have been unheard-of and shocking. But with her "quiet way of holding her ground" Sophia Jane then decided, for reasons of pleasure as well as justice, that henceforth Nannie would breastfeed only her own babies and she would do the same. "I understand now," she tells her sister Keziah, "why the black mammies love their foster children. I love mine" (*CS* 334). She asserts her will to defy foolish customs of race and sex.

By force of example, these three unlikely hero-women show Miranda that her own life, too, can exceed the limits of the socially approved ideals.

5
Seizing the Moment
Endless Memory and "Noon Wine"

All the things I write of I have first known, and they are real to me.
—Katherine Anne Porter, "Why I Write about Mexico"

Porter's years in Paris in the early 1930s were a time of achievement, especially with the completion and publication of "The Old Order." They were also a tense time, fraught with concern over German rearmament. In addition, Porter had health problems, and her disposition suffered. Nevertheless, this trying period ended with the 1935 publication of the first "Old Order" and a revised and enlarged edition of *Flowering Judas,* retitled *Flowering Judas and Other Stories.* It led directly, moreover, to her miracle year, 1936, when the elements of her long preparation came together in the writing of two masterworks about Texas.

In April 1932, only seven months after her arrival in Germany and three months after she settled in Paris, Porter fell ill with bronchitis and, fearing a relapse into tuberculosis, checked into a hospital for a short stay. She then, in June, joined Eugene Pressly in Basel, Switzerland, where he was working as a translator at a three-month disarmament conference. While in Basel she wrote the introduction for *The Itching Parrot* and the germs of two of her finest works, "Noon Wine" and "Pale Horse, Pale Rider." At the end of Gene's three months they returned to Paris, where he had a job as a clerk at the U.S. Embassy. On March 11, 1933, despite considerable rockiness in their relationship, they were married.

According to pattern, Porter's letters to friends and family proclaimed her undying love for this wonderful man, and she plunged into housekeeping, even taking a class to develop her cooking skills in exotic ways. But soon she tired of housework, and their continual money problems, which she complained of to her family in Depression-wracked America, frayed her nerves. They argued. That fall, however, brought a dramatic change in her fortunes: Donald Brace proposed to publish an enlarged and more widely distributed edition of *Flowering Judas.*

Her respiratory problems continued, however, and in early 1934, in an effort to help her recover and also to soothe obvious problems in her marriage, Barbara Harrison invited her to Davos, Switzerland, for a few weeks at a sanitarium. Soon Barbara, Monroe Wheeler, and his life companion Glenway Wescott all left for New York. Badly missing them when she returned to Paris, and determined to get some distance from the frequently glum and dreary Pressly, she located a six-room house that would give her space to work and allow them separate bedrooms. That summer, despite having extracted several "Old Order" stories from the manuscript called "Many Redeemers," she returned to work on it, still wanting to succeed with the novel that continued to elude her.

The year 1935 proved to be a golden one. Two of the finest of the "Old Order" stories appeared in print, "The Grave" in April and "The Circus" in July. Distance of both miles and time had given her the necessary perspective to begin re-creating her early life in Texas. Then in October *Flowering Judas and Other Stories* was published. The first *Flowering Judas,* five years before, had been a limited edition of six hundred copies containing only six stories: "María Concepción," "Magic," "Rope," "He," "The Jilting of Granny Weatherall," and "Flowering Judas." It had made her reputation among a literary in-group but not with a larger public. The new version added "Theft," "That Tree," "The Cracked Looking-Glass," and "Hacienda," making it a substantial volume that not only was released in a larger initial print run but went into subsequent printings. This was a major milestone in Porter's career, and she recognized that she needed to seize the moment.

Fastening her frustration with the novel on Gene, she managed to get him out of the way by persuading him to make a two-month visit to his family in the States. Unfortunately, Josephine Herbst arrived for a visit just before he left, draining away the quiet time Porter had meant to use for immersing herself in her work. Now divorced from John Herrmann, Josie stayed for several days before going on to Germany, then came back through Paris while Gene was still away. Although Herbst's accounts indicate that she and Porter enjoyed their time together, Porter's do not. Besides feeling distracted and stymied in her work, she no longer fully trusted her old friend, who had used some of her earlier confidences for a story in which Porter and Ernest Stock appear in thin disguise. Too, they may have argued politics, since Porter was pulling back toward the center while Herbst retained her radical convictions.[1] But the main factor in the cooling of Porter's friendship toward Herbst seems to have been that Josie made a sexual move on her, or in Unrue's words, "let Katherine Anne know that she herself would not mind a little 'physical comfort'" (*Life* 157). Lesbians were anathema to Porter.

Almost forty-five now, she felt, as Unrue correctly observes, the kind of fear of becoming unattractive and lonely that Mrs. Treadwell expresses in *Ship of Fools* at the same age (*Life* 157). Europe was moving toward cataclysm. She needed to return to her own country and complete, at last, the major works that had been too long pending.

Soon after Pressly returned, she began planning a visit of her own. Having wangled yet another advance on the defunct Cotton Mather book, she sailed for Boston on February 6, 1936, then took a bus to Houston and her sister Baby's house. There she enjoyed herself, visiting and playing games and impressing her family with her beauty and sophistication, but nevertheless found that her feelings toward Texas were as conflicted as ever. Writing from Houston on April 10, she told Pressly she couldn't possibly ever live there again—though she may have been exaggerating her dissatisfaction in order to soothe his feelings. Later that month, she and Baby took their father to Indian Creek, the first time any of them had been back since 1892. At her mother's grave, she was overcome by sadness and nostalgia. She sat in the grass beside the stone marker and wrote what is probably her finest poem, beginning "This time of year, this year of all years, brought / The homeless one, home again."

When she returned to Paris, she and Gene began preparations to leave Europe permanently. After five years as expatriates, they returned to the United States in October 1936. By then their life together was quite obviously in disarray. Matthew Josephson, who ran into them soon after they landed in New York, said that he was surprised at the level of open hostility between them and thought he detected a "'mean streak'" in Porter that he hadn't seen before (*KAP* 298). She had tried out the word "divorce" in a letter to Ford Madox Ford and Janice Biala in January, and the marriage would not last another year. What kept her hanging fire was uncertainty as to how she would support herself alone— though Pressly's professional future was also in some doubt at the time they returned.

The same letter to Ford and Biala that intimates her simmering intention to leave Eugene also puts its finger very precisely on her state of mind as an artist at the time of her return. She told them that she believed she had arrived at a moment in her development as a writer that would determine her entire future. She was right. She returned ready to produce her finest work, the center of her oeuvre, and she at once addressed herself to it. While Pressly went to make arrangements for a job, she took a piece of friendly advice from Carl Van Doren and retired to the Water Wheel Tavern in Doylestown, Pennsylvania, for a period of quiet work. In short order she completed two (not the three she claimed) novellas that were now "familiar and complete in her mind" (*KAP* 298–99), pulling together drafts she had written while in Europe. One of these, "Noon Wine," often thought to be her finest single work, had been begun in Basel and significantly advanced when she made a breakthrough just before leaving Paris for her spring 1936 visit to Texas. That would seem not to have been a mere co-incidence. In "Noon Wine" she made her most direct return to the Texas of her childhood.

Porter arrived at the Water Wheel Tavern contract in hand. When Donald Brace suggested bringing out the enlarged *Flowering Judas and Other Stories,* he had also revised her existing contract for a novel to read, instead, a volume of five short novels or long stories. The five were to be "Noon Wine," "Old Mortality," "Pale Horse, Pale Rider," "The Man in the Tree," and "Promised Land." They would become three. "Promised Land" would be incorporated into *Ship of Fools,* and "The Man in the Tree," drawing on very troubling material from Porter's Texas past, was never finished. But by late December she had finished "Noon Wine" and "Old Mortality" and was well along on "Pale Horse, Pale Rider"— a remarkable trio indeed. She later liked to say that she had produced the three gem-like works in seven days each. This was not quite true. But "Old Mortality" and "Noon Wine" were sent to the publisher before she left the inn and appeared in journals in the spring and summer of 1937. Her few weeks in Doylestown may well have been the most rewarding time of her life.

While there, she wrote Gene that she would not live with him again but then did an about-face and took an apartment with him in New York until he left for a job in South America. At that point she received word of a $2,500 award from the Book of the Month Club but still hesitated to file for divorce. In late spring, learning that Pressly had found his job in South America unacceptable and was coming back, she set out for another visit to Texas in order to avoid him.

There was also another good reason to go. A celebration of her father's eightieth birthday was planned for June 28 at the Old Settlers Reunion in San Marcos. The event gave her a fuller opportunity than her visit the previous year to observe and mingle with people who had spent their lives in central Texas and known her as a child, and she responded with a warmth of affection that led her even to think she might move back and live there. A letter she wrote to Josephine Herbst later in the summer, which I will discuss at some length, provides extraordinary insight into her feelings about Texas at this important time in her life.[2]

Being back, she said, brought her "no regrets and no wrenchings of the heart for any part of the past" because "everything had moved back, taken shape, was something whole and finished" (*SL* 149). "Shape" was a word Porter often used

9. Katherine Anne Porter at age forty-seven, with her father beside a road in central Texas, 1937. Even in relatively advanced years, the tall, slim Harrison Boone Porter maintained the good looks that Katherine always admired in him and in other men. Katherine Anne Porter Papers, Special Collections, University of Maryland Libraries.

as more or less an equivalent for "meaning." She continued, "I could look at it with complete detachment except for a pleasurable sense of possession; what had been was mine because I really could remember, and now understand, something of what had happened not only to me but to all these people."[3] Struggling to express the emotions awakened by her return, she added, "I felt myself *part* of a society, and not alien or wanderer at all" (149). On the contrary, Porter in fact felt like an "alien or wanderer" all her adult life. After rejecting her original home—for good reasons—she persistently tried, without success, to replace it. Even during her period of intense work in Pennsylvania the fall before attending the Old Settlers Reunion she had taken time to look at real estate, imagining she might buy a house even though she wasn't sure how she was going to feed herself.

If she had not already completed "Old Mortality," we would believe it came together here at San Marcos. There are also connections of a sort with the not yet finished "Pale Horse, Pale Rider." Adam in that story may have become clearer in her mind as she took "snapshots" of her father with "old ladies he had danced with in his youth." She told Herbst that she had been asked to speak and was introduced by "an old gentleman" as "the littlest Porter girl, the curly haired one" (*SL* 149–50). Of course she was not the "littlest," or youngest, among her siblings at all, as any old gentleman who remembered the family would have known. Even though the littlest, Baby, never appears in Porter's fiction, it is surprising to find her erased this way in a letter. Another old gentleman she spoke with, she wrote, had known her grandparents and remembered her "beautiful" dead aunts. Everyone had "such vitality, such impassioned memories, and had lived so fully and at such high tension I felt that everything I had ever written about them was very pale and out of focus." Perhaps she was feeling needlessly jittery about the work she had recently finished writing at the Water Wheel Tavern.

Her upbringing might have taught her "nothing about the world [she] was to live in," Porter wrote, but as she looked around she thought, "These people are strong, and they are my people, and I have their toughness in me, and that is what I can rely upon . . . I loved them, really with my heart. I liked the precision of their old fashioned language, their good simple manners that would be good manners anywhere, and their absolutely innate code of morals that shows itself in their manners." It was at this point that, carried away by enthusiasm, she hazarded a claim to "feel pretty certain that I could live, now, in San Marcos, Texas, and have a good life and go on writing the way I have begun . . . I'd be willing to risk it" (*CL* 150). Even at the moment of making the claim, however, she returned to clearer sight: "BUT—they are a disappearing race, soon they will all be dead, and the young people are scattering out as far as they can go." Her quick juxtaposition of the picture of her father in his youth against the advanced age of the Old Settlers points clearly to nostalgia as the source of her impulse to return. The central Texas she was momentarily moved to consider a potential home was the central Texas of a past even longer ago than when she lived there and felt desperate to get away.

Despite her nostalgic rush during her visit to San Marcos, Porter also saw negatives, such as the farmland "impoverished" and neglected. "I saw all our fields lying full of weeds, (my grandmother owned six thousand acres of good thick black land in that country once, and it was said you could plant a walking stick and it would sprout in that land) and the present owners don't know enough to plant the fields to clover for a few seasons to bring it back." In a litany of social criticisms, she identified the villain as mechanization and large companies that pay no heed to the actual producers on the land—a reflection of her renewed friendships among the Southern Agrarians. "I am not writing about political theory," she insisted, "but of what I saw in the south" (*SL* 150). Not "Texas" but "the south."

At this point it might appear that Porter's ambivalence toward Texas was simply an expression of a more general duality in her nature between wishful idealization of her memories and hardheaded recognition of fact, part of an amalgam of a split entailing past and present, willful forgetting and equally willful remembering of old hurts. As we have already seen, it was more complicated than that. Her visit to the Old Settlers Reunion did not touch on her feelings about either violence or racial injustice, nor did she summon up her reserves of an independent mind-set when enjoying the company of various old gentlemen or the sight of her father dancing.

~

At the invitation of Allen Tate and Caroline Gordon, Porter went directly from the Old Settlers Reunion in San Marcos to the Olivet College Writers' Conference in Michigan, her first of her many stints of lecturing at colleges. She then rode back to Tennessee with Tate and Gordon for a long visit at their country home, Benfolly, where she had once thought of building a cabin. The visit provoked the flare-up of her Southern agrarianism that enters the letter to Herbst that she wrote there. Six years before, in November 1930, another of the unregenerate Agrarians, Andrew Lytle, had written her a letter opening "My Dearest" and reporting on having had "a fine time" with Tate et al. "discussing the old Confederacy and its legitimate off-spring." In turn, she commended Lytle to her father in a letter of June 26, 1931, as a "throw-back" who "whoops her up for the Old South," well knowing he would find that appealing. Now, her regional feelings fueled by the Old Settlers Reunion in San Marcos, she again engaged in passionate discourses about such proofs of the South's mistreatment by the North after the Civil War as disparate rail rates.

Porter was never so fully committed to this reactionary Southern position as her Fugitive and Agrarian friends; her enthusiasm sometimes heated up, sometimes cooled off. Moreover, she tried to maintain a distinction between the South and Texas. Even when she vilified Texas she praised Southern ways, and she fell into rhapsodies about Texas only at moments when she could think of it as Southern—as she did when writing to Herbst about the reunion. Yet there were also times when she threw them together and vilified both. In an April 1, 1920, letter to her father and her sister Gay she avowed, "I hate like the devil to think of the south again for a residence." In another letter to Gay eight years later she said that she could not "bear to remember" any part of her early life until she "left the south"—not "left Texas," as we might expect. But such times were the exceptions.

She now enjoyed settling into Benfolly's country life, picking tomatoes and making jams and jellies and playing with barn kittens. She also enjoyed the company of a number of Tate's and Gordon's friends—Robert Penn Warren, with whom she had corresponded about the stories published in the *Southern Review,* novelist Brainard Cheney and his wife, Frances, Andrew Lytle, Cleanth and Edith ("Tinkum") Brooks—all of them true Southerners. Warren's good-looking young graduate student at Louisiana State University, Albert Erskine, who worked as business manager of the *Southern Review,* also came to visit. Porter was then forty-seven. Erskine was twenty-six. It was instant romance. Allen Tate later told Joan Givner that the two of them sat on the wide front gallery and talked until 4:00 A.M., keeping him awake, and he guessed right then that they would have an affair (*KAP* 305). If so, his intuition hadn't reached quite far enough. On March 19, 1938, six months after the fateful night, he wrote Lytle with bemused surprise:

> Katherine Anne and Albert Erskine have announced their intention of getting married in April.
> Let it sink in.
> I am convinced that even this isn't the last attempt.
> There will be others. And they get younger all the time.

In September, with $400 borrowed from Monroe Wheeler, Porter paid shipment charges on possessions Eugene Pressly had unexpectedly sent back and moved into an apartment on Jackson Square in New Orleans, a city she always liked to claim as part of her personal myth. Her letter asking for the money referred implausibly to operas and performances by great actors she had seen there in childhood. But her main purpose in making the move was to be close enough, yet not too close, to Albert Erskine in Baton Rouge. Soon they did indeed, as Tate said he expected, become lovers.

Of more significance to readers, she also soon finished "Pale Horse, Pale Rider." It appeared in the *Southern Review* in the winter 1938 issue, and *Pale Horse, Pale Rider: Three Short Novels* was published in 1939. Her annus mirabilis, stretched out to a little more than a year, was done. She had seized the moment and made the most of it.

~

In "Noon Wine" Porter returned to the period in her late childhood between the death of her grandmother and her year at the Thomas School in San Antonio. A taut, vivid novella set among the plain farming people of central Texas, it has at times been extravagantly praised for its compelling rendition of a social class of which Porter had no direct experience. Only in recent years has it become known that her own social class was not so exalted as she claimed and that she knew the social class of the characters in "Noon Wine" quite well. The Thompsons of the story were directly modeled on Harrison Porter's cousin Ellen Skaggs Thompson and her husband, Gene. Harrison had parked three of his four children with them for some unknown period after their grandmother died while he "looked around," as the saying goes. Either he and Gay (the eldest) or he and Harry Ray (the only boy) visited around and tried to formulate a plan for where to go next.[4] These Thompsons and their farm were the unnamed autobiographical source for "Noon Wine." They even had a hired man named Helton, as in the story. Indeed, Givner reports having received a letter from a descendent of the Thompsons indicating that both the Thompson and the Skaggs family wanted to sue Porter. For what, one wonders—defamation? Or simply the story's nearness to fact, making it a kind of violation of privacy?

"Noon Wine" is easily summarized though not so readily understood. It is set at the Thompsons' somewhat ramshackle central Texas farm. Mrs. Thompson is in weak health and rather whiney. Her tobacco-chewing husband is something of a big talker who thinks highly of himself and would rather go into town for a nip than work. Seemingly out of nowhere, a mysteriously uncommunicative Swede named Helton arrives and sets things right, repairing the front gate, cleaning the springhouse, making neat balls of butter. His only apparent fault is his devotion to a collection of harmonicas on which he plays a single tune over and over; when the Thompsons' two boys meddle with the harmonicas, he shakes them with a silent, menacing fury. But the incident goes unaddressed since the farm has become profitable, allowing Mr. Thompson to be ever less occupied in hard work and ever prouder of what he has accomplished. Years later another mysterious stranger, Mr. Hatch, as garrulous as Mr. Helton is taciturn, shows up and reveals an intention to take Helton back north to stand trial for murder. When Helton approaches, the understandably distressed Mr. Thompson, as concerned to protect his prosperity as he is to protect his hired man, sees or thinks he sees Hatch pull a knife on him. Taking up a handy ax, he brings it down on Hatch's head, killing him on the spot. Helton, not wounded at all, runs away. The knifing had been a hallucination. Mr. Thompson is found not guilty of murder but knows his neighbors and ultimately even his family no longer trusts him, and he kills himself.

In this stark outline, the story sounds excessively plot-driven. But in fact, as in most of Porter's work, the plot is the merest vehicle for subtle probing of character, motive, culture, and ultimate mystery. The story is pervasively inflected, for example, by social class. Her time at her cousins' farm as a child seems to have caused Porter strong discomfort about her family's social standing. As Givner puts it, she was shocked at finding there were such low-class people among her kin, living in such an unmannerly way. Staying with them, Givner believes, drove her to "reassess the quality of her own family and the atmosphere of her family life, for not only did the farm closely resemble the Porter farm but Mr. and Mrs. Thompson closely resembled her own parents" (*KAP* 74). How she could have known about a resemblance to her mother is not clear; she had only hearsay and the evidence of a single indistinct tintype to go on. Otherwise, Givner's reading is convincingly plausible.

In 1956, when the *Yale Review* invited Porter to submit an essay explaining the genesis and process of composition of any one of her stories, she chose "Noon Wine." The essay that resulted, which plays so important a role here, is a masterwork in its own right, probably the most frequently read of any of her essays. It is also an intriguing example of how she at once drew on and disguised her personal past. In language of grace and polish, clarity yet elusiveness, "'Noon Wine'. The Sources" explains why she cannot explain how the story came to be—and in doing so, of course, explains. At any rate, it affords us glimpses of the long-past impressions and episodes that contributed to her conception of the story. Her choice of "Noon Wine" as the work whose sources she would probe, plus the fact that she "came so close and yet could still not acknowledge her relationship to her own place and her own people"—emphatically denying that she even knew the Thompsons—is a powerful expression of her "fatal ambivalence" about her Texas roots (*KAP* 77).

Although the opening of the essay has been partially quoted before, I want to quote it more fully here:

> By the time a writer has reached the end of a story, he has lived it at least three times over—first in the series of actual events that, directly or indirectly, have combined to set up that commotion in his mind and senses that causes him to write the story; second, in memory; and third, in recreation of this chaotic stuff. One might think this is enough; but no, the writer now finds himself challenged to trace his clues to their sources and to expose the roots of his work in his own most secret and private life; and is asked to live again this sometimes exhausting experience for the fourth time! (*CE* 467)

Focusing on both the process and the content of memory, the passage displays the balance between personal and slightly formal tones that Porter typically struck in her best work. Notable, too, is its deferral of any reference to violence, though that is a pervasive theme second only to the power of memory. This deferral, I believe, reflects the powerful anxiety that violence caused Porter. From long

reading of both her personal story and her fiction, I am convinced that the violence she sensed in the society around her, both personal and public, was the
second of the two main reasons she left Texas—second, that is, after ambition.

Although I have called the *Yale Review* piece an essay and it is collected among
her nonfiction, its genre is not entirely clear. Porter herself calls the point into
question, musing that it might better be thought of as "a meditation rather than
an exposition" (*CE* 468). In fact, it might better not be thought of not as "nonfiction" but as "apparent nonfiction." Both here and elsewhere, when she wrote
about her early years and her family she slid very easily between memory and
imagination. In the case of "'Noon Wine': The Sources," skepticism is particularly warranted when she not once but twice disclaims any acquaintance with the
Thompsons at whose farm the novella is set. "Let me give you a glimpse of Mr.
and Mrs. Thompson, not as they were in their real lives, for I never knew them,"
she claims, and refers to "the woman I have called Mrs. Thompson—I never
knew her name" (*CE* 478, 481). Yet she did know them. In a letter to Gay dated
October 8, 1956, she acknowledged that she had retained the name Thompson
from the originals and indeed "the only thing in that piece that is not fact as I remember it" is the change of Mr. Thompson's first name from "Gene" to "Royal."

Like "Noon Wine" itself, the essay also raises issues of social class, though in
general rather than personal terms. In a long aside about an older generation that
she labels "good society," as distinct from the middle class of her own day, Porter
states that the Texas of her childhood "was not really a democratic society," but
"if everybody had his place, sometimes very narrowly defined, at least he knew
where it was, and so did everybody else." A paragraph on "humble ancestors"
and "rising in the world" follows, ending, "Aspiration to higher and better things
was natural to all men, and a sign of proper respect for true blood and birth.
Pride and hope may be denied to no one" (*CE* 471–72). This far and no further
will she go toward her family's social standing. She prefers celebrating the "summer country of my childhood" to writing in any factual way about her own or
her story's origins. And it is because of the idyllic nature of her tribute that we
are brought up so short by the intrusion of violence.

We know from the way she describes her "own place" that the setting of
the essay, as distinct from the story, conflates her grandmother's farm in Hays
County with her birthplace in Brown County. Beginning in Hays County, she
shifts midway to recall that "small clear branch of the Rio Blanco, full of colored
pebbles, Indian Creek, the place where I was born" (*CE* 470)—an impossibility,
since she was taken away to her grandmother's house in Kyle before she was old
enough to see these colored pebbles, or at any rate to remember them—and at

some point, without making it clear, shifts back.[5] Only a reader acquainted with Porter's life story will recognize that the place where she and her siblings ramble and catch crawfish, and where there is an Uncle Jimbilly who had "once been my grandparent's [*sic*] slave," must be Hays County. But the presence of Uncle Jimbilly is actually another fiction. Givner states flatly, on the basis of what appear to be firm foundations of research, that there were "no Negro servants attached to the household" in Porter's day, though a former servant called Aunt Jane (who became, of course, Aunt Nannie) sometimes visited.

In much the same way as she blurs the two *places,* Porter blurs the location of her memories *in time.* They come to her, she says, from "certainly before my third year." We could quibble over whether that means when she was two or still one, since technically one's third year begins the day after one's second birthday, but in any event it is doubtful that she would have such elaborate memories from so early a point in life. Her blurring of both place and time moves us into a space of reverie, an idealized essence of childhood itself, but also serves as one of the factors leading us to question whether the events she relates ever actually happened.

Barely has she established this "state of instinctive bliss which children only know" when her child self hears "like a blow of thunder" the "explosion of a shotgun, not very far away," followed by "a high, thin, long-drawn scream" (*CE* 474). We have been prepared for this moment by an earlier passage (partially quoted above) describing a grim perception that she says has been with her from her earliest years, her awareness of

> the underlying, perpetual ominous presence of violence; violence potential that broke through the smooth surface almost without warning, or maybe just without warning to children, who learned later to know the signs. There were old cruel customs, the feud, for one, gradually dying out among the good families . . . and country life, ranch life, was rough in Texas, at least. I remember tall bearded booted men striding about with clanking spurs, and carrying loaded pistols inside their shirts next to their ribs, even to church. It was quite matter of course that you opened a closet door in a bedroom and stared down into the cold eyes of shotguns and rifles, stacked there because there was no more room in the gun closet. (*CE* 472–73)

Porter typically wrote in a spare style. The piling up of adjectives here ("underlying, perpetual ominous") before the phrase "presence of violence" signifies an unusually strong emphasis. The long guns stacked in a bedroom closet because the gun cabinet was already full indicate not merely a potential for violence but an excess of that potential—even if one does not question whether a full gun cabinet is excessive in the first place. When she then makes reference, almost as a throwaway, to "living . . . all our summers among loaded guns and dangerous cutting edges" (*CE* 473), the everyday ordinariness of weapons is expanded to include knives as well as guns. These implements of violence, remembered as having been omnipresent in her earliest years, now become acutely, visually present for her readers as well.

With the sound of a gunshot and a scream, potential violence abruptly becomes actual. That instant—that "spot of clear light and color and sound, of immense, mysterious illumination of feeling against a horizon of total darkness"— is later reinforced in her childhood awareness by a bit of overheard adult gossip about someone named Pink Hodges being "got" by "old man A——," name unremembered, just A. This, Porter tells us, is the source of the episode in "Noon Wine" when Mr. Thompson drives around the countryside vowing to his neighbors that he killed the curiously sinister Mr. Hatch because he charged Helton with a knife. Over and over Mrs. Thompson sits listening to him give this explanation until he reaches the point of telling neighbor after neighbor that they can ask her, she "won't lie"—implying that they probably think he would. At that point she "never fail[s] to say: 'Yes, that's right, that's the truth'" or "'It's true, I saw it'" (*CS* 262, 264). According to the essay, the woman who actually stopped at Grandmother Porter's house to vouch for her husband, the Mr. A—— of the forgotten name, was a "poor sad pale beaten-looking woman" (*CE* 476). "Beaten-looking": a pointer to yet another kind of violence and one with particular significance for Porter.

In the story, Mr. Thompson despairs of ever fully exonerating himself and commits suicide—in a way that closely resembles the suicide of Mr. Shimerda in Willa Cather's *My Ántonia*, published eighteen years before Porter completed "Noon Wine." The essay does not mention a suicide but adds another detail from her claimed memory of the visit made by Mr. A—— and his wife. She recalls her grandmother's saying afterward—and she puts the words in quotation marks, as if that long-dead voice were actually speaking—"I was never asked to condone a murder before." Note that she does not claim she never heard of a murder in the area before. Porter's father is quoted as replying, "Yes, and a cold-blooded murder too if there ever was one" (*CE* 477).

"So," Porter adds, in a statement that seems to extend far beyond the story itself, "there was the dreary tale of violence again" (*CE* 477).

It is not clear whether a killing such as the one referred to in the essay actually occurred or if so whether the names were those she cites, Pink Hodges shot by a Mr. A——. The only Hodges I have found listed among early settlers was at Dripping Springs, several miles northwest of Kyle. Barkley's community history of Hays County mentions various "hangings . . . shootings and killings" at an abandoned house on a hilltop near there (145) but nothing to validate Porter's essay. A "Pink" Hodges does turn up, though, in the later history of Kyle.[6] A man by that name married the daughter of Thomas Green Martin, owner of the first saloon in town, whose parents had settled on a farm north of the community in 1868. Thomas Martin was born in January 1879, and his daughter Lula was his fourth child, which would seem to make her earliest possible year of birth about 1903 to 1905. Her marriage to "Pink" Hodges, then, would not likely have come before, say, 1920. Was this "Pink" an offspring of the Hodges family of Dripping Springs, and was he named or called after one of his ancestors? If so, it would still be possible that a man by that name was killed during Porter's childhood. Or she might have heard the name when she attended the Old Settlers Reunion in 1937, liked it, and used it almost two decades later when she wrote her essay. Since it is clear that "'Noon Wine': The Sources" is not strictly speaking nonfiction but an example of a genre somewhere between the essay and the story, she might well have incorporated names and other details much as she did in fiction.

I suggested earlier that the chillingly matter-of-fact reportage of Mr. Thompson's suicide may have been modeled on the suicide in Cather's *My Ántonia*. Compare the two:

Mr. Shimerda "pulled the trigger with his big toe. He layed over on his side and put the end of the barrel in his mouth, then he drew up one foot and felt for the trigger. He found it all right!"

Mr. Thompson "lay down flat on the earth on his side, drew the barrel under his chin and fumbled for the trigger with his great toe. That way he could work it."

There is another parallel with *My Ántonia* as well. In "Noon Wine" Mr. Thompson kills Hatch by bringing an ax down on his head "as if he were stunning a beef" because he thought Hatch "made a pass at Mr. Helton with his bowie knife" (*CS* 256, 260). The bowie knife hardly needs explanation; its association with Texas through the Jim Bowie who died at the Alamo is familiar. But the ax has precedents both in Cather's novel and in fact. In *My Ántonia* after the Burdens' hired man explains his theory of how Mr. Shimerda might have carried out his suicide (with his toe), he adds that nevertheless there was "something mighty queer about it": "I found Krajiek's axe under the manger, and I picks it up and carries it over to the corpse, and I take my oath it just fit the gash in the front of the old man's face" (93). The implication is that the death already ruled a suicide may have been murder. Doubt is cast on the finding of the court.[7] But the precedent from fact is even more interesting: a series of ax murders in 1911 and 1912. (We will return to these in chapter 6.)

All this violence had entered Porter's life, or at any rate her perception of her life, before she left Texas. We can only guess that she was likely to have read about the ax murders in newspapers, but in any event—or so "'Noon Wine': The Sources" retrospectively indicates—she had come to think of Texas as a place where the guns or the knives or the axes were always ready to hand. However much she sometimes idealized the Southern aspects of Texas, the problem also creeps into her fiction. In Gary Ciuba's words, violence was "always just below the surface of the South's old order" and "just seems to erupt" in her stories (73). It erupts in "Noon Wine" without warning on an ordinary day in August as easily as Mr. Hatch, the mysterious stranger who drives up to Mr. Thompson's farm unannounced, drops the astonishing news that quiet Mr. Helton once killed his brother with a pitchfork on just such a hot summer day, or as easily as Mr. Thompson could somehow find an ax handle in his hand and, as if without volition, feel his arms "go up over his head and bring the ax down on Mr. Hatch's head as if he were stunning a beef" (CS 242, 251, 255–56). And as a result, Mrs. Thompson becomes afraid of him.

The character of Mrs. Thompson occupies a great deal of visual attention in the story, much as her prototype—whom Porter claims she did not know except for a single glimpse—does in the essay. She is seen "lying down, with the green shades drawn" and "a wet cloth over her eyes," "shading her eyes," "one hand supporting her flat, pained side," as "a little frail woman with long thick brown hair in a braid, a suffering patient mouth and diseased eyes which cried easily" (CS 225–27), and more. When she and Mr. Thompson return home from his compulsive attempts to convince neighbors of his innocence after he kills Mr. Hatch, her face is "gray with dust and weariness." Stepping down from the buggy, she shakes out her "light flower-sprigged dress. She wore her smoked glasses, and her wide shady leghorn hat with the wreath of exhausted pink and blue forget-me-nots hid her forehead, fixed in a knot of distress" (CS 256). In the essay, Mrs. A——— is described in strikingly similar language: wearing a "faded cotton print dress" and a "wretched little straw hat with a wreath of wilted forgetmenots," and with "dark glasses" (CE 476). When Mrs. A——— arrives to help her husband explain away his guilt, it is the grandmother whose "brows [are] knitted in painful inquiry" like the "knot of distress" in Mrs. Thompson's forehead. Otherwise the two passages are closely parallel. But the essay adds an important detail: Mrs. A—— is "beaten-looking"; she is "a poor sad pale beaten-looking woman" who "looked as if she had never eaten a good dinner, or slept in a comfortable bed" (*CE* 476). Both the fictional Mrs. Thompson and the possibly factual Mrs. A—— are victims. At minimum, we see them being pressured by their husbands to sacrifice their integrity, but a victimhood of long standing is implied in their weakness, pallor, and wiltedness, and certainly in Mrs. A——'s being "beaten-looking."

Porter's state of health at various times prior to the writing of "Noon Wine" or even the long process of making notes and drafts for it would certainly have made her "pale." She appears pale in her pictures from those years. She had two bouts of tuberculosis in the 1910s, she sometimes did not have enough to eat, and she suffered a nearly fatal bout of the killing flu of 1918, leaving her with a tendency toward bronchitis ever after. More to the point, she was actually beaten, and if John Koontz's abusive episodes have been reported with anything like accuracy she must at times have looked it. Little wonder the domestic violence Porter suffered during her early adulthood in Texas would merge with her early childhood memories of lurking violence or that she would want to leave a place she associated with fear of bodily harm.

Explaining how she came to write "Noon Wine," Porter says in her essay, "I used this scene"—the peculiar scene at her grandmother's house that she witnessed as a child—"in 'Noon Wine.'" But for the character of Mrs. Thompson, who at the end of "Noon Wine" is or seems to be afraid of her husband, she did not have to turn to a Mrs. A—— going about with her husband, trying to explain a murder. The figure she describes so empathetically as a "pale beaten-looking woman" was, or was also, herself.

∾

One more point before we leave "'Noon Wine': The Sources." A particularly incongruous statement in the essay is Porter's declaration that it captures "the whole society in which I was born and brought up" (*CE* 468). If so, her "whole" social world was among plain folk and included few if any amenities or high-culture artifacts. This is directly contrary to her claims of an upbringing among a defeated aristocracy with relics of their past still in evidence. Particularly in "Old Mortality" and parts of "The Old Order," she presents a society replete with fancy-dress balls, complete editions of Dickens and Scott bound in leather, excursions to florist shops and plays and concerts. None of these markers of high culture appears in the bare world of "Noon Wine." The statement (admission?) that *this* was "the whole society" of her childhood throws into high relief the contrast between these subsistence farming people of no elegance and little grace and her claims of origins among an aristocracy reduced in circumstances but still enjoying refined comforts, including evenings of good theater and music.

Such refined entertainments would not have been entirely unavailable in the Texas of her childhood. The network of "opera houses" that afforded experience of the performing arts to people in small towns all around the country also extended into Texas. Joseph Gallegly points out in his meticulous history of theater in Texas that Houston enjoyed its first theatrical performance in June 1838, in the early years of the republic, when the raw city's population was "some two thousand souls" (170). *Richard III* was performed there in 1839 and other great plays—*Othello, The School for Scandal, Romeo and Juliet,* and *Macbeth*—in 1840. Galveston saw its first theater performance in 1839 and in the 1890s, the first decade of Callie Russell Porter's life, witnessed performances by Sarah Bernhardt, Helena Modjeska, Richard Mansfield, and Minnie Maddern Fiske—all four generally counted among the greatest performers of their time. Ignace Paderewski played a recital in Houston in January 1896 (Gallegly 176, 162–63)—perhaps the source of Porter's reference to Miranda's cousins' having seen him in a concert transplanted to "their city," in "Old Mortality" (*CS* 179).

Porter insisted that she and her family attended such performances and specifically mentioned a production of *Hamlet* in San Antonio in 1900. Library copies of the *San Antonio Daily Express* do show frequent theatrical performances but not at so elevated a level. Since information on her early years is in some respects sketchy, one is hesitant to reject Porter's claims out of hand, but they appear to be exaggerations if not untruths, based more on wish than on fact, motivated by a desire to enhance her family's social standing.

As we have seen, if she sometimes exaggerated the wonders of her childhood, then, she apparently also "confronted" her childhood memories with degrees of anger and resentment that also exaggerated their bases in fact. At other times she spoke of her childhood indirectly, either by way of fictional characters (as in "The Downward Path to Knowledge") or by pointing out in the lives of other people (or attributing to them) qualities and experiences that reflected her own. At such moments, in the words of Emily Dickinson, she told the truth but told it "slant." Two examples of this selective empathy with fellow writers are her characterization of Katherine Mansfield's work as "a triumph of discipline over the unruly circumstances and confusions of her personal life and over certain destructive elements in her own nature" and her description of the young Willa

Cather as a "lonely" girl who "happened to be an artist . . . sitting by the fireplace to talk down an assertive brood of brothers and sisters, practicing her art on them, refusing to be lost among them" (*CE* 50, 32). What she wrote was not inaccurate of either, but it could equally well have been written about herself. She was seeing bits and pieces of her own struggle in those of her sister writers.

At times Porter's "endless process of remembering" could lead her into descriptions of an idealized rural Texas that sounds almost like an Eden. For instance, in "'Noon Wine': The Sources": "This summer country of my childhood, this place of memory, is filled with landscapes shimmering in light and color . . . that soft blackland farming country, full of fruits and flowers and birds . . . the smells and flavors of roses and melons, and peach bloom and ripe peaches, of cape jessamine in hedges blooming like popcorn, and the sickly sweetness of chinaberry florets, of honeysuckle in great swags on a trellised gallery; heavy tomatoes dead ripe and warm with the midday sun, eaten there, at the vines; the delicious milky green corn" (*CE* 470–71). Yet in a letter to William Goyen of May 19, 1951, that same country of her childhood sounds like an Eden badly fallen, with "every plant and tree" holding "a thorn or spike or needle." Recalling the general "prickliness of things: cactus, grass burrs, cockleburrs," she labels it a "purgatory" and concludes, "the great overwhelming advantage of being grown up is that blessed be God, one can never be a child again." Which version is accurate? Under the pressure of inner conflict, truth and fiction mix. When she breaks the illusion of Eden[8] to reveal her accumulated bitterness, as she does in complaints to her sister or with the sound of the gunshot in "'Noon Wine': The Sources," the shattering of the remembered moment comes as a shock.

With so much variation in the way Porter writes out her "endless remembering," we rarely know whether she is writing truthfully—though experienced readers can sometimes identify passages even in her letters when it is clear she is falsifying.[9] It is always important, then, if we are to reach an understanding of her subtle and evasive mind that is at all reliable, to read both her fiction and her nonfiction alongside letters and external biographical or historical information. In attempting to plumb the mysteries of how Texas shaped her and how she shaped Texas in her writing, "Noon Wine" and "'Noon Wine': The Sources," together, provide a valuable opportunity for this kind of multidimensional reading.

6

Awakening the Southern Belle from Her Dream of a Horse Race

In the literary marketplace, the role Porter played was that of an artistic Southern belle, a sort of Scarlett O'Hara who was also a literary genius.
—Don Graham, "A Southern Writer in Texas"

Their stories were almost always love stories against a bright blank heavenly blue sky.
—Katherine Anne Porter, "Old Mortality"

"Old Mortality" and "Pale Horse, Pale Rider," two of the three impressive novellas Porter completed in 1936 and 1937 as she "seized the day" of her artistic readiness, follow Miranda's awakening from her relentless conditioning as a latter-day Southern belle. In addressing this essentially feminist theme, Porter was taking up a subject as deeply rooted in her early life in Texas as the mysteries she treated in "Noon Wine."

All through her life Porter struggled with the fact of her sex and the need to adopt appropriate gender roles. Her grandmother's expectations remained with her as an ingrained set of prescriptive standards that her urge for freedom repeatedly led her to violate. As a girl she observed and admired her beautiful aunts and cousins as models of the true (which is to say, mythicized) Southern belle—a figure totally at odds with her powerful drive for achievement. She never reached a satisfactory resolution of this dilemma, which Joan Givner, in her essay "Problems of Personal Identity," labels a conflict between "her female self and her artist self." On the one hand she defined herself in terms of feminine beauty and seductiveness, and on the other in terms of an absorbing commitment to her artistic discipline. She needed a self-definition that could encompass both these personas, but they remained at war. Her sexual acting-out of her need for male attention continually violated the norms of propriety inculcated by her grandmother, while her drive for professional achievement and recognition on an equal plane with men invalidated both. Her departure from Texas and her development of a driving commitment to her career enacted a rejection of the Southern sense of the female self, yet she clung to an insistence on femininity drawn from that very amalgam of ideas.

In Anne Goodwyn Jones's formulation of the problem, Porter was not alone in facing the conflicts she did: "The very act of writing evoked . . . a sense of self-contradiction" for women writers in the South because "southern ladies were expected to defer to men's opinions, yet writing required an independent mind" (xi). But with her conspicuous glamour and compulsive love affairs, Porter faced it with particular intensity, enacting a role of tortuous femininity even as she was reaping the harvest of a long artistic apprenticeship. Her struggles against early social inequality and problems of gender identity were painful ones that hampered her development as a person and an intellectual. She lived in a perpetual inner disharmony.

In the society in which Porter grew up, male and female gender roles were sharply differentiated. Young women were supposed to attract husbands, and mature women were supposed to limit themselves to domestic matters and good deeds, usually through their churches. The emotional and behavioral problems that impeded Porter in her work as an adult were in large part rooted in the tensions generated by these restrictive ideas. She seems to have recognized herself early on as an artist (actress? dancer? writer?) and to have felt herself suspect for that reason. Whether this arose solely from her father's resistance to the idea of women having careers (he actually does seem to have told her, as she claimed, that if she wanted to write she could write letters) or from a more generalized cultural suspicion, she felt she was regarded as a "freak" in Texas because she wanted to write (*Refugee* 39). Certainly gender was not the only problem from her early years that stretched its hidden hand into her adult life. We have seen her awareness of the daily presence of tools of violence, and her first marriage made her only too aware of a personal dimension to the potential they represented. She was also quite aware of the element of racism in Texas (and the South more largely).[1] But the dissonance that was most inclusive and longest lasting was that between traditional expectations of an upper-class white woman—held up for her emulation even though the family was no longer upper class—and her powerful urge to break free of those constraints. When she made her escape from Texas and the unhappiness she had experienced there, she was also seeking to escape limiting models of womanhood.

The obvious fact that Porter was very beautiful made this all the harder. In one of her later columns in the *Rocky Mountain News* (July 13, 1919), she complained of the "ideal of prettiness, nauseating and eternal" as an impediment to seriousness both in the theater (her nominal subject) and for a woman. She understood that taking physical attractiveness as a measure of worth debased women's self-respect and potentially ensnared them in self-betrayal. Yet she never stopped measuring herself by that standard and presenting herself as a glamorous beauty. Even in her later years she appeared at readings in evening gowns and long gloves (which Flannery O'Connor slyly observed somewhat "interfered with her turning the pages").[2]

Porter's desperate if unconscious determination to use her beauty to win love was acted out in a long series of turbulent involvements with men. I have already traced the series up to 1936–37 (though with no claim of exhaustiveness). At the time she and Albert Erskine became lovers, in the fall of 1937, she had been married four times, not including the debated Ernest Stock. When Erskine quickly began urging her to marry him, she had to explain that she would first have to get a divorce from Eugene Pressly, who was then in Russia. She fended off Erskine's proposal until Christmastime, then made a retreat to her sister's house in Houston and wrote her acceptance from there. One might suppose she would then fly back to her lover's arms, but she lingered in Houston, waiting for the complicated divorce to come through and writing him long letters fantasizing about the house they would build. Meanwhile, she enjoyed the company of fun-loving Gay, Gay's daughter Anna Gay, and brother Paul's good-looking seventeen-year-old son Paul, who had admired her extravagantly when she visited in 1936.[3] When the divorce from Pressly became final on April 9, 1938, she could no longer put Erskine off. He drove to Houston to pick her up, and ten days later they were married by a judge in New Orleans, Robert Penn Warren serving as best man. It was only then, apparently, that Erskine learned her actual age.

In a legal sense, the marriage lasted three and a half years but in any real sense less than two. Predictably, Porter rushed into domesticity, then realized (as if she had not already known) that it was hard to write while also cooking and cleaning. In July, less than three months into the marriage, she again went to the Olivet Writers' Conference, over Erskine's objections.[4] She did not stay away; she did come back after the conference; and neither Eudora Welty nor W. H. Auden, both of whom visited Baton Rouge during this period, observed any problem in the marriage. But when the April 1939 publication of *Pale Horse, Pale Rider* was greeted with critical acclaim, her standing in the literary world became such that she received—and accepted—more and more invitations to speak at colleges, which took her more and more away from Erskine. On May 15, her forty-ninth birthday, she wrote Erskine from New York that although she truly loved him she did not want to live in Baton Rouge. Nevertheless, she again returned, partly for what Unrue calls a "half-hearted reconciliation" (*Life* 177) and partly to finish paying for the land she had bought for their house, in order to sell it at a profit of $650 two days later. But in July she again went to Olivet over Albert's objections.

That fall, on September 1, 1939, Adolf Hitler's Germany invaded Poland, launching World War II. Porter had witnessed the Nazi rise to power while she was in Europe—including some of the mass rallies—and her reaction to the onset of war was highly fraught with emotion as well as opinion.[5] Like most Americans, however, she did not become fully aroused about the war until after Pearl Harbor.

In the meantime, she was more occupied with other matters, such as ending her marriage. In January 1940 she and Erskine began making preparations to separate. She applied for a two-month residency at the writers' and artists' retreat Yaddo, at Saratoga Springs, New York. When she arrived there in June, the director, Elizabeth Ames, quickly extended her stay to a full year, providing her a secure base of operations from which to make speaking trips to writing workshops and colleges. She and Erskine maintained a friendly correspondence, but in the spring of 1942, at his request, she established residency in Reno and obtained a divorce. This was her last marriage, though by no means her last romance. In May 1944, while living in Washington, D.C., at the home of painter Marcella Comés Winslow, she met a handsome soldier named Charles Shannon, twenty-nine years old in comparison to her fifty-four, with whom she had an intensely emotional affair. Others followed, including a brief, turbulent relationship with bisexual Texas novelist William Goyen. Again and again her dream of the belle cum siren turned into nightmare. She was never able to awaken herself fully from that dream. Yet when she could distance its effects on her life by addressing it through her imagination, she wrote stories that issue powerful wake-up calls.

We have seen that even some of her earliest works demonstrate a deep interest in women's social roles. "María Concepción" presents a woman of strength even to the point of ruthlessness, and "Flowering Judas" shows us, in Laura, a woman with strength of another kind, able to keep herself functioning and maintain an outward calm even though actually terrified of her social environment.[6] But it is in the Miranda stories that Porter most fully explores her own tangled feelings about being a woman, through scrutiny and rejection of the traditional roles of Southern belle and Southern lady—roles she herself never stopped playing. Along with "The Old Order," the two novellas "Old Mortality" and "Pale Horse, Pale Rider" offer Porter's "most complex and interesting gender-thinking" (Titus 178).

∽

In a letter to Porter of January 12, 1972, Southern novelist and poet Robert Penn Warren recognized "Old Mortality" as having "few peers in any language." It is indeed a work of superlative artistry both in its human and cultural insights and in such technical aspects as structure, tautness of language, and subtle manipulation of narrative point of view—measures of craft that were of supreme importance to Porter. What strikes me as most remarkable, however, as I read it again and again, is Porter's use of dual intersecting plot lines as a way to reach, and to engage the reader in reaching, a significant set of insights. Both narrative lines derive from Porter's own life and stresses: one her attempts as a child in Texas, in reduced and unstable circumstances, to understand her family and its Southern heritage, the other her conflicted drives toward mutually exclusive models of female life. Both narrative lines are launched in the first of the novella's three parts, labeled 1885–1902.[7]

The setting was declared by Porter, in her 1943 letter to fellow-novelist George Sessions Perry, to be between San Marcos and Austin—a siting that draws a small circle around Kyle. But that is scarcely plausible. Neither the fancy-dress Mardi Gras ball at which Amy is established as a three-dimensional character nor the two-story grandeur of the house where she comes sweeping down the stairs reflects the Porter family's quality of life in Kyle. Yet the story is clearly autobiographical. The ball may to some degree reflect a carnival in Houston called No-Tsu-Oh, "patterned after the New Orleans Mardi Gras," that was "celebrated annually" from 1899 to World War I. Porter would have had an opportunity to take part in or observe No-Tsu-Oh when she and John Henry Koontz lived in Houston.[8] Primarily, though, the ball is redolent of New Orleans. This is one of those times when Porter blurred, rather than emphasized, the distinction between Texas and the South. But her own struggle to understand her elders and forebears and the significance of their Southern origins certainly took place in Kyle.

The primary narrative line of "Old Mortality" follows the story of the beautiful but doomed Aunt Amy, quite literally the belle of every ball. A fixture in the family's obsessive remembering, Amy has also been a presence in the girls' lives from earliest memory as a "sad, pretty story from old times" (CS 173). But as Miranda will learn, her story is in fact not "pretty" at all. Blood runs through it, as it does through "Old Mortality" as a whole, in a series of progressively more disturbing images. The model of an opposite kind of female life, also introduced in Part I, is Cousin Eva, a kind of anti-belle, "shy and chinless, straining her upper lip over two enormous teeth" (CS 178). Unlike Amy, who is sought after for every dance at balls, Eva sits "in corners" and watches her "unnatural" mother,

Cousin Molly Parrington, an over-age belle of dyed hair and inappropriate flirtations. Unwilling or unable to progress to the stage of Southern lady, Molly forestalls any possibility of social pleasure or courtship Eva might have had by openly referring to her as an "old maid." Perhaps, then, by necessity or perhaps by choice, Eva has embraced alternative roles. Going to family parties in "her mother's old clothes, made over," she has a career teaching Latin in a "Female Seminary" and "believe[s] in votes for women"—indeed, is an activist in the cause, a speaker at rallies, unafraid to assert her opinions (CS 178).

Although Amy is described in the family myth as "spirited-looking," the extent of her spiritedness, actually rebellion, is not openly discussed but is revealed in the episode of the Mardi Gras ball. Defying her father's direct order to dress more modestly, she flirts so outrageously with a former fiancé named Raymond that her cousin Gabriel, hopelessly in love with her, challenges him to a duel and her brother Harry takes a shot at Raymond without bothering with the niceties of a challenge. Amy, we realize, may be even more rejecting of the role of the belle than Eva is, in that even while acting it out, she parodies it. But this strategy for achieving selfhood proves—as Amy has fully realized—self-destructive. The whiffs of scandal that hover about her story may be ignored in official retellings of her legend, but the family cannot deny that she was "unhappy" and "died young" (CS 173). Those facts are socially acceptable; they make her story Poe-esque and Amy herself a tragic heroine. But by taking the role of the belle to its logical extreme while defying its strictures of decorum, Amy demonstrates that the myth itself has a dark side. It places needless stress on the young, like Maria and Miranda, who have unrealistic patterns held up to them for emulation, and it blights the lives of women like Eva who are not beautiful or do not subscribe to the goals expected of a belle.

The second narrative line in "Old Mortality" is of course Miranda's long effort to understand the family myths in which she has been brought up, primarily the story of Aunt Amy, her father's favorite sister. Porter had earlier traced the formation of Miranda's independent mind in "The Old Order," but the story begins anew in "Old Mortality." Eight years old as the novella begins, she is again presented as a lively, curious child—so emotionally volatile that at one point she throws herself flat on the floor in despair over arithmetic—and her sister Maria, four years older, as a well-behaved and keenly observant girl. Their grandmother remains a figure of strength and influence. This time there is no brother Paul. The issue is female acculturation.

Although the Miranda and Maria we see in Part I have trouble reconciling what they have been told (the family myth) with what they observe, they fully understand and accept the defining requirements for assuming the role of the belle: "There were points of beauty by which one was judged severely. First, a beauty must be tall; whatever color the eyes, the hair must be dark, the darker the better; the skin must be pale and smooth. Lightness and swiftness of movement were important points. A beauty must be a good dancer, superb on horseback, with a serene manner, an amiable gaiety tempered with dignity at all hours. Beautiful teeth and hands, of course, and over and above all this, some mysterious crown of enchantment that attracted and held the heart" (*CS* 176). What they do not at all understand—though readers do—is that even the beautiful Amy felt pressured by these expectations. We see her solidifying her status as Belle Supreme as if it were hard labor, going to every ball and dancing all night even when feverish. Returning exhausted and sick from the "lark" of riding horseback to the Mexican border to get her brother out of the country after he shoots Raymond, she quips, "And if I am to be the heroine of this novel, why shouldn't I make the most of it?" That is, she recognizes herself as a character in the South's social fiction, but not so much its "fairest flower" as its "ornamental victim."[9]

To Miranda and Maria, the long-dead Aunt Amy, modeled jointly on Porter's aunts Annie Porter Gay and Ione Porter, is only a "ghost in a frame" that they gaze at in puzzlement. Not yet questioning their adults' veracity as tellers of the story, they simply wish they understood. But to their father, if they express their perception of a disparity between the legend of Amy and the evidence of their own eyes, it is the legend that is true and the evidence that plays it false. The picture they puzzle over in the opening paragraphs does not do Amy justice, he explains; she was much more beautiful than that and more slender and graceful than the girls' cousins, even though these present-day belles whom they see for themselves "all boas[t] of their eighteen-inch waists." A better horsewoman, too, he insists. But they begin to notice that their father tells other stories that are clearly and obviously at variance from observable fact. He declares that "there were never any fat women in the family," whereas they know of two—our friend Great-Aunt Eliza, from "The Old Order," and Great-Aunt Keziah, whose husband "refused to allow her to ride his good horses after she had achieved two hundred and twenty pounds" (*CS* 174).

Their grandmother, too, seems to find no reason to discard the myth of the ideal Southern woman just because her daughter died before completing it. Twice a year she goes through a ritual of grieving for Amy (apparently based on Porter's father's similar rituals), sitting in the attic and going through keepsakes of Amy such as gloves, ornaments, and dresses as if they were precious relics. To

Miranda and Maria, who are allowed to witness these bouts of mourning as long as they stay quiet and don't touch anything, the keepsakes she treasures are merely "moth-eaten bunches of pink ostrich feathers for the hair . . . clumsy big breast pins and bracelets . . . silly-looking combs, standing up on tall teeth"—a collection of "faded" and "misshapen" things scarcely worth keeping, let alone crying over (CS 175). Not only do they strike the girls as "dowdy," they confirm the melancholy strain in the legend.

"Amy's wedding dress," Grandmother sighs, and spreads open an "immense cloak of dove-colored cut velvet, spreading beside it a silver-gray watered-silk frock, and a small gray velvet toque with a dark red breast of feathers" (CS 182). She had tried to persuade Amy to wear white satin, she explains, but Amy insisted, "'I shall wear mourning if I like . . . it is *my* funeral, you know.'" In the funereal gray clothes with dark red feathers like a bleeding wound in the breast, beauty and sexuality, marriage and death are inextricably entangled. Trying to pick up "floating ends of narrative" and patch them together, the girls quiz family members for details that may explain. "Tell me again how Aunt Amy went away when she was married," they ask an aunt, whose reply pictures marriage as a kind of doom: "She ran into the gray cold and stepped into the carriage and turned and smiled with her face as pale as death, and called out 'Good-by, good-by,' and refused her cloak, and said, 'Give me a glass of wine.' And none of us saw her alive again" (176).

Part II, dated 1904, continues the narrative thread of the girls' efforts to understand. Now fourteen and ten, they have been sent to a convent school. Still under the influence of the family romance, reinforced by their reading of romantic pulp fiction, they enjoy thinking of their lives in the lurid terms of anti-Catholic tales in which "unlucky maidens" are "'immured' in convents" and "forced to take the veil—an appalling rite during which the victims shrieked dreadfully" (CS 193). Here as elsewhere, the narrative voice gently mocks even as it identifies with the girls. Myth and reality are again at variance; their own convent school has "no dungeons" and the nuns are only "very dull good-natured women" (193–94). Throughout the school week the girls long for weekend outings, but often, after preparing for such visits, they are left sitting in their dress-up clothes as a punishment for poor grades or misbehavior. Resembling Amy in one way, at least, they tend to resist authority.

On the day that constitutes the narrative present of Part II, however, their wait is not in vain. Their father comes to take them to the horse races, where their uncle Gabriel is "running a mare" named Miss Lucy. The girls know of Gabriel as a character in the story of Amy, where he is cast as a romantic youth so desperately in love with her that he takes to racehorses for consolation when she spurns him (until he becomes dishonored and loses his inheritance, whereupon she marries him). Now, at the racetrack, just after they have placed their one-dollar bets on the filly, a "vast bulging man with a red face" appears and their father exclaims, "Bless my soul, there's Gabriel." Silently they wonder how this "shabby fat man with bloodshot blue eyes" can be Aunt Amy's "handsome romantic beau" who wrote poetry about her: "Oh, what did grown-up people *mean* when they talked, anyway?" (*CS* 197). Gabriel's horse, a long shot, wins, thrilling them to screams and tears and winning them a hundred dollars apiece (which their father confiscates to put into their bank accounts). But afterward, as they stand in the winners' circle, they see the dark side of the victory that had seemed so glorious:

> The horses were coming in, looking as if their hides had been drenched and rubbed with soap, their ribs heaving, their nostrils flaring and closing. . . . Miss Lucy came in last, and a little handful of winners applauded her and cheered the jockey. He smiled and lifted his whip, his eyes and shriveled brown face perfectly serene. Miss Lucy was bleeding at the nose, two thick red rivulets were stiffening her tender mouth and chin, the round velvet chin that Miranda thought the nicest kind of chin in the world. Her eyes were wild and her knees were trembling, and she snored when she drew her breath.
>
> Miranda stood staring. That was winning, too. Her heart clinched tight; that was winning, for Miss Lucy. So instantly and completely did her heart reject that victory, she did not know when it happened, but she hated it, and was ashamed that she had screamed and shed tears for joy when Miss Lucy, with her bloodied nose and bursting heart had gone past the judges' stand a neck ahead. (*CS* 199)

Even worse, the filly's condition is no surprise to Gabriel. He admits to Harry that she had had nosebleed since the previous day but he ran her nevertheless because he so desperately needed a win.

The horse race episode is a much-noted parable of the victimization of young women. As a filly, a young female horse not yet bred, Miss Lucy is a counterpart of Miranda and Maria or of the belles they have been taught to admire—all of them, ironically, fine horsewomen. The blood coursing from Miss Lucy's nostrils echoes the dark red feathers on Aunt Amy's gray hat and, as we learn later, her lung hemorrhages after overexerting herself at dances and parties, the figurative horse races in which she and other young belles had to compete for husbands. As Cousin Eva later says in Part III, the premarital social whirl was a "market" in which girls were pitted as rivals for the prize, and as she says so she arches her neck "like a cavalry horse getting a whiff of the battlefield" (CS 216).

This reading of the horse race episode of "Old Mortality" was first formulated by critic Jane Flanders in her 1976 essay "Katherine Anne Porter and the Ordeal of Southern Womanhood." Porter quickly made it clear to Flanders that she rejected the feminist interpretation. Responding in conciliatory terms in a letter dated September 4, 1976, Flanders assured Porter that she understood her dislike of the word *feminism* and respected her wish not to be labeled feminist, but even so, remained convinced of the validity of her reading. Later, when she sent Porter a draft of a paper on Porter's early book reviews to demonstrate the logic she had brought to her interpretation, Porter marked it up, changing the word *feminist* to *feminine* and at one point writing in the margin, "I am not anything ending in -ist . . . but *very* feminine." The stunning self-contradiction of her comment is evident when it is compared with a letter written in 1963, where she recalled as "beyond tiresome" an exchange with Hemingway scholar Carlos Baker in which she felt she was being labeled feminine (S/T 174–75).

Despite her claim to be "*very* feminine" and her devotion to stunning clothes and personal beauty, Porter did recognize—at any rate, during the years when she was making notes for "Old Mortality" and then writing it—the pernicious implications of such standards of female value and identity. The story powerfully demonstrates that measuring young women by their beauty and charm was destructive and that elevating such attributes as goals to which girls should aspire was both daunting and crippling. This theme of the destructiveness, let alone artificiality, of the South's idealization of the belle is the focus of Part III, dated 1912.

Here, in a long conversation between a now eighteen-year-old Miranda and Cousin Eva, the two narrative lines of the story converge. In Part II, the independent-mindedness we have seen developing in Miranda from childhood has culminated in her small act of "mov[ing] away coldly" from her father after he refused to answer her question about whether Gabriel was a drunkard (CS 200). Freighted with meaning, this small action prefigures the real break she has now made by eloping and not seeing him for almost a year. Nevertheless, she is now on a train going home for the funeral of Uncle Gabriel, who has at last drunk himself to death. It would seem that the last vestige of the family myth has died and that only clarification, followed by liberated departure into fully enlightened adulthood, awaits Miranda.

By chance her seatmate is Cousin Eva, whose story has never, until now, engaged Miranda's attention. Recognizable by the features we heard about in Part I, "two immense front teeth and a receding chin," Eva proves to have a story of her own. She has become a genuinely eccentric, intimidating old woman with "choleric black eyes" and a look of "disapproval," but as Miranda realizes, an old woman who "did not lack character" (*CS* 206). After the two identify themselves to each other, they begin a conversation that often puts Miranda into a mental whirl but leads to a warm mutual regard. Eva remembers her as a "lively little girl" and "very opinionated"—a judgment she voices with approval, however, because she believes in having strong opinions. Eva also remembers Miranda as having unconventional aspirations: "The last thing I heard about you, you were planning to be a tight-rope walker. You were going to play the violin and walk the tight rope at the same time," a recollection Miranda confirms, though now she would prefer to be "an air pilot" (207–8). At any rate, despite having achieved the conventionally approved status of married woman, albeit through the unconventional method of elopement, she no longer aspires to be either a belle or a lady.

As they talk, Eva seems to Miranda to pick up and voice her very thoughts, as if their minds were fusing. It is a not only uncanny experience but frightening prospect, since Miranda devoutly hopes never to become so unattractive and forbidding as her cousin. Yet she recognizes and admires Eva's energetic efforts for woman suffrage, a cause she also believes in. And as Eva thaws toward the lively girl who came in and sat on her hat only a few minutes before, she now calls her "my dear." Speaking of Gabriel, as they naturally do, leads them to Amy. But how different Eva's version of the story is! Despite declaring that she loved Amy, she calls her "a devil and a mischief-maker" and declares her "reputation" wasn't worth a snap of the fingers and her departure after her wedding was "to scandal and to death" (*CS* 211). Seemingly intent on debunking the myth, she gives Miranda an entirely new version of the story:

> "I never believed for one moment . . . that Amy was an impure woman. Never! But let me tell you, there were plenty who did believe it. There were plenty to pity poor Gabriel for being so completely blinded by her. A great many persons were not surprised when they heard that Gabriel was perfectly miserable all the time, on their honeymoon, in New Orleans. Jealousy. And why not? But I used to say to such persons that, no matter what the appearances were, I had faith in Amy's virtue. Wild, I said, indiscreet, I said, heartless, I said, but *virtuous,* I felt certain. But you could

hardly blame anyone for being mystified. The way she rose up suddenly from death's door to marry Gabriel Breaux, after refusing him and treating him like a dog for years. . . . And there was something very mysterious about her death, only six weeks after marriage." (211–12)

Placing little credibility in this strangely obsessed cousin, Miranda insists that Amy "died of a hemorrhage from the lungs"—that is, of tuberculosis. (The trail of blood continues.) But Eva dismisses the idea as "the official account" and urges her not to "live in a romantic haze about life" (212).

Miranda has thought, of course, that she was trying all along to break free of that very haze and thought she had succeeded. But not only does she find herself defending Aunt Amy, but when Eva asks her if in eloping she at least married into money, Miranda scoffs inwardly, "As if anyone could have stopped to think of such a thing!" (*CS* 213). That is, she still clings to the accompanying myth of the love story. Eva, of course, has had no part to play in that story, but now shows, by the very intensity of her effort to replace it with a more lurid version, that she is still a victim of the family romance: "Cousin Eva strained her lips tightly over her teeth, let them fly again and leaned over, gripping Miranda's arm. 'What I ask myself, what I ask myself over and over again,' she whispered, 'is, what connection did this man Raymond from Calcasieu have with Amy's sudden marriage to Gabriel, and *what* did Amy do to make away with herself so soon afterward? For mark my words, child, Amy wasn't so ill as all that. She'd been flying around for years after the doctors said her lungs were weak. Amy did away with herself to escape some disgrace, some exposure that she faced'" (214). Her version is that Amy was pregnant by Raymond and in order to escape the notoriety of it committed suicide by overdosing on the medication she was given "to keep her quiet after a hemorrhage." Blood again.

Because Eva has been defined as a free, independent woman committed to intellectual pursuits, it is tempting to read this concluding section as Miranda's awakening. If so, we are falling for a narrative trick. Porter has set us up to think in terms of a dichotomy, but the story Miranda must interpret is not a simple either/or. Eva's version of the legend of Amy is as romanticized as the traditional one but in the mode of dark romanticism, akin to Miranda's and Maria's fascination with immurement, dungeons, and screaming novices. When Miranda stammers vaguely that at any rate Amy was very beautiful, Eva denies even that part of the myth. "I for one never thought so," she says. "And her illness wasn't romantic either . . . though to hear them tell it she faded like a lily. Well, she coughed blood, if that's romantic" (*CS* 215).

This harsh statement is still not the end of the trail of blood, however, because Eva goes on from the coughing of blood to the primal taboo of menstrual bleeding: "She had a lovely complexion . . . perfectly transparent with a flush on each cheekbone. But it was tuberculosis, and is disease beautiful? And she brought it on herself by drinking lemon and salt to stop her periods when she wanted to go to dances. There was a superstition among young girls about that. They fancied that young men could tell what ailed them by touching their hands, or even by looking at them. As if it mattered?" (*CS* 215). Miranda, still clinging to her belief in her own enlightened state, comments coolly, "I should have thought they'd have stayed at home if they couldn't manage better than that." But Eva knows better: "Those parties and dances were their market, a girl couldn't afford to miss out, there were always rivals waiting to cut the ground from under her" (216). Like fillies being run in a race, they had to do what they could to stanch their bleeding so they could go on running.

Miranda has wondered earlier why Eva seems to have hated Aunt Amy so. Her silent question shows insight, but not a fullness of insight. At this point in the story we readers can answer, though she cannot, that Eva hates the system that sets up such an ideal as the Southern belle. But we, too, still have more to learn. In a spate of bitterness Eva reveals that her hate is both principled and personal:

> "'Hold your chin up, Eva,' Amy used to tell me," she began, doubling up both her fists and shaking them a little. "All my life the whole family bedeviled me about my chin. My entire girlhood was spoiled by it. Can you imagine . . . people who call themselves civilized spoiling life for a young girl because she had one unlucky feature? Of course, you understand perfectly it was all in the very best humor, everybody was very amusing about it, no harm meant—oh, no, no harm at all. That is the hellish thing about it. It is that I can't forgive," she cried out, and she twisted her hands together as if they were rags. "Ah, the family . . . the whole hideous institution should be wiped from the face of the earth. It is the root of all human wrongs." (*CS* 217)

And the next minute she is saying, "Tomorrow we'll be at home again. I'm looking forward to it, aren't you?"

There is after all no escaping the bonds of family. Stepping down onto the train platform the next morning, Eva is incongruously happy to see Harry, and Miranda is painfully aware that her father has not forgiven her for her elopement. Like Eva, but silently, she, too, denounces family: "*I will be free of them, I shall not even remember them*" (*CS* 219). Wanting to be free of all bonds, she means to "run away from marriage" just as she earlier ran away *to* marriage. "I won't be romantic about myself," she promises herself. "Let them tell their stories to each other. Let them go on explaining how things happened. I don't care. At least I can know the truth about what happens to me." But the last word comes in the narrator's detached voice, a word of chilling recognition: "At least I can know the truth about what happens to me, she assured herself silently, making a promise to herself, in her hopefulness, her ignorance" (221).

It is hard to decide whether Porter meant by this ending that none of us can ever know the truth of our experience, or just that Miranda did not yet have that capacity, or if the story only raises the question. It is hard even to know whether an older Miranda achieves clarity of judgment at the end of "Pale Horse, Pale Rider" or "The Grave." In the course of both, she gains maturity and some measure of wisdom. One thing we can see at the devastatingly ambiguous end of "Old Mortality" is how deeply Porter drew on her own experience in writing the novella. By using the structure of two intersecting story lines, she not only explored both her early efforts to understand her Southern heritage and her mature tension between conflicting goals of career and romance but also made it evident that the quest for understanding was, and needed to be, directed precisely at the myths of gender.

Further, the blood motif in "Old Mortality," both menstrual blood and blood coughed up, reflects not merely Porter's normal cycles but her experience of abortion and possible stillbirth, her own case of tuberculosis, and possibly her mother's as well. Miranda's youthful elopement and her determination to run away from her marriage reflect Porter's all-too-early marriage and her escape from it, while her father, like Miranda's father, stood at a disapproving distance. And Miranda's return home, not to stay but to visit, reflects Porter's own returns to Texas, never to stay but only to visit. She had returned from Europe to visit her family only six months before she completed "Old Mortality." During her visit she went, if not to a funeral, to the evidence of one: her mother's grave. Perhaps it was that most recent of her few returns, combined with her first visit to the grave, that sparked the final *click* with which the scattered notes and drafts for the novella came together in her mind, allowing her to write it all down in one week, the second week of November 1936.

∼

Just as "Old Mortality" demythicizes the figure of the Southern belle, so "Pale Horse, Pale Rider" demonstrates the vulnerability of the related myth of romantic love to the world's slings and arrows. It is set in Denver at the time of Porter's newspaper work there in 1918, when two twentieth-century disasters,

World War I and the flu pandemic, converged. In a later chapter we will examine this second novella about Miranda in connection with Porter's reaction to war. Here I want to consider very briefly its resolution of the theme of the Southern belle.

In "The Fig Tree," we saw Miranda as a small child, lacking the knowledge she needed in order to rid herself of a false sense of guilt over having buried a chick alive. By giving her that knowledge and a sense of the wonder of a universe where "nobody knows," Great-Aunt Eliza manifested her heroic stature as a guide to maturation. In "The Grave" we saw Miranda—still a child, still lively and independent—wanting to *see,* to know. In all of the "Old Order" stories and in "Old Mortality" her saving quest for knowledge holds her back from the brink of surrender to the South's rigid expectations. Yet the figure of the belle continues to interest and challenge her. In "Pale Horse, Pale Rider" she carries out the belle's task of seeming spirited and appealing even while things happen *to* her. As an "ornamental victim" on whom society presses its dictates, the belle does not so much initiate action as accept her bloodied fate. But Miranda continues to muster her resistance to victimhood and at the end pulls back from a brink of a different kind.

The Miranda we see here is, like the classic Southern belle, beautiful, a good dancer, and a good horsewoman, and she is in love with a young man who epitomizes the South's traditional ideal of chivalric heroism. At the same time, she has in many ways freed herself of the restrictive myth. She is a career woman, she smokes openly, she speaks with a savvy modern irony, and she is onto the falsity of values surrounding her. Much like Porter herself, the Miranda of "Pale Horse, Pale Rider" has chosen the Eva-like path of a career without entirely rejecting the role of the belle.

As the story opens, Miranda is trapped in a nightmarish dream—the first in a series—of Texas. In the daytime her waking self is also immersed in a dream, but this one of romantic love. Adam, her young soldier, is also a Texan. Both his name and his regional identity, paired as it is with hers, announce that this is to be a story of return to beginnings. As Gary Ciuba points out, Adam embodies a male perfection very much in keeping with the "southern military tradition" of handsome officers with polished manners in beautifully tailored uniforms (104). But this seeming return to a fresh beginning is not immaculately Edenic. In truth, none of us can reach back to unfallen beginnings; they are always already tainted by societal customs and pressures and, more profoundly, by death. In the same way, even as she tries to hold onto this new love, she is already infected by the flu virus.

In her first dream, Miranda takes advantage of everyone's being asleep to escape from a home that would bend her to its will:

> Now I must get up and go while they are all quiet. Where are my things? Things have a will of their own in this place and hide where they like. Daylight will strike a sudden blow on the roof startling them all up to their feet; faces will beam asking, Where are you going, What are you doing, What are you thinking, How do you feel, Why do you say such things, What do you mean? No more sleep. Where are my boots and what horse shall I ride? Fiddler or Graylie or Miss Lucy with the long nose and the wicked eye? How I have loved this house in the morning before we are all awake and tangled together like badly cast fishing lines. (*CS* 269)

Her "things" (clothes) and clothing in general are a prominent motif throughout the story, representing, as Mary Titus writes, "the tight social control of individual activity, particularly gender activity," and particularly in wartime (164). Two of the horses her dreaming self considers riding have familiar names—Fiddler, the Grandmother's aging saddle horse in "The Old Order," and Miss Lucy, the filly in "Old Mortality." And the imaging of the family as "badly cast fishing lines" aptly represents the tangled confusion of emotions Porter experienced in her own family.

Miranda chooses to ride Graylie, reminiscent of the pale horse of the Apocalypse, "because he is not afraid of bridges"—that is, of transitions, whether from one bank of a stream to another or figuratively from one state or condition to another or from life toward death, as this dream ride will be. Also, as a no-color color reminiscent of Amy's gray wedding clothes with the dark red mark of death on the breast, gray anticipates her choice of plain, colorless clothes at the end when she goes back into the world as one of the living dead. Mounting Graylie, she rides at a run, leaping a hedge and a ditch, while a stranger on another gray horse, Death personified, keeps pace. At last, reining Graylie in, she rises in her stirrups and shouts to the now vaguely familiar stranger, "I'm not going with you this time—ride on!" (*CS* 270). Not this time but another. With that, she awakens.

While she bathes and dresses we see retrospectively her previous day when she was tasked with visiting wounded soldiers—a conventional role for a woman in wartime. As both Titus and Ciuba emphasize, that is one of the things war traditionally did through its ideology of the home front: it made gender roles more rigid: "Like the old-time daughters of Dixie, the women left behind by World War I were supposed to defend civilization by sacrifice . . . in works of home-front charity [that] perpetuate[d] . . . sexism" (Ciuba 103; Titus 164–65).[10] Miranda had carried a basket of flowers and treats to distribute—a detail marking the femininity of her "war work." Knowing what a false gesture she was making, she had felt "miserably embarrassed" by it and, walking quickly through the ward, had set the whole basket down on the bed of one particularly hostile soldier and hurried outside. At that point she made herself a promise—much as she did at the end of "Old Mortality" but this time more firmly grounded: "Never again will I come here, this is no sort of thing to be doing" (*CS* 277). Later, into the post-midnight hours, she went dancing with Adam.

Now, headachy and flushed from the advent of the flu on the day the story begins, she makes herself look as pleasing as she can and leaves to meet Adam, who waits just outside the door of her room to walk her to work. As they go, they see reminders of war and death, including a passing funeral. Adam speaks of trying to get used to wearing the prescribed wristwatch though it seems effeminate to "southern and southwestern" boys like himself. Before parting at the newspaper building, they stop for coffee and exchange terse patter about the "perfect nonsense" of the war—patter designed to mask their actual sense of impending disaster (*CS* 283). At the end of this day, Miranda has to review a stage show. As if in a world of their own or a capsule through which they can see others yet remain apart, they go to the show together, have dinner, and dance a little, all the while sharing their witty demurral from the war fervor all about them.

On the second day of the story Miranda wakes up seriously ill. Needing to be hospitalized but with no hospital beds available, she stays in her room despite the landlady's alarm. Adam has received word that his deployment is being sped up and has been at camp for processing. When he comes back, he takes care of her, disregarding the danger to himself, until an ambulance comes twenty-four hours later. These are their last hours together and the time when, in spite of her nausea and fever and delirium, they most fully express their love. Then, while he is out getting supplies, she is taken to the hospital. Even with the aggressive treatment this affords her, which many flu sufferers did not receive, she very nearly dies—indeed, has what we now call a near-death experience. A month passes before she fully regains consciousness and learns that Adam is dead—not on the battlefield but of the flu, presumably caught from her.

The role of the belle has died in her; she no longer pretends to be chipper and charming, nor does she care about bright, pretty clothes. True to the sense of style she had shared with Adam, she wants an elegant minimalism of her own devising. When her friends come to help her get ready to leave the hospital, she writes out a list of what she needs:

"One lipstick, medium, one ounce flask Bois d'Hiver perfume, one pair of gray suède gauntlets without straps, two pairs gray sheer stockings without clocks—"

Towney, reading after her, said, "Everything without something so that it will be almost impossible to get?"

"Try it, though," said Miranda, "they're nicer without. One walking stick of silvery wood with a silver knob."

"That's going to be expensive," warned Towney. "Walking is hardly worth it."

"You're right," said Miranda, and wrote in the margin, "a nice one to match my other things. Ask Chuck to look for this, Mary. Good looking and not too heavy." Lazarus, come forth. Not unless you bring me my top hat and stick. Stay where you are then, you snob. Not at all. I'm coming forth. (*CS* 316)

The last five sentences, beginning with "Lazarus, come forth," are often misread as more of the conversation with Towney, but the absence of quotation marks tells us that they are not in fact spoken. Instead, they are an imagined conversation with the dead Adam, couched in the stiff-upper-lip style they adopted before losing each other. Terse and superficially simple, they are nevertheless an ambiguous exchange. Which one calls the other Lazarus? Does Miranda summon Adam from the grave, or does he summon her to his side from her living death, "one foot in either world"?

There is no ambiguity at all, however, in the imagined conversation that follows—still without quotation marks and thus still entirely in her mind:

Adam, she said, now you need not die again, but still I wish you were here; I wish you had come back, what do you think I came back for, Adam, to be deceived like this?

At once he was there beside her, invisible but urgently present, a ghost but more alive than she was, the last intolerable cheat of her heart; for knowing it was false she still clung to the lie, the unpardonable lie of her bitter desire. She said, "I love you," and stood up trembling, trying by the mere act of her will to bring him to sight before her. If I could call you up from the grave I would, she said, if I could see your ghost I would say, I believe . . . "I believe," she said aloud. "Oh, let me see you once more." The room was silent, empty, the shade was gone from it, struck away by the sudden violence of her rising and speaking aloud. She came to herself as if out of sleep. Oh, no, that is not the way, I must never do that, she warned herself. (*CS* 317)

The clarity with which Adam's shade appears to Miranda's wishful inner sense, a product of the intensity of her love for him, again draws on Porter's experience. She was in Denver when her intense beloved little niece died, and her account to Gay of how the child "came back to her," in a letter of April 1, 1920, is in language much like this passage.

The love Porter felt for her niece was an emotion free of artifice or convention, very different from the romantic but self-interested love to which the Southern belle aspired as her proper goal. Miranda's love for Adam is seen as an equally authentic one. Poet Allen Tate thought "Pale Horse, Pale Rider" verged on "sentimentality," but most readers have seen in it, instead, a tense reserve that steels the emotional tone (*S/T* 27–28). Though a love story, it has none of the "bright blank heavenly blue sky" quality attributed to Miranda's conventional elders' love stories in "Old Mortality" (*CS* 175).

The significance of the grayness and plainness of the clothes Miranda asks for at the end of the story goes beyond overt femininity or refusal of cheerfulness. By rejecting ornamentation in favor of plainness and grayness, she chooses a costume—and it is indeed a costume in an almost theatrical sense—pointedly expressive of her rejection of the role of the belle, with its obligatory gaiety and charm and its aim of matrimony. When she experiences a compelling hallucination of Adam's return but rejects such a willed summoning of the dead as a temptation to madness, she fully and finally rejects the myth of romantic love and then dresses the solemn part she expects to play. The abnegation expressed in the grayness of her clothes indicates the resignation with which she goes out to a life without love.

Mary Titus sees Miranda's outfit at the end of "Pale Horse, Pale Rider" as both a costume of minimalism and a costume of androgyny. "Even costumed as a woman, with makeup and perfume," she writes, "Miranda will remain marked by an absence; she is incomplete, external lack pointing to internal lack." That much is true. But in going on to state that Miranda "jokingly calls for a 'top hat and stick,'" Titus goes astray. The top hat and stick are outside the quotation marks that indicate her words with Towney. Miranda does call for a walking stick to support her in her weakness; the kind she wants is an elegant though simple one, a "walking stick of silvery wood with a silver knob." By carrying a traditionally masculine walking stick, Titus argues, and one of such style, Miranda will be "in the costume of the 1920s women who most rebelled against gender conventions. . . . In such garb she would resemble the transvestite women painted by Romaine Brooks," the figure of the fop or dandy who became "one cultural role and potential stereotype for homosexuals" (166). What is important about Miranda's chosen costume at the end, however, is not so much its emulation of the fop or dandy as its reconceptualizing of gender itself. She turns against traditional ways of presenting female gender even as she turns against that most traditional of Southern ways of gendering, the belle.

The very first critic to develop an influential overall view of Porter's work was William J. Nance in his *Katherine Anne Porter and the Art of Rejection* (1964), a book she intensely disliked. Nance saw the Miranda stories, in particular, as being grounded in a principle of rejection, a certain withdrawal from life or from joy. Drawing heavily on the passage about her choice of clothes after her near-death from the flu, he saw this "principle of rejection" as the essence of Miranda's character and perhaps Porter's own. Nance's interpretation was persuasive and was long deferred to but was ultimately, I believe, a distortion, just as Unrue's totalizing view of her work as a search for "truth" is, in my view, a distortion, and for much the same reason: Porter's thought and sensibility were not driven by *any* single meta-belief or truth-statement but by variance and contradiction (*S/T* 270). But I invoke Nance's argument for another reason as well. His idea of "rejection" is conceived altogether in private terms, as a matter of personality or personal predilection. My point is that Miranda's negative choices, while they do have a basis in personal experience, represent more. The ending of "Pale Horse, Pale Rider" represents a rejection of a social and cultural idea. The "principle of rejection" at work here is a rejection of a limiting and fundamentally condescending concept of women. The part of Miranda that does, finally and fully, die is the part that was intrigued by Aunt Amy and the role of the belle. When she returns to life, it is as a woman who no longer hopes to live a love story.

There is yet one more thing to be said about her plain, gray costume. Miranda's rejection of ornamentation in favor of an elegant minimalism is a fine metaphor for Porter's art itself. It was in fact toward the end of her time in Denver—the time setting of "Pale Horse, Pale Rider"—that she began working to eliminate extraneous ornamentation from her writing. The prose she then began to write was directed toward more serious subjects in a style more compressed and disciplined, a prose of surface simplicity joined to depth of implied meaning. In rejecting the Southern belle, with all her elaborations and frills, Porter achieved her potential as an artist.

7

Racial Nightmares and
"The Man in the Tree"

Southern trees bear strange fruit.

—Abel Meeropol, "Strange Fruit," recorded by Billie Holliday in 1936

The only direct account of racial violence in any of Katherine Anne Porter's published fiction comes in "The Witness," where Uncle Jimbilly recounts the abuse inflicted by white masters during slavery:

> "Dey used to take 'em out and tie 'em down and whup 'em," he muttered, "wid gret big leather strops inch thick long as yo' ahm, wid round holes bored in 'em so's evey time dey hit 'em de hide and de meat done come off dey bones in little round chunks. And wen dey had whupped 'em wid de strop till dey backs was all raw and bloody, dey spread dry cawnshucks on dey backs and set 'em afiire and pahched 'em, and den dey poured vinega all ovah 'em . . . Yassuh. And den, the ve'y next day dey'd got to git back to work in the fiels or dey'd do the same thing right ovah agin. Yassuh. Dat was it. If dey didn't git back to work dey got it all right ovah agin."
> (*CS* 341)

It is a hair-raising account for readers but apparently less so for the three children to whom he speaks. They feel "faint tinglings of embarrassment" and "wriggle" a little with "guilt," and Paul wishes to change the subject. But Miranda characteristically "want[s] to know the worst." "Did they act like that to you, Uncle Jimbilly?" His answer seems intended as testimony that Miss Sophia Jane, the children's grandmother, was too good a mistress for that, or it may simply demonstrate that Jimbilly knows not to go too far. Now it is Paul who pushes the question: "Didn't they ever die, Uncle Jimbilly?" "Cose dey died,' said Uncle Jimbilly, 'cose dey died—dey died . . . by de thousands and tens upon thousands'" (*CS* 341–42). But the children are intent on another kind of death, that of a jackrabbit they are planning to bury, and they redirect him toward his whit-tling of a wooden headstone. As usual, he "gets right back to work"—perhaps like the beaten slaves who knew they had better "git back to work" at once? While he whittles, though, he pursues purposes of his own—the tale of white cruelty. Indeed, whatever the work he was engaged in, Uncle Jimbilly "dwelt much on the horrors of slave times" (341).

In "The Journey," another of the "Old Order" stories, it appears that the three children easily shrug off the horrors Uncle Jimbilly dwells on. But in an unpub-lished manuscript usually referred to as "The Man in the Tree," Porter raises the possibility that a child who sees or perhaps only hears of such atrocities is likely to carry the trauma for life.

Porter herself was an example. Brought up in Texas at a time when lynching was practiced frequently and with increasing cruelty, she remained torn between guilt and her own entrenched prejudices. In letters and other scattered jottings we see a deep inner conflict between awareness of racial injustice and claims that it was deserved, anxiety about the threat of racial equality or mixing and fear of the violent natures of white men who carried out lynchings. Joined with distress over racial injustice and fear of other whites who could find it in themselves to inflict such cruelty, in "The Man in the Tree," is a sense that a small-town lynch-ing is a kind of violence in the family—perhaps, given the realities of interracial sex in the South, literally so.

It is one of American history's great ironies that white people, especially but not solely Southerners, developed such an unreasoning conviction that black men were always lusting after white women and girls. The far more usual practice was the other way around. Racial mixing was an inseparable part of slavery. Many white masters (Thomas Jefferson, for instance) had concubines in the slave cabins or commandeered female slaves for sex on impulse. Maria, the narrative center of the "Man in the Tree" fragment, reveals the shadow of a long tradition, then, in her anxiety about violence that occurs practically in the family. At some points in the rambling manuscript we find indications, in fact, that this story, like "Old Mortality," "Pale Horse, Pale Rider," and "The Old Order," may have be-gun its life as part of Porter's intended novel of family history. She never finished the novel, nor was she able to bring the material on lynching sufficiently under control to complete it.

Gary Ciuba's explanation of her inability to do so is that as a "daughter of the Old South" she was "still too limited" by its "racial prejudices" to gain needed distance (60). But this explanation, sound though it is, does not go nearly far enough to account for the complex contrary memories and impulses underlying that limitation or the depth of emotion evident in the draft. Porter was attempting to deal with a topic for which Texas provided abundant usable background but also abundant horror and white guilt. If we take her most fully autobiographical fiction as an indicator (as it usually *is* taken), she was also dealing with a topic of significant concern in her own family. In "The Journey," which most fully recounts the tie between Grandmother Sophia Jane and the ex-slave Aunt Nannie,[1] the Gay family inhabits a "tangled world, half white, half-black, mingling steadily . . . the confusion growing ever deeper." The Grandmother worried "whenever a child was born in the Negro quarters" whether it would be black or light-colored. Although she "learned early to keep silent and give no sign of uneasiness," she perpetuates the unspoken concern to later generations by sending her granddaughter "to see whether the newly born would turn black after the proper interval" (*CS* 337).[2] I do not offer this as evidence that Porter had black relatives but only that she might have had and that she was fully aware of this dimension of the society into which she was born.

Before turning to "The Man in the Tree," I will return briefly to "Noon Wine" to indicate an unexpected connection, then summarize the historic record of lynchings in Texas as background and Porter's racial attitudes as indicated in a number of scattered unpublished statements.

At the center of "Noon Wine" is an artfully rendered scene of masculine competition that culminates in murder. Mr. Hatch, the verbose and faintly sinister intruder on Mr. Thompson's farm, pretends to let slip by accident the startling news that Mr. Helton, the Thompsons' peculiar but competent hired man, is an escaped mental patient from North Dakota who killed his own brother on a summer day as hot as this very hot summer day in Texas. As they talk, the two engage in a kind of parrying for dominance, a covert contest under the guise of social interaction that ranges from which of them has better taste in chewing tobacco to which laughs louder at jokes and which knows better how to handle a "complainin'" woman. To Mr. Thompson it is an unsettling exchange, especially as Hatch willfully misconstrues several of his remarks. Revealing an intention to take Mr. Helton back north to stand trial, Hatch pulls a knife on the just-arriving Helton and stabs him—or so Mr. Thompson believes, or imagines, or perhaps wants to believe. At that point, acting almost as an automaton or as if in a dream, Mr. Thompson raises an ax that seems to have appeared in his hand almost without his volition and kills the would-be bounty hunter. In the same moment he sees Mr. Helton, not even wounded, run away and realizes, as do we, that he has not killed a man in defense of his hired man or to keep Helton's supposed killer from getting away but for no real reason at all.

"Noon Wine" is an especially fine example of the characteristic limpidness of Porter's style. Her words are almost like a kind of transparency overlaid upon a set of objects and scenes that they do not so much name as reveal. Robert Penn Warren spoke of this quality in her writing as "a kind of indicative poetry." Yet behind these clearly revealed objects and actions lurk uncertainties such as the mystery of Mr. Thompson's motivation. Was it concern for Helton or an acting out of his irritation? Or perhaps a panicked defense of his own economic status when threatened with the loss of his excellent hired man, the agent of his recent rise in prosperity? We sense that the devil has appeared and made trouble, but we don't understand why or how.[3]

Mr. Thompson's ax is one of the most vivid and surprising of the story's concrete details but also something of a mystery. Why choose an ax as the murder weapon? Possibly for reasons of realism, since a farm like the Thompsons' would necessarily have an ax, and it is ready to hand at the story's climax because the two men have been sitting on a couple of large stumps, one of which serves as the chopping block. Or Porter could have chosen the ax as a complement to the surrealistic atmosphere of the story, the common but faintly sinister object becomes part of a dreamlike sequence when Mr. Thompson's perceptions veer off from reality. Another possibility, alluded to earlier, links the incident to a piece of Texas history: a series of ax murders that occurred in south-central Texas some twenty-five years before she completed "Noon Wine," though not nearly that long before she began making drafts for it. We know that Porter's imagination characteristically drew its central power from memory. We know, too, that she was alert to current events. Considering this alertness, as well as how attuned she was to the newspaper as a social institution, it seems likely she would have read about these murders, which occurred between April 1911 and August 1912, in the papers.

During the period of these serial killings Porter and her first husband, John Koontz, were living in Houston and Corpus Christi. The first in the series of ax murders took place in San Antonio, where the Porters had lived less than a decade before: five members of a mulatto family were axed to death in their sleep. Ten months passed. Then in February 1912 a mulatto woman and her three children were axed to death in their beds in Beaumont, east of Houston. On March 27 six members of, again, a mulatto family were axed to death in their sleep in Colorado County, between San Antonio and Houston. Two more murders occurred in April 1912, just a week apart. Three mulattoes were axed to death in their sleep in Hempstead, near Houston, on April 4, and five members of the William Burton family, all mulattoes, were killed in the same way in San Antonio on April 11. The grisly series came to an end in August 1912 with a "bungled attack" on another mulatto family, the Dashiells, in San Antonio when their home was invaded by (reportedly) a black man who hacked off the mother's arm and fled when her screams awoke the others.[4] A bizarre new chapter had been added to the history of violence in Texas. And the common thread that runs through the series of ax murders was race.

"Noon Wine" is directly linked to this history by the detail of the ax and indirectly linked to it by its emphasis on ethnic difference. Mr. Helton arrives from a far-off place, he is ethnically marked as a Swede, and his behaviors are distinctly odd. Then Mr. Hatch also arrives unexpectedly from afar, and he, too, is marked as being different, a stranger, not so much ethnically as behaviorally. Perhaps not as odd as the hired man, he is far more sinister. Hatch imputes blood-guilt to Helton, and then Mr. Thompson imputes bloodguilt, or an imagined bloodguilt, to Hatch. The violence that ensues takes on a surrealistic quality as a sequence of actions whose elements are recognizable, emerging from a hallucinatory logic in the course of a disguised contest for masculine dominance. These are the elements involved in the social ritual of lynching.

～

The Southerners who brought an ideology of white supremacy into eastern and central Texas along with slavery also brought a social order that produced frequent violence. Historian William Carrigan writes that the slave system in itself entailed a "high level of day-to-day violence," and Cynthia Nevels, in *Lynching to Belong,* finds that European immigrants to Texas adopted racist practices as a strategy for assimilation. Brazos County, she writes, was one of the "most southern" counties in the state, not by location but because of its high rate of violence.[5] Located in the center of the slaveholding region of Texas, the county had more than its share of lynchings.

Between 1890 and 1930 hundreds of black people in Texas and thousands in the United States as a whole, as well as smaller numbers of Mexicans and a few whites accused or convicted of crimes, were killed by lynching.[6] The usual method was hanging, often preceded by torture and mutilation, perhaps after removing the victim from a jail. Sometimes mutilation was inflicted after death. Increasingly as time went on, lynch mobs burned their victims alive. To explain in any ultimate sense how people who were, or considered themselves to be, civilized could commit such acts would require explaining evil itself. Trudier Harris proposes that lynchings were "rites of exorcism" in which white Americans shifted their own potential for evil onto people of color in "scapegoat rituals" (xiii, 13). But it is possible to find more limited explanations without venturing into the mysteries of souls.

One cause of lynching was the extreme power disparity embedded in the practice of slavery. To this was joined the social acceptability of violent traditions such as dueling and feuding in the South. Another element was fear. By 1825, only a year after Stephen F. Austin's first allotment had been completely settled, there were 443 slaves among the Old Three Hundred settler families; by 1860 slaves constituted one-third of the population of central Texas, in Brazos County 1,000 out of a total population of 2,500 (Carrigan 28, 50; Nevels 15). Slave owners and other whites could not evade the knowledge that slaves nursed resentments, however compliant and cheerful they might seem, and if they reflected on it for even a moment they must have realized that however valiantly they might attempt to articulate a justification of the "peculiar institution," those resentments were well-founded. Slave uprisings had occurred at various times and places in the South, and the large slave population in Texas could have been a prodigious force exacting vengeance if slaves organized themselves to that end. The magnitude of white atrocity toward the dark people they owned as property threatened to be their downfall. Through the spectacle or "drama" of lynching, they could teach "all southerners, male and female, black and white, precisely where in the social hierarchy they stood"—and that they had better stay there (Brundage 11).

The practice of lynching, then, reflected a determination to retain power in the existing hierarchy. Members of the planter class meant to stay at the top. As for whites of lower standing or out-and-out poverty, it has often been reasoned that they were eager to demonstrate their bare superiority to the enslaved or formerly enslaved. With only rare individual exceptions, all classes of whites were intent on maintaining their racial superiority. In addition, they could always hope that collaboration with the elite by carrying out their filthiest work might gain them some particle of favor and thus a way to rise in the social order.

It is at this point that the common thread identified in the series of ax murders, mixed racial heritage, becomes pertinent. The ideology of racism seeks to maintain clarity and separation—to define clear categories of racial identity and behavior even at the cost of ignoring obvious human commonalities. Mulattoes, by their very identity as an intermediate group, undermined such clarity on both sides, for blacks and for whites. It is possible, in fact, that the bloody ax murders were not crimes of white against black at all, since at least one assailant was reported to have been a black man. But then, that could have been another instance of scapegoating.

William Carrigan adds two other important but less obvious reasons for the development of a "lynching culture" in Texas. The first is "historical memory" in local communities. Because Texas had been established as a political entity through a process of widespread violence between settlers and Indians, whites remembered "extralegal violence" as a "just and necessary part of their history" (3, 13). A sense of valorous tradition characterized by violence against a darker people was carried forward and extended to lynching of blacks and Mexicans. Second, Carrigan cites official tolerance. Texas was "a contested place" with multiple ethnic and economic groups in contention, and "mob violence rose and fell according to the degree to which constituted authorities, especially the courts, tolerated it" (13). Whites who committed lynch murders were rarely treated as criminals. When that tide turned, lynching nearly disappeared.

The practice of lynching also drew on a strong element of sexual politics. It was a display of white male power over black males that positioned women as the ostensible cause. If black men had lynched whites every time a black woman was violated under slavery, there would have been a shortage of rope and kindling, but the protection of white women from blacks became a supposed imperative and a matter of honor. As Trudier Harris writes, rape was "the one 'crime' for which lynching became the only punishment." Any black male accused of familiar or aggressive behavior toward a white woman or girl was regularly assumed to be guilty, and a featured part of the ritual of punishment was castration (Harris 5–7). The subtext of such actions was a warning to all black males that they should not consider themselves fully men with power to protect or to satisfy their own women.

Although accurate tallies of lynchings were not kept until the 1880s, we know that the practice began before the Civil War, accelerated during Reconstruction, and peaked in the thirty-year period between 1890, the year of Porter's birth, and 1920, two years after she left Texas. In the seven-county area of central Texas that Carrigan studies there were 64 lynchings of blacks between 1860 and 1929, with 20 in the 1890s alone (113)—that is, in just 7 out of the present 254 counties in the state. What follows is an attempt, drawing on Newton and Newton's *Racial and Religious Violence in America,* to give some sense of the prevalence and nature of lynching in Texas beginning with the year of Porter's birth as a context indicating the social environment before examining her writings on race and lynching. A few incidents are discussed in some detail.

1890: fifteen lynchings, all of blacks, in nine counties: Anderson, De Leon, Grimes, Harris, Limestone, Polk, Red River, Robertson, and San Augustine. Offenses cited as provocations: attempted murder or suspicion of murder (five), suspicion of rape (six), suspicion of arson (one), gambling (one), theft (one), no apparent reason (two).

1891: ten lynchings, nine of blacks and one of a Mexican. Counties: Burnet, Cass, Polk, Rusk, Smith, and Tom Green. Offenses cited: rape (two), suspected robbery (two), being a "desperado" (one), suspected murder (one), "being troublesome" (two), "insulting whites" (one), no apparent reason (two).

1892: ten, all of blacks, in five counties: Bastrop, Grimes, Lamar, McLennan, and Tyler. Reasons cited: suspicion of murder (one), accusation of or suspicion of rape (seven), participating in a riot (three).

1893: four, all of blacks, in Grimes, Hunt, Lamar (in Paris), and McLennan (in Waco) counties. Reasons cited: suspicion of rape (one), rape and murder (one), no apparent reason (two). The lynching in Paris was one of the more unusual and gruesome incidents of the period. Henry Smith was arrested for raping and murdering a three-year-old white girl named Myrtle Vance. He escaped but was located in Arkansas by a search party and brought back to be killed. A crowd of about ten thousand came to watch him die, some "by specially arranged railroad junkets" (Goldsby 12). That in itself sets this act of mob murder apart, but it is also exceptional in its cruelty and the extent to which it entered a wide public awareness. The father of the murdered child was given the honor of setting Henry Smith on fire but first burned him on the arms, legs, chest, back, and mouth with heated irons. The event was reported in newspapers nationally and even internationally. Photographs were copyrighted and sold. A sound recording was made both for sale and for synchronized exhibit along with the photographs. One local citizen boasted afterward that Paris had now achieved fame and a reputation for "moral stamina and worth" (Goldsby 13).

1894: ten lynchings, all of blacks, in Cameron, Coryell, Freestone, Harris, Hopkins, Lavaca, Marion, McLennan, and Tyler counties. Offenses cited: suspicion of wrecking trains (one), suspicion or accusation of murder (one), suspicion of rape (one), attempted rape (one), suspicion of arson (four), writing a letter to a white woman (one), no apparent reason (one, in McLennan County, which includes Waco).

1895: fourteen, thirteen of which were of blacks and one of a Native American. Counties: Angelina, Henderson, Lamar, Lee, Liberty, Madison, Morris, Navarro, Smith, Washington, and Wharton. Offenses cited: murder of a white woman (one), injury to a white woman (one), suspicion of murder (two), suspicion of rape (one), unknown (six), no apparent cause (four), "for the color of his skin" (one). The incident in Smith County on October 29 was another burning alive.

1896: four, three of blacks and one of a Mexican. Counties: Bexar (where the one Mexican lynched was shot eight times and his body burned as punishment for courting an Anglo girl), Brazos (two, on suspicion of rape), and Jefferson, in the town of Beaumont (for suspicion of murder).

Out of thirty-seven counties shown for the period 1890–96, thirty-three lie east of the I-35 line, running southward through Fort Worth, Austin, and San Antonio to Corpus Christi—the line commonly considered the break point between the South and the West. Two others, Burnet and Coryell, would be east of I-35 if it ran straight north-south. Only Tom Green County and Cameron County are truly outside the region we have identified with the South. This pattern of distribution, with the great majority of lynchings concentrated in the eastern and east-central parts of the state that had been slave territory, would continue.

After declining in 1896, the number of lynching incidents rose again to eleven in 1897 (but with twenty-nine victims), then declined sharply in the following three years. In 1900 there was only one lynching, of three black men accused of attempted murder. Then in 1901 the number rose again (to eight incidents with twelve victims) and varied erratically through 1918, the year Porter left Texas. Of the twelve killed by mobs in 1901, eleven were blacks lynched for causes ranging from murder to "insulting a white woman" to no apparent cause at all (on Christmas Day in the already notorious Paris). In Corsicana, south of Dallas, a black man charged with killing a white woman was publicly burned before five thousand witnesses. In 1902 another black male, charged with criminal assault, was burned at the stake before a crowd of four thousand.

From 1906 to 1908, when Porter was living in Louisiana after her first marriage, there were twenty lynchings in that state and twenty-one in Texas. In 1914, when she visited Louisiana again after her abortive escape to Chicago, there were nine lynchings there including a burning at the stake. By that time there had been three more lynchings by burning alive in Texas, including one of a Mexican American. In 1914, of course, Porter was desperate because of poverty and her sister's problems, and it is possible that she was not attentive to the news. Even so, we can see from this summary that her years in Texas and Louisiana gave her abundant opportunity to know that the society in which she lived was shot through with racial violence.

One of the most notorious of all lynchings in either Texas or U.S. history occurred on Porter's birthday, May 15, in 1916. She was hospitalized for tuberculosis in far west Texas at the time, and we can hope she was not aware of it, since as Unrue has pointed out she always attached great importance to her birthdays.[7] Yet that would probably be a false hope, since recently published evidence indicates she was not merely reading but writing for newspapers even while hospitalized.[8] The setting was Waco (a city that later gained additional notoriety for the Branch Davidian incident), and the lynching there on May 15, 1916, is commonly called the "Waco Horror." A mentally handicapped black youth of seventeen named Jesse Washington who had been tried, convicted, and sentenced to hang for killing a white woman was dragged from the courtroom by a mob, stabbed, mutilated, and burned alive before a crowd variously reported to have numbered between five and fifteen thousand. Policemen who watched made no attempt to interrupt the atrocity. Even if Porter did not know about it when it was first reported, details in "The Man in the Tree" indicate that she probably became aware of it at some point, perhaps by having seen some of the numerous and widely circulated picture postcards of the burning and the charred corpse. A direct reference in the manuscript makes it clear that when she thought about lynching she thought about Waco.

Such violence feeds on itself and creates, through laws of competition and mass behavior, an impetus to spread and worsen. On Christmas Day 1917 eight Texas Rangers and four volunteers who were terrorizing the town of Porvenir (in Presidio County) in an attempt to locate bandits tortured twenty-five Mexicans and shot two to intimidate the rest. Fifteen more were assembled and killed by a posse. Porter left the state only a few months after this incident but returned in 1921. On July 6, 1920, in Fort Worth, where the Ku Klux Klan was quite dominant in politics, two black brothers suspected of murder were burned alive. As if not to be outdone, Klansmen in the rival city of Dallas branded KKK on a black man's forehead with acid on April 2, 1921. On October 21 of that year, after a black man wounded two whites in the course of labor violence during a strike at the Armour meat plant in Fort Worth, he was dragged out of the hospital where he was being treated for a fractured skull by a gang of thirty men and hanged. At the time of this last incident Porter was temporarily living in Fort Worth; thus it seems very likely she would have read about it.

The year 1922 was a pinnacle of sorts, with fifteen black men lynched in Texas. One of these was burned alive in Conroe (just north of Houston) in April. Three were burned at the stake in a single incident on May 6 in the small town of Kirven (in Freestone County, far east Texas) on charges of murdering a white girl—a crime for which two white men were later convicted. That same month a

10. Charred corpse of Jesse Washington, lynched in Waco, Texas, on May 15, 1916 (Porter's twenty-sixth birthday), with jubilant crowd members still gathered around. Library of Congress, Washington, DC.

black man was whipped to death by a group of whites in Bryan (Brazos County). And between October and December that year, in three separate incidents in or near Streetman (in Freestone and Navarro counties), three blacks were burned to death by mobs. In a fourth incident during that same period the uncle of a black man suspected of rape was hanged when a mob was unable to locate his nephew.

After that year lynching erratically dwindled. Maybe public opinion was turning against the obvious brutality. But there were two other reasons of which we can be more confident. First, there had been an active antilynching movement both in fact and in literature ever since 1892, led by journalist Ida B. Wells-Barnett. Second, lynching was starting to be prosecuted and punished as a crime. Four whites were indicted in Upshur County, Texas, on August 2, 1919; three white men were charged with murder in Fort Worth on February 13, 1922, for the hanging of the man dragged from a hospital; and in 1924 a hundred whites were arrested for an attempted lynching of two blacks in Dallas.[9]

The 1922 lynching in Kirven has been studied in detail by Monte Akers, whose account of it, *Flames after Midnight,* was published in 1999 by the University of Texas Press. It is not an easy book to read. While living in Freestone

County from 1981 to 1990 as a managerial employee of Dow Chemical Company, Akers became aware that the county had a past people did not talk about when he heard a fellow employee whisper, "Kirven is where they burned the niggers." When he was elected to public office in 1986, he set himself the task of interviewing older residents of the county in order to put together the story of the county's history, including the Kirven lynching.

The area of Limestone and Freestone counties had grown rapidly during the Mexia oil boom and was already considered so lawless that the governor had declared martial law. The crime that launched the sequence of events leading to the lynching was the exceptionally brutal murder of Eula Ausley, a seventeen-year-old white girl from a wealthy family. Waylaid on her way home from school the day before her high school graduation, Eula was raped in a peculiar and peculiarly monstrous fashion involving genital mutilation with a board, she was stabbed multiple times, her throat was cut, and her face and head were stomped flat. A crime such as this in Texas in 1922 could be counted on to provoke violence by whites assuming the perpetrator or perpetrators to be black. By the next morning "armed men from three counties" were in Kirven (49). A black man of twenty-two named Curry, who worked for Eula's uncle, joined one of the posses but became the prime suspect when his wife told another posse that he had come in with blood on his clothes the night before. By that time the sheriff had arrested two white men for the crime, but word of the arrests had not reached the posses. Curry had slipped away into the woods when he began to sense hostility, but he was found and taken to jail in the nearby town of Fairfield. He quickly implicated two others, and they, too, were seized and taken to the Fairfield jail. When the crowd found out, they broke into the jail and drove all three to Kirven to be killed. Local people came out to watch, some waking up their children to see the spectacle.

It was conducted quite systematically. Leaders first prepared firewood, then either castrated Curry or cut off all his sexual organs; a Baptist and a Methodist minister prayed for the three men's souls; and with that Curry was tied to an iron plow and burned (64). The second man was burned in the same way. Some in the crowd then said the third man should be let off because his father was known to be white. But instead of groveling and pleading, he cursed at them, so he was burned too. "His death," Akers writes, "might be viewed as a microcosm of early-twentieth-century Southern racism. A black man with the right connections would be protected even when associated with a heinous crime but only as long as he respected the codes, acted docile, and kept his place" (67).

The incident was reported in newspapers all over the country, including Chicago and New York. The *Houston Chronicle* reported that "the general feeling [in Kirven] was that the mob of six hundred did a 'good job.'" The Socialist *New York Call,* where Porter had published an article the previous year, reported the incident with a dateline of Fairfield and the headline "Sheriff Holds 2 Whites in Crime That 3 Burned For."

∽

The experience of growing up in a lynching culture might affect one in a variety of ways—perhaps pulling one into the eddy of racism and racial cruelty as a participant or perhaps provoking a struggle to expunge every trace of prejudice from one's mind. Neither was entirely true of Porter. Her racial attitudes were often contradictory and fluctuating.[10] From earliest childhood she had heard laments for the South's loss of the Civil War. Yet it is clear that she was at least sporadically able to stand back and take an independent view of the South and Texas. Her adherence to the ideology of the Old South waxed and waned.

By quoting selectively, it would be possible to place Porter, at various times in her life, at virtually any point on the spectrum of racial attitudes. In a 1927 book review published in the *New Republic* she indicated dissent from her region's exploitation of black people with the ironic quip, "In the South we persist in the aristocratic old tradition of Negro peonage." We might take this for the crucial (if cryptic) statement. Or we might decide she most clearly and meaningfully indicated her racial attitudes through the black characters in her fiction of the 1930s. Aunt Nannie, self-possessed, direct, and loyal though never subservient, is one of the strongest and most fully human characters she ever created. Uncle Jimbilly, with his determination that white abuse of slaves not be forgotten (he "meant one to hear"; *CS* 341), is equally compelling if less fully rounded. It would seem that Porter must have felt a strong essential sympathy in order to create these figures. In "The Journey," when the Grandmother and Nannie encounter an eighty-five-year-old judge from back in Kentucky and he refers to Nannie as "that strip of crowbait I sold to your father for twenty dollars," Nannie objects, after they drive on, "Look lak a jedge might had better raisin', look lak he didn't keer how much he hurt a body's feelins." It is not the judge who retains dignity in the exchange (*CS* 332).

Yet even though she could write of black people in ways that indicate respect, Porter was at times so tone-deaf that (as reported by *Time* magazine in 1961) she could refer to her family's "wonderful old slaves" as "companions." After mouthing this variant of the Happy Plantation myth she received a letter from Pauline Young of the NAACP, protesting that she found it impossible to "reconcile the two terms" *slave* and *companion*. Givner, who quotes Young's letter, points out that in the wake of this protest or reprimand Porter offered a rather different version of her position on race: "I [told a reporter] that I was horrified at the Negro people in this country having to riot to gain something they should have had all along" (*KAP* 452–53).

For various negative comments on blacks and for the "virulent anti-Semitism" evidenced in *Ship of Fools* and in marginal notations in certain books in her personal library, Givner calls Porter flatly a racist (*KAP* 450). And there is a good deal of evidence (some of which I will cite here) to support this conclusion. Yet it strikes me as an oversimplification of a quite complex matter. I hope, instead, to demonstrate in more specific terms how Porter's views varied at different times and how they reflect other motivating factors, including the history of Texas.

Porter seems to have enjoyed "darky" humor all her life. It was a trait she shared with her Agrarian friends, as in the merry tone of Caroline Gordon's letter to her from Andrew Lytle's estate Merry Mont, in Kentucky: "My dear, you *must* come down here. You can live for next to nothing. There are still plenty of good niggers left, thank God," who are "extraordinarily uncorrupted" and "still 'wrop' their hair!" (March 11, 1928). In similar though less humorous way, Allen Tate wrote on November 24, 1930, that he hoped the South's Negroes could be kept in a state of backwardness until their distinctive character could be captured in literature. He seems to have meant captured by white writers like himself apparently unaware of black writers who had already done so through direct insight.

Porter began writing fiction set in the South soon after meeting the Tates. Her persistent emphasis on the existence of "good" classes of Southern people, their natural graciousness, their love of leisure and calm—as in "Portrait: Old South," where these qualities are attributed to her grandmother—readily accorded with the Agrarians' allegiance to the idea of a natural aristocracy. Her first completed story about the South was "He," published in the *New Masses* in October 1927. As time went on, and especially after her visit to Benally in 1937, she increasingly adopted the Agrarians' rhetoric of a Southern rural life imperiled by the North's industrialism. It was a rhetoric fundamentally rooted in an ideology of white supremacy, and when she expounded such views her concern was strictly for the South's whites.[11]

Her fiction and her fictionalized accounts of her own life had always paid service to a romanticized plantation ideology based on black labor, and like others of the Agrarians she liked to espouse the stale and patently spurious argument that slavery had actually benefited slaves and burdened their owners. In a letter to Gordon on November 5, 1964, she cited her grandmother to the effect that it was the slave owners who remained in bondage after Emancipation because they continued to bear the responsibility of caring for affectionate former slaves who refused to be on their own. One wonders how she knew what her grandmother had said upon hearing of Emancipation, but maybe that, too, was part of the family legend. Certainly it was not something Porter had just thought up when she was writing to Gordon, since more than three decades earlier she had told Herbst much the same, that in the South your "help" is like a dead weight around your neck.[12] It was a form of scapegoating of blacks by no means unique to Porter.

In Mexico in the 1920s, as one element in her left-of-liberal principles then, Porter had been genuinely respectful of the Indian population and sympathetic to their cause. She had also, as we have noted, created Aunt Nannie and Uncle Jimbilly as persons of dignity. But by 1936, when she resumed work on the lynching story for which she had earlier made preparatory notes, her feelings had bifurcated into a conflict between racial guilt and acceptance of racial stereotypes. It is unfortunate that we have no way of dating specific parts of the disconnected scraps that make up the manuscript to see where they fit into this evolution. In any event, though its general trend seems to have been toward illiberality, the pattern was not consistent. In 1935 when her father wrote that Baby's son Breck had "killed a negro and wounded another in the longshoremen strike at Galveston while a Texas Ranger" she replied that "poor negroes" were "mistreated in too many ways anyhow" (March 30, 1935). Scattered notes found among her papers, labeled as having been intended for Glenway Wescott and probably written about this same time, insightfully identify economic insecurity as at least part of the cause of American racial prejudice. Yet in other undated notes her own prejudice emerges unmistakably and with particular focus on racial mixing; mixed-race blacks, she said, were "worse" than others and had no right to social equality. At some point she assigned these notes the date 1937, which if accurate would coincide with a period of known work on "The Man in the Tree." Either then or whenever she made the annotation, she called her statements about blacks' unreadiness for full civil rights an understatement.

In 1958 Porter told an interviewer with the *Richmond News Leader* that the Supreme Court ruling against segregation was "reckless and irresponsible," and "that thing was taking care of itself very well" (*Conv.* 39). One wonders if the parents of children still attending inferior segregated schools thought the situation was resolving itself well without interference. Throughout the 1960s she and her sister Gay exchanged letters that again and again returned to the topic of the "Negro race" and black people's laziness, untrustworthiness, and so forth.

Katherine Anne's side of the correspondence includes references to no-good hired help who didn't do a fourth of the work a white person did and her determination not to put up with "them" any more. She also expressed vexation at the rising middle class of blacks (but she used another word) whom one was expected to address as Mr. or Mrs.[13] In a letter of June 15, 1963, to Cyrilly Abels, she referred to Washington, D.C., as being "infested" with blacks. It would seem that the emergence of black Americans from deferential silence during the civil rights movement aroused Porter's wrath much as it did that of many other, seemingly less enlightened whites. She preferred black folks like the domestic help she remembered from long ago in Texas.

In 1965 Porter stated in a *Book Week* symposium that "no witch was ever burned in New England or anywhere else in America, and *even no Negro* except among the New England Puritans in the seventeenth century" (*CE* 87; emphasis added). The claim connects to her long-past work on Cotton Mather and the Salem witch hysteria, which she must have believed made her an expert, but not only is it appallingly insensitive, implying as it does that the burning of Negroes might be less heinous than the burning of white women regarded as witches, it is historically incorrect.

❧

"The Man in the Tree" was one of the five novellas or long stories for which Porter had a contract in hand when she retreated to Doylestown, Pennsylvania, in 1936 for the most intense and productive period of work in her career. The sixty-seven-page manuscript now found among her papers is a collection of disconnected pages, some typed, some scrawled, that start, break off, repeat, and start over. Except for a few brief sequences, the pages are unnumbered. It is impossible to make a coherent story by merely moving them around. The manuscript could not be published with just a little touching up. Even the title is inconsistent; "The Man in the Tree" is shown eight times, but two sheets show "Never-Ending Wrong" (the title ultimately used for her Sacco and Vanzetti memoir), "All the Evidence" is shown once as a possibility to be considered, and four times, more as references than as possible titles, she calls her work-in-progress simply "the southern story" or "the lynching story." Another confusion for anyone who reads the fragment or set of fragments is the recurrence of similar or identical phrases, sentences, and even whole paragraphs on multiple pages in different contexts. Characters change names, and the setting moves about. Only the site of the lynching, the unnamed town's square, remains consistent.

One page out of the sixty-seven bears the scrawled note "Written in Paris." If so, Porter had been working on this material (along with the "Noon Wine" and

"Old Mortality" material) well before her retreat in the fall of 1936. This supports the idea that the lynching story was conceived as part of the multigenerational family novel she began trying to write in the 1920s. And indeed the manuscript twice makes passing reference to a relationship of blood between the white and the black characters.

The character through whose central consciousness events are viewed is called Maria, usually Maria Townsend but sometimes Maria Gay or Maria Beauregard. Married and living in a small town in the South, she seems to be a grown-up version of the older sister in the Miranda stories. She is the mother of a little girl named Gabriella or Gabrielle, and on two of the sixty-seven pages she also has a baby boy called either Buffins or Stuffins. Her husband, Courtney or Court, is the prosecuting attorney of the town, possibly (or possibly not—indications vary) with aspirations to be a gentleman farmer. At one point, in a scene with a sister called Gabriella (the same name as used elsewhere for the child), Maria is referred to as Miranda. Once she is referred to as "Miss Kathin Ann." Unlike the rest of the manuscript, this latter scene is told in the first person for a few lines before the I's are crossed out and it returns to third-person narration centered in Maria's consciousness.

Among the black characters, who mostly speak a broad dialect, are two household servants, one the cook and the other a housekeeper who also serves meals. These women are referred to with three different names—Anna, Caroline, and Marty—assigned sometimes to one, sometimes to the other. A thirteen-year-old girl called either Loute or Lute runs errands and does miscellaneous small tasks. One fragment begins the morning after the lynching with Lute being sent off to take Gabrielle to school (a convent school). In some versions Lute sees the man hanging in the tree when she returns by way of the square. In others she takes that route *to* the school, and both she and the child see the body of the lynched man. In these versions Lute at first insists that Gabrielle did not see the body—an important point in Maria's mind since she is convinced that such a sight will scar a child for life.[14] Either way, after Lute returns she falls into hysterical screaming behind the house.

The young black man whose body hangs in the tree is usually called Hasty Bunting or Bunton. Interestingly, and perhaps in keeping with a statement elsewhere in the draft that the lynching had happened practically in the family, "Bunton" is a last name borrowed from some of Porter's relatives. Given the intertwined but usually unacknowledged family relations among whites and blacks in the South, it might be said of many lynchings that they were practically in the family. Hasty (once called Skid) is the grandson of Aunt Nanny, usually spelled with a *y* here rather than the *ie* of the equivalent character in "The Old Order." Like the Nannie we already know, this Nanny is clearly the family's center of gravity. We know that in the one instance "Skid" denotes "Hasty" because there are two versions, one with each name, of the scene in which he is delivered to jail. Elsewhere, however, Skid appears as a separate, little-developed character briefly seen mowing the Townsends' (or Gays' or Beauregards') lawn. As he works, he sings:

> You gointa git somethin you don' expeck
> It aint no money and it aint no check
> And you're goin home all wrapped up in
> A wooden kimona trimmed with tin.

Death is very much on the minds of the black people. Except for Nanny, they are all constantly afraid. And even with the story in so minimally developed a state, we can see that they should be. Maria at one point acknowledges to herself that the black people around her, including Lute, probably live in constant fear of what even she, weak and self-doubting as she is, can do to them.

Porter takes their fear seriously but nevertheless presents Lute, Hasty, and Skid as foolish, laughable people. Lute is given big, splayed feet that flap as she walks, and she is unreasonably terrified of sleeping in a bed. When Hasty is driven to jail in another town the classic but classically inadequate effort to protect him from lynching—he enjoys getting to have a ride in a car even though he vaguely knows what may await him. The corresponding scene with Skid is more serious; he looks at the strong bars of his cell and tells himself the new jail will be adequate to protect him from the mob sure to come. We know he will be proven wrong.

Two major scenes sketched out repeatedly in varying versions are the discovery of the body hanging in the tree and a visit Maria pays to Aunt Nanny after the lynching has become generally known. The lynched body has apparently only been hanged, not burned. Perhaps Porter could not bring herself to write in any detail so appalling a scene as a live burning. Nevertheless, hints of burning hang about the story. At one point it is directly asserted that the body has not been disfigured, but in some variants Lute sees a group of white men doing something to it—the inescapable implication being that they are castrating it. If so, it is surprising only in that they have not done so before the hanging, a common practice for any offense involving a white woman, as in one way or another this one does. In one version a slatternly white woman believed to be a prostitute runs into the street screaming that she has been raped. In other versions she sells Hasty an orange for a quarter, then claims he did not pay for it.

Perhaps this is a stretch, but I wonder if the fruit stand motif so intimately linked with the lynching is an allusion to "Strange Fruit" the song about American racism and lynching most famously performed by Billie Holiday starting in 1936, first recorded by her in 1939. The absence of dates of the manuscript sheets of "The Man in the Tree" or any statement to that effect by Porter means we cannot know with certainty whether that is plausible, but we have other indications that she may have worked on the material on into the 1940s.

In the other major scene, Maria's visit to Aunt Nanny, we see the venerable old woman on her deathbed. One reason for Maria's making the visit is her natural concern for Nanny's feelings, since it was her grandson who was lynched, but another is her threatened sense of their long relationship. Nanny has refused to accept the mourning clothes Maria sent over on any basis other than a purchase. She sent back a message that she would come work out their value when she got a little better. Hurt and offended, Maria wonders why this old woman she has known all her life will not accept the gift as just that, a gift. But Nanny reiterates her refusal. She is resolved to take "no mo' favors fum white folks" ever again because "fust thing you know they turn on you, they say you stole it"—a reference to the accusation that Hasty did not pay for the orange. But the larger explanation, left tacit, is that acceptance of gifts implies friendship. Maria's reply, that Nanny has worked enough and more than enough to pay for anything she ever received, all her life, is an echo of "The Last Leaf," where Aunt Nannie moves away to a small cabin of her own after the Grandmother dies and only years afterward does Maria realize that they "had not really been so very nice to Aunt Nannie" but had let her "work harder than she should have" (*CS* 348).

The scene between Nanny and Maria is curiously marked by echoes of a similar scene in Willa Cather's *Sapphira and the Slave Girl* (1940) when Sapphira goes to visit a venerable slave named Jezebel on her deathbed. Despite her distress and weakness, Nanny's eyes remain hard and bright and she displays a sly facetiousness much like Jezebel's. Both Sapphira and Maria, as they go to pay their visits, recall that the dying black woman had planted all the flowers on the place. In both, a younger black woman present at the bedside tries to insist that the old woman is wandering in her mind and should not be taken seriously. Nevertheless, both old women are implicitly recognized as sibylline figures.[15] It is these echoes I referred to earlier as indicating that work on "The Man in the Tree" continued sporadically at least into the 1940s or after. *Sapphira and the Slave Girl* was published in 1940. We know that Porter worked on "The Man in the Tree" *before* her near-miraculous completion of two major works at the Water Wheel Tavern, and these echoes or borrowings are indications that she worked on it again in the 1940s or after. Her compulsion to try to engage the material stayed with her.

In the scene at Nanny's bedside and elsewhere, Maria appears overwhelmed by guilt, both societal and individual. White guilt is the central theme running through the "Man in the Tree" drafts in all variations, but Maria also feels she may have failed to be as attentive to Aunt Nanny's needs as she should have been; she may somehow have let Nanny imagine the family has turned its back on her. There are other failings, too, for which Maria feels inadequate and guilty, all of them in some way pointing to a failure to live up to her role as Southern lady, able to manage those around her while also inspiring their love. She feels inadequate in her housekeeping, in her supervision of children and servants, and even in the management of her dog. She has failed to discipline any of them. On the other hand, she cannot bear the way the black women are always thrashing their children, and she refuses to inflict corporal punishment on anyone, so what is she to do? She is trapped and tormented by her role of mistress of the household.

At one point in the manuscript pages Maria is referred to as a flower of Southern womanhood, a familiar phrase implying that a married woman is competent and beautiful and has a governing sense of tradition. Besides feeling incompetent, however, Maria neither fulfills nor is entirely loyal to tradition. She might better be called the flower of *enlightened* Southern womanhood, or Southern womanhood struggling toward enlightenment. She is caught inside contradictions between tradition and family loyalty, on the one hand, and on the other an inner recognition that her slave-owning society has been in the wrong of it. Even as she tries to excuse herself by recalling her family's kindness to the "negroes" who worked for them, she remembers that her grandmother's boasts of never having actually whipped "their people" had an added proviso indicating that small blows with sticks or boxing of ears didn't count—as if those were acceptable. To Maria, striking others is never acceptable. And now a black man has been hanged from a tree in the town square. It all brings her a realization that she has been complicit in a system that fully justifies the fear or hatred of the black people around her. Yet she is not so fearful of them, in return, as she is of the town's white men.

Maria's plight, caught between contending ideologies, reflects Porter's own, mouthing excuses like the master-as-victim idea and picturing Lute and other characters in racist terms, even while denouncing the practice of lynching in a way that demonstrates long concern. A number of details in "The Man in the

Tree" indicate that she was well-informed about the practice, almost certainly from newspapers.[16] Her introduction of the question of whether the body in the tree has been mutilated shows that she knew about the common practices of beating, branding, or castrating before finishing the victim off. It is also clear that she realized lynching was an atrocity from which white male perpetrators got a sexual charge as they exhibited their power over black men and, by implication, women. Two details, in particular, provide compelling evidence that Porter knew at least some parts of the history of lynching in Texas. First, one of the servants brings Maria a postcard bearing the picture of the lynched boy, saying that she bought it for a quarter (the same price that Hasty paid, or was accused of not having paid, for an orange). Though it seems scarcely believable now, the practice of selling such postcard images was widespread, including postcards of the live burning of Jesse Washington in Waco. Second, a single pointed reference in the scene where the sheriff and Court drive Hasty to jail shows that she was aware of Waco's record as a hotbed of lynching: the sheriff tells Court, Maria's husband who is riding along, that they really ought to take him to Waco and let the people there handle it. Court says that "there'll be a lynching all right," and the sheriff's agreement expresses an aspect of the lynching that Porter's draft draws back from suggesting in any other way: "And there aint no question but there's gointa be a hot time in the old town tonight." The reference to Waco appears only three lines later. Waco and burning: the "Waco Horror."

If Porter had been able to finish her lynching story, she might have achieved a reputation for tormented ambivalence about the South comparable to that of William Faulkner. But her own inner turmoil was apparently too great to allow finality about this painful subject, even a final ambivalence. The jumbled manuscript repeatedly gives evidence of her depth of thought and feeling about race relations in the South, and indeed at one point directly echoes Faulkner. On the page where the name Miranda creeps into the story, just after Miranda vows she will not stay in "this filthy country" and is accused by her sister of hating "us all," she bursts out, "I don't hate you, . . . I love all of you too much"—much as Quentin Compson cries out, when asked at the end of *Absalom, Absalom!* why he hates the South, "I dont hate it, . . . I dont hate it . . . . *I dont. I dont! I dont hate it! I dont hate it!*"

Steeped in the culture and traditions of the South and in its literature, Porter had given long and uncomfortable thought both to what she loved about the South and to what she hated about it. What she seems to have found ugliest of all was its racial violence. Her uncompleted manuscript ponders racial guilt, the havoc wreaked on families by conflicting opinions on race, and the permanent harm to children who "see" the evidence of the South's racial hatred. Her sense of revulsion is eloquently conveyed in a sentence that appears multiple times in variant versions, usually embedded in paragraphs. Just once, on an otherwise clean page, free of the jumble that characterizes most of the draft, this sentence appears as the beginning of the story. Unlike the other beginnings, it is simple and stark, its simplicity stating with perhaps the greatest depth she ever achieved Porter's understanding of the tragedy of the South's—and Texas's—history: "He hangs there, dark among the dark branches, a reproach and a witness, not only against his murderers, but to the shame of those who believed they were his friends."

∾

It is scarcely believable that the same person who could perceive the tragedy of race so keenly as to write this sentence and who was so conflicted about the horrors of lynching that she could not complete what might have been a major work about it could also set her hand to an another uncompleted manuscript, equally disordered and duplicative, bearing the title "The Negro Question." This set of drafts and notes (for an essay) is as forceful in its expression of racial hatred as "The Man in the Tree" is in its expression of grief and guilt.

The draft begins with a statement of satisfaction at having seen, during a visit to Texas and Louisiana, a change for the better in the living standard among blacks. Many seemed to have better jobs than they did when she lived there and to be sharing to a greater extent in the American standard of living, for instance, driving their own cars to work. Their children seemed better clothed and nourished: "It was not the Millennium, by a long shot, but it was all going in the right direction." But her enlightened satisfaction in the material progress of blacks is vitiated on the very first page by endorsements of segregation. She observes that the Negroes had a separate movie theater to attend and that as a group they were "staying reassuringly black." What can this mean except that Porter, a representative of the white master class, is satisfied ("reassured") by these black people's willingness to stay in their place and not mix carnally or in any other way with whites? "I am one of those," she states, who believe that both races are "better for not mixing at all."[17]

She goes on to denounce the "fallacy of modern egalitarianism," saying that equality "quite simply is something that exists between equals." Clearly she assumes that white and black are inherent non-equals, one superior and the other inferior. She has no patience, she writes, with people who decry the African American's condition but say nothing about the American Indian, "who is much worse treated by his government and his society." Lest we believe she thinks the Indian should be treated as an equal, however, she quickly adds, "He is of course a

savage with no written history or literature—but so is the Negro." And contrary
to the evidence of "The Man in the Tree," she here denies that she feels "one
trace of guilt because my grandparents and all my known ancestors were slaveholders." That only meant, she repeats, "their slavery to slaves."

The draft labeled "The Negro Question" begins as a roughly typed manuscript and ends as a set of scrawled notes on irregular slips of paper. Near the
end—inescapably recalling the scrawled note in Joseph Conrad's "Heart of
Darkness"—she drew a heavy black line across the page and entered the following: "They were savages and all they Brought to this Count[r]y was their Sav-
agery. Their former good manners were the manners taught them by their white
masters. Sometimes with the whip." Then another heavy black line. It is hard to
resist the inference that the isolation of these curt sentences by two black lines
represents their encapsulation as her definitive statement on race. While denying
the guilt she expressed in "The Man in the Tree," she also denies by omission the
ultimate wrong of lynching.

8

War's Alarms

Three Texans, Two Wars

Imagine that it has really taken me all this time to understand that recurring war, every generation, is the constant, the one thing we can depend upon in this world.

—Katherine Anne Porter to Donald Elder, January 30, 1941

In her caustic essay about Gertrude Stein "The Wooden Umbrella," Porter characterized the "literary young" who gathered around Stein in Paris, "snatching" at her every word, as "children . . . between two wars in a falling world" (*CE* 257). It is an apt characterization of the period when Porter was in Europe. As early as 1931 she was expressing in letters her apprehensiveness about the likelihood of renewed war. The Nazis were seizing power (Hitler was named chancellor on January 30, 1933), and everyone, she said, was talking about the prospect of war. Everyone, that is, but Stein, whom she acidly sketched as being impervious to the threat. In indirect quotation (a device that allows for considerable liberty) she has Stein say "there was not, of course, going to be another war" and adds an astonished "this was in 1937!" (*CE* 266). Even in 1938, so the essay implies, the approach of war had barely registered on Stein's awareness. But then, "she could not be expected to know that war was near. They had only been sounding practice *alerts* in Paris against expected German bombers since 1935" (*CE* 269).

Since Porter had left Paris in 1936, it is hard to think how she could have known what Stein was saying at her salons in 1937 and 1938. The hostile tone of her essay (not published until 1947) was partly driven by private, postwar grievances that honed her retrospective indignation. But it is nonetheless true that her own foreboding is evident in letters she wrote during her years in Europe, and if she genuinely believed Stein was heedless of the approach of war her mockery was well-founded.

The Europe to which Porter sailed from Mexico in 1931 was still trying to put the pieces back together from World War I. The most pressing international issue seemed to be the failure of the Western world's economic system, and her own most pressing political concern was how fully to commit to the

Communist Party. She had been interested in communism since her early days in New York when the Bolshevik Revolution was exciting news. During the last of her four stays in Mexico she had felt bitterly disillusioned by the failure of the largely communist-led revolution to curtail exploitation of the poor by the rich and powerful. Yet even as she prepared to leave for Europe she retained (as she told her father in a letter of June 26, 1931) her sympathetic feeling for Russia and a vague intention of going to Moscow to see for herself how communism was working out there. At the same time, she admitted to feeling uncertain whether she could ever be a fully committed communist and a year later was still wobblingly perched on that same fence. In a letter of August 3, 1932, she shared her dilemma with John Herrmann, telling him she had long considered going to Russia to study Marxism thoroughly but continued to feel reluctant on grounds of artistic autonomy.[1]

Not long after her arrival in Europe, the nature of Porter's primary political concern began to shift. She was still interested in communism, and as she witnessed rallies by both the Nazi Party and the Communist Party she knew she preferred the latter. But having found Germany more devastated by postwar issues than she expected so long after the war, she now saw it as part of a larger *pre*war world and felt the rumblings of what was to come.[2] She referred to "the next war" in a letter to Peggy Cowley on October 1, 1931, only ten days after reaching Berlin, and on December 27 wrote Eugene Pressly that war seemed to be just over the horizon. When she mentioned her hope to go to Russia to an unnamed news correspondent she'd happened to meet, she said, he warned her that she would be going straight into the middle of a war. Between late 1931 and the fall of 1936, when she returned to the United States from Europe, the likelihood of renewed war was never far from her mind. Her letters to friends and family in the States frequently mention her anxiety over it.

During this period Porter thought more carefully and in a more informed way about the larger world than she ever had before. The opportunity to do so had not been her motivation for travel either to Mexico or to Europe; each time, she had sought a pleasant but inexpensive place to live so that she could write. In Mexico she developed a sense of what could be achieved through an art firmly rooted in its own place, and may also (during her first visit especially) have sharpened the awareness of violence that she would later attach so forcefully to her Texas childhood in "'Noon Wine': The Sources." She brought her own localized art to fruition in Europe. But having at last completed the "Old Order" stories she had struggled with for so long before coming to a realization of their right shape, she returned to her own country to pull together and polish the three novellas usually regarded as her triumphs. One of these was, of course, her story of the doomed belle in a world of death, her World War I story "Pale Horse, Pale Rider." Another was an allegorical story of the world's voyage toward World War II called "No Safe Harbour," a proposed novella that would not be finished until years later in the enormously expanded form of *Ship of Fools*. Having promised Harcourt, Brace five long stories but having completed only three, she might reasonably have added one that was not mentioned in the contract, "The Leaning Tower." She had begun making notes and drafts for this story of the coming of war as early as 1932. Completed in September 1940,[3] it has been less often read and admired than "Old Mortality" or "Pale Horse, Pale Rider" but deserves to be better known. Wescott, whose steady encouragement helped her finish it, wrote in his diary for April 16, 1941, and in a letter to Porter the following day that it was "rather godlike."

These, then, are Porter's three works of fiction directly related to war: "Pale Horse, Pale Rider," "The Leaning Tower," and *Ship of Fools*. Differing markedly in tone and method, they are nevertheless complementary, not only in addressing the general theme of war's social ramifications but also in their emphasis on the causes and effects of war in the human soul.

Apt as it is, the phrase "between two wars in a falling world" does not really reflect Porter's own sense of the times or how her life had been marked by war.[4] In the January 1941 letter to Donald Elder quoted in the epigraph to this chapter, in which she mocked her own slowness to realize that wars were the most reliable thing we can count on in this world, she mentioned three—the "disgraceful" Spanish-American War, the Great War (or World War I), and "now this one." She reached back to the Spanish-American War to make her point because it was the first American war actually fought in her lifetime, launched when she was seven years old. But she might well have invoked the Civil War, because growing up in a society and a family that cherished the memory of the Lost Cause, she was aware of that internecine war as a precondition of her life long before the age of seven. And she might have mentioned several others between the Spanish-American War and the world war of 1914–18.

Directly on the heels of the Spanish-American War, which ended in 1898, came the Philippine-American War (1899–1902).[5] Little known by Americans now, it drew considerable press coverage and public opposition at the time. There was also the Russo-Japanese War (1904–5), but the United States was not directly involved, though the working out of the peace treaty on American soil by President Theodore Roosevelt drew a good deal of attention. Since the United

States did not enter World War I until April 1917, Porter might have taken the view that her life was unburdened by active involvement in warfare for a stretch of nearly a decade and a half, even if she had thought to mention the three-year engagement in the Philippines. But that would not have been strictly true, because combat between the United States and some of the rebel ethnic groups in the Philippines did not end until 1913, only a year before the Great War began with Germany's invasion of Belgium on August 1, 1914. Between then and U.S. declaration of war in the spring of 1917 Americans were still not free from the murk of war. Most were keenly attentive to its course and the shocking casualties on both the Western and Eastern fronts throughout 1915 and 1916,[6] and from March 1916 until spring 1917 American troops were fighting in Mexico in a punitive military expedition launched from Fort Bliss, Texas, as a pursuit of Pancho Villa.

By the time the Great War ended with armistice on November 11, 1918, the Russian Civil War had been underway for over a year and would continue until 1923, with U.S. intervention on the side of the Whites beginning in 1918. Considering her keen interest in the Russian experiment, we can feel confident that Porter would have been aware of this struggle between Bolsheviks and anti-Bolsheviks. Certainly she was aware of the continuation of sporadic fighting in the Mexican Revolution into the 1920s. Between the end of these two conflicts and the outbreak of World War II in 1939, attentive people throughout the world were only too aware that Japan had invaded Manchuria in 1931, Mussolini attacked Ethiopia in 1935, the Spanish Civil War broke out in 1936 (the year Porter left Europe), and the Sino-Japanese War broke out in 1937. She was almost literally correct, then, when she declared to Donald Elder in 1941 that war had been "the constant, the one thing" she could "depend upon," as she put it with sadly beautiful irony, throughout almost her entire life up to that point.

During the few months she spent in Berlin in 1931 and 1932 Porter felt the disheartening sense of déjà vu that many of her contemporaries were writing about (for instance, in London, Louis MacNeice in "Autumn Journal"). Porter made this feeling compellingly real in "The Leaning Tower" and sporadically so in *Ship of Fools,* begun by at least 1931. Both are deeply involved with the approach of World War II. This means that her work on both actually overlapped by some five years her writing about the final weeks of World War I.

"Pale Horse, Pale Rider" is both a love story and a story about the stateside atmosphere at the end of World War I when the great flu pandemic struck. By giving it so specific a time setting, Porter made its distinctively clipped dialogue, in particular, an anticipation of the world-weariness of the 1920s. At the same time, from the retrospective vantage of 1936 and after, the lovers' sense of a doom unique to their own historic moment becomes deeply ironic, as both Porter and her later readers viewed their unawareness from an informed perspective. Retrospective vision was characteristic of Porter's writing at its best and most compelling; she typically looked back toward the past through the screen of later experience. But while the retrospective vision plays an important role in all three of her works about war, it does so in strikingly different ways and with drastically different degrees of success. One attribute they share is that each in its own way draws a connection with Texas. One of our questions in this chapter will be, why?

⟨≈⟩

It is not known whether Porter participated in any active protests against the Great War; probably not, since to do so would have been to risk arrest and possibly imprisonment. The Sedition Act of 1918 empowered the U.S. attorney general to prosecute anyone accused of making "disloyal utterances" (Kennedy 80 82). Even before that, the post office was refusing to deliver mailings of socialist, therefore pacifist, print materials. It was a dark time in the nation's history for tolerance and civil liberties. Those who were against the war were for the most part quiet.

It does appear that in Porter's private views she dissented from the war fever that swept the country as virulently as the flu epidemic.[7] She would claim in an August 1963 letter to her nephew Paul that even in 1914 she "wondered why the USA interfered in the European war—only another war such as they had been having for two thousand years." Of course, the United States did not intervene in 1914, not until 1917. Porter's after-the-fact statements about her opinions are never very reliable. At times she claimed to have been a lifelong pacifist, but the evidence from the 1940s, at any rate, does not support that claim. It is true, however, that she had an early inclination toward socialism, and pacifism was a bedrock principle of the Socialist Party.[8] "Pale Horse, Pale Rider," perhaps *because* it was written through the lens of later experience and therefore was not topical but timeless, expresses dissent from war itself more eloquently than any direct political statement she could have made.

Miranda is among those caught between opposition to the war and fear of openly expressing her views. A frantically nervous young newspaper reporter in Denver, as Porter herself was in 1918, earning very little in a time of inflated prices, she can scarcely pay her rent and buy food yet is being pressured to purchase government bonds. But her quandary goes beyond the financial issue. To buy bonds would be to contribute to a war she considers "filthy." If she buys bonds, then, she is false to her real opinions, yet she must do so in order to avoid intolerable penalties for maintaining those opinions. Committed by her ideals of citizenship to free speech and committed by her profession as a reporter to free publication of information, she is doubly silenced. "Suppose I were not a coward, but said what I really thought?" she asks herself when two faceless government men invade the newspaper office demanding to know why she hasn't bought a bond. "Suppose I said to hell with this filthy war?" (CS 273). But she can't risk it. All she can say is that she can't afford to.

Concerned as it is with the war's threat to civil liberties, "Pale Horse, Pale Rider" is also deeply concerned with war's debasement of language.[9] To a serious writer, purity of language is the essence of life; the wrenching of language into double-speech or non-speech is intolerable. But the governmental watchmen who menace Miranda at the newspaper office, as well as a bond salesman she sees later, exemplify just that. A cant language of super-patriotism made up of conventionalized chunks of language like "our American boys fighting and dying in Belleau Wood" (CS 273) blares at her from every side. As she and her soldier sweetheart Adam make their way through the two fragmentary days they have together, they adopt such prefab language in a patently mocking, ironic way that demonstrates both their trust in each other and their resistance to mob pressure. Their recourse to a speech of conscious, tight-lipped irony as a way of resisting the distortions of cant and false sentiment conveys what might be called (borrowing from Ernest Hemingway) emotion under pressure.

The story is structured around a series of dreams. In the first of these, as we have seen, Miranda dreams herself back in Texas (though not named as such), slipping away from her family home to race the apocalyptic pale horseman of death. She is aware only of the pervasively ominous nature of the dream, but in fact she is falling ill with the flu. After this opening dream of the race with death and her worry over the previous day while she bathes and dresses, Miranda finds Adam waiting outside her door with the happy news that he doesn't have to return to camp that day. As the day progresses, she senses that she is falling ill but determinedly pushes that awareness aside, knowing only too well how little time remains before Adam is sent to the trenches of the Western Front. There, he tells her, the life expectancy of a "sapping party" is "just nine minutes." "Make it ten and I'll come along," she quips (CS 283)—a fair sample of their tone together.

Though they try to protect the private space of their love from the world outside, their talk keeps circling back to the war. It takes over and alters every aspect of life. Over her coffee Miranda starts by talking about having to take it without cream and ends by claiming she is going to "get in good shape for the next round. No war is going to sneak up on me again." Parodying the official line, Adam replies that "there won't be any more wars, don't you read the newspapers? . . . We're going to mop 'em up this time, and they're going to stay mopped, and this is going to be all" (CS 281). Through the logic of irony, he is saying in effect (as Porter would later say) that "recurring war" is likely to be "the constant" of their lives.

Both Miranda and Adam quip that the war is "funny" or "simply too good to be true," knowing they mean the opposite. Nevertheless, he has adopted the traditional masculine idea that he couldn't respect himself if he didn't fight. Miranda does not accept this but knows there is no use trying to argue the point. It is one of the ways in which she is doomed and one way in which she is ultimately the voice of wisdom in the story—a helpless kind of wisdom.

At the theater that night Miranda and Adam sit with enforced patience while a Liberty Bond salesman delivers "the same old moldy speech" they have heard before (CS 293). Miranda tries to block out his voice, but as the fragmentation of the speech indicates, she hears the usual phrases rolling past: "vile Huns— glorious Belleau Wood—our keyword is Sacrifice—Martyred Belgium—give till it hurts—our noble boys Over There—Big Berthas—the death of civilization— the Boche." "Oh, why won't he hush?" she whispers, but the cant rhetoric pours unstoppably on: "atrocities, innocent babes hoisted on Boche bayonets—your child and my child—if our children are spared these things, then let us say with all reverence that these dead have not died in vain—the war, the *war*, the war, the war to end war." Mentally, she calls the speaker's bluff: "What about Adam, you little pig? Coal, oil, iron, gold, international finance, why don't you tell us about them, you little liar?" But she and Adam join in, grinning "shamefacedly" at each other, when others in the audience stand up and sing "There's a Long, Long Trail a-Winding."

Porter's depictions of the bond salesman and the enforcers at the office are as accurate a representation of the times as her choice of the audience-participation song.[10] The term Liberty Bond or Liberty Loan was coined by Secretary of the Treasury William McAdoo in 1917 for the purpose, in his own words, of "capitaliz[ing] the profound impulse called patriotism." To do so, he employed such hard-sell methods as "Four-Minute Men" who appeared at movies, on stages, at lodges, and elsewhere, "fervently urging" people to buy bonds. McAdoo himself labeled anyone who did not buy bonds "a friend of Germany."[11] Miranda's fear of the agents of such a policy would have been valid. Her counting up of her few dollars as against the cost of necessities is entirely convincing; such a woman would undoubtedly have had trouble getting by—as Porter well knew. The pressure to buy bonds and the judgment that failure to do so indicated a lack of patriotism took no heed of people's finances. Miranda's fears of being accused of disloyalty are also entirely realistic. The glances she and Adam exchange at the theater are their only way to communicate their distaste for the speaker, since words can be overheard.

The next day, she wakes up late, seriously ill and aware that a doctor has come and left a prescription. When Adam returns from his day at camp and finds her feverish, he dashes out to get the medicine, and while she lies half asleep waiting for him she dreams again. This second dream sequence, more compact than the first, is rendered with a brilliant surrealism as it sweeps her from Colorado's mountains to a still-unnamed Texas, which then morphs into a jungle:

> I must have warmth—and her memory turned and roved after another place she had known first and loved best, that now she could see only in drifting fragments of palm and cedar, dark shadows and a sky that warmed without dazzling . . . there was the long slow wavering of gray moss in the drowsy oak shade, the spacious hovering of buzzards overhead, the smell of crushed water herbs along a bank . . . and the slender ship spread its wings and sailed away into the jungle. The air trembled with the shattering scream and the hoarse bellow of voices all crying together. . . . Danger, danger, danger, the voices said, and War, war, war. (*CS* 299)

She is roused by Adam's return from the pharmacy and the sound of the landlady's voice threatening to put her out on the sidewalk because of her contagion. But Adam shuts the landlady out and insists that he will take care of Miranda himself. It will prove to be his voluntary death sentence.

While they wait through the night for an ambulance to come, they talk about the things they have loved about simply being alive—in the past tense, as if they have already accepted their doom. As they sing "Pale horse, pale rider, done taken my lover away," we learn that Adam is also a Texan. He "heard Negroes in Texas sing it, in an oil field," he says, while Miranda had "heard them sing it in a cotton field" (*CS* 302–3). Comforted by this commonality, which strikes them both as confirming that they belong together, Miranda drifts off to sleep again and dreams her third, ultimately prophetic dream, in which Adam is shot through by numerous arrows and dies while she lives.

Even beyond its stylized language—so smartly clipped in Miranda and Adam's dialogue, so powerfully elaborated in the dream sequences—the real brilliance of "Pale Horse, Pale Rider" is its intertwining of war with pathology. Making this same point—how "effectively" Porter "evokes the dual menace of war and epidemic"—Gary Ciuba calls attention to a comment by Alfred W. Crosby in *Epidemic and Peace, 1918,* that the story is "the most accurate depiction of American society in the fall of 1918 in literature. It synthesizes what is otherwise only obtainable by reading hundreds of pages of newspapers" (318). Both Ciuba and Crosby are quite right, yet it is not so much that the menace is "dual" as that Porter presents war as the social *equivalent* of contagion and the flu epidemic shown with such realism in its own right; it is also metaphoric of the collective pathology of a war mentality. War's infection of language and of the fundamental honesty of relationships is a kind of poisoning of society. Indeed, soon after she is taken to the hospital Miranda dreams another, yet more devastating dream in which war and the flu epidemic come together in an act of poisoning.

The ambulance crew that takes her to the hospital has included a remarkably caring young doctor with the German name Hildesheim. In her fourth dream, again set in the landscape of Texas, Miranda's sickness unto death becomes an infection of her mind by the cant rhetoric she has so steadfastly rejected:

> Across the field came Dr. Hildesheim, his face a skull beneath his German helmet, carrying a naked infant writhing on the point of his bayonet, and a huge stone pot marked Poison in Gothic letters. He stopped before the well that Miranda remembered in a pasture on her father's farm, a well once dry but now bubbling with living water, and into its pure depths he threw the child and the poison, and the violated water sank back soundlessly into the earth. Miranda, screaming, ran with her arms above her head; her voice echoed and came back to her like a wolf's howl, Hildesheim is a Boche, a spy, a Hun, kill him, kill him before he kills you.

Awakened by Dr. Hildesheim himself, she begs his forgiveness for what she has just said. It is perhaps the strongest rejection of war's hatred in any of Porter's writing that at this point the good German-descended doctor takes no notice whatever of her accusation. He knows that it is her sickness speaking and quietly goes about his business of healing (*CS* 309).

Miranda's final dream sequence is of the approach to death. In a version of the beatific vision that Porter always said she experienced during her near-death from the flu, she passes down a long passage to an "overwhelming deep sky where it was always morning." Yet even in that pleasant "sea and sky and meadow" she feels a "thin frost" of apprehension and realizes that she has not found the dead who have gone before her (*CS* 311–12). The dead are missing, and she unwillingly returns to the world of the living, now strangely empty and inert compared to the eternal world she had envisioned in her dream. It is a "dull world to which she was condemned, where the light seemed filmed over with cobwebs . . . all objects and beings meaningless, ah, dead and withered things that believed themselves alive!" (314). The war has ended, but rather than rejoicing at her restoration to a postwar world she feels only that her doctor and nurses have "set her once more safely in the road that would lead her again to death." At the end, knowing that Adam is dead, she leaves the hospital seeing ahead of her a kind of living death: "No more war, no more plague, only the dazed silence that follows the ceasing of the heavy guns' noiseless houses with the shades drawn, empty streets, the dead cold light of tomorrow" (317). Her language here conveys much the same bleakness as Wilfred Owen's vision of the postwar world of the bereaved: "And each slow dusk a drawing-down of blinds." Whether by an independent road or by having read the great poet of the Great War, Porter had arrived at the same point and adopted the same numbed tone.

～

At the time World War II began in Europe, Porter was calling herself a pacifist. After December 8, 1941, when the United States declared war on Japan, her thinking about the war moved from avowed opposition to wartime patriotism. Letters to her then husband Albert Erskine, as well as others, demonstrate this shift. On March 13, 1938, shortly after the Anschluss (the forcible union of Germany and Austria), she called herself a confirmed pacifist. On June 14, 1940, she wrote Glenway Wescott that she was so "stunned" she couldn't sleep or work and called the war a "disaster" and a "majestic and terrible Nemesis" (*SL* 179). That same day, she wrote Erskine that it had been a hard blow to her. Four days later, on the eighteenth, she told him she would be willing to die if that would avail to defeat Germany, then wrote again the next day apologizing for having expressed violent impulses that did not represent her essential beliefs. Also writing on the nineteenth, in a letter that must have crossed hers, Erskine insisted that if any good came out of the war it would be in spite of the fighting, not as a result of it. He did not "intend to take part," he declared, but meant to "miss no chances to talk against the war—and finally, if necessary, to go to jail." On June 21 she joined him in denouncing both America's political leaders and its financial powers as having systematically engineered the war for no good end and urged that they not be, either of them, co opted by it. In short, they were agreed in opposing the war. Four months later, on October 13, 1940, Erskine wrote that he was registering for the draft. Subsequently more and more of Porter's letters expressed wartime zeal, and on the Fourth of July 1942, she made a radio speech

11. Katherine Anne Porter, age fifty-two, celebrating her divorce from Albert Erskine, June 19, 1942, in Reno, Nevada. The inscription on the back in Porter's hand reads, "Unbride tosses unwedding bouquet." Katherine Anne Porter Papers, Special Collections, University of Maryland Libraries.

proclaiming the war in which America's soldiers were fighting as "my war" (*CE* 193–96).

It was in the fall of 1940, toward the end of her correspondence with Erskine (from whom she was divorced in 1942) and three years after finishing "Pale Horse, Pale Rider," that she completed "The Leaning Tower." Her long novel about the coming of war, *Ship of Fools,* would not appear until 1962. Since the time setting of *Ship of Fools* precedes that of "The Leaning Tower" by a few months, I will take up the novel first. Neither work treats the actual, declared war or its effects; both concern the approach of war.

The record of Porter's work on *Ship of Fools* is one of the most frightful accounts of writer's block in all literature. The germ of the work was the long diary-letter she kept during her voyage to Europe in 1931. She worked on the material sporadically, often at wide intervals, from that time until its publication in 1962—over thirty years. The great turning point that enabled her to complete it came in 1955, when after prolonged and unpleasant negotiations with William

Jovanovich, the new president of Harcourt, Brace, during which he referred to her as the company's "property," she signed a contract for the long-awaited novel with Seymour Lawrence, of Atlantic Monthly Press. Lawrence provided financial help that freed her from the Harcourt, Brace contract, an advance of $2,500, and a monthly stipend. With that, he entered a seven-year regimen of coaxing, encouraging, and reassuring her.

Taking a three-year lease on a house in Connecticut, Porter settled into her work. Her nephew Paul came from New York on weekends to do chores, her niece Ann and family were nearby, and Gay visited from Texas. For a while she made progress. But Lawrence's expectation that *Ship of Fools* (the new title) would be finished for publication in November 1956 was far off the mark. He had encouraged her to accept a speaking tour that fall as publicity for the novel, but with no novel out it only meant more delay. When her lease on the house ended in early 1958 the book was still not finished. She had committed herself to the University of Virginia as writer-in-residence for the fall semester (following William Faulkner in that role) and to Washington and Lee for the spring of 1959. Hoping to complete the book before she went, she asked Lawrence to find her another secluded place to work. He booked her into an inn in Ridgefield, Connecticut, for a month, but after three weeks of hard work she had to say she could not finish before leaving for Virginia.

The retrospective vision that was always at the heart of Porter's fiction had served her well in "Pale Horse, Pale Rider." But in *Ship of Fools* memory hardened into mere hindsight. She liked to believe that she had foreseen the coming of World War II from the time she arrived in Germany or even before, as she observed the German passengers on the *Werra*. And indeed, as we have seen, her letters do document anxiety about the likelihood of another war as early as 1931. But the prolonged delay in publishing the novel drained that fact of any value. If she had published *Ship of Fools* in 1933 it would have been timely and controversial. If she had published it in 1940 or 1945, perhaps even in 1950, it would have been read as a deeply thought-through book possibly demonstrating prescience. But by 1962 its themes had been combed through too many times for it to claim any depth or newness of thought. A blatant example of Porter's attempt to maintain a claim of prescience based on the 1931 time-setting occurs early in the allegorical voyage in an exchange between two of the many anti-Semites among the characters, Herr Rieber and Lizzi Spöckenkieker:

Lizzi screamed out to little Frau Otto Schmitt . . . "Oh, what do you think of this dreadful fellow? Can you guess what he just said? I was saying,

'Oh, these poor people [she means the lower-class Spaniards in steerage] what can be done for them?' and this monster"—she gave a kind of whinny between hysteria and indignation—"he said, 'I would do this for them: I would put them all in a big oven and turn on the gas.' Oh," she said weakly, doubling over with laughter, "isn't that the most original idea you ever heard?"

Herr Rieber stood by smiling broadly, quite pleased with himself. Frau Schmitt went a little pale, and said in a motherly, severe tone, "There may be such a thing as too much originality—for shame, I don't think that is funny!" Herr Rieber's face fell, he pouted.

Lizzi said, "Oh, he did not mean any harm, of course; only to fumigate them, isn't it so?"

"No, I did not mean fumigate," said Herr Rieber, stubbornly. (58–59)

Porter seems to have supposed the passage would have ironic impact, as an anticipation of the gas chambers her readers all, by 1962, knew about, where fumigation was used as a ploy to facilitate the process. But it is simply too obvious. There is no discovery in such a dialogue staged in 1931 from a perspective thirty years afterward. There is even less discovery in Herr Hutten's suggestion that Jews "should have special quarters on ships and other public conveyances. They should not be allowed the run of things, annoying other people" (246). Essentially he is suggesting a mobile ghetto. But the Jews of Europe had lived in ghettos for centuries. Despite its portentous air, the novel cannot maintain a claim to profundity. It was a great commercial success, but was simply too far after the fact to convey genuine insight.

Another issue at the heart of any critical judgment of *Ship of Fools* is genre. Porter had willed herself to produce a novel, the genre of the literary big boys, but it was not congenial to her. We rightly expect some kind of development or unfolding to occur in the characters of a novel, and we expect a structure of action in which one event or episode leads to another in a way that shows characters or ideas in new ways and carries forward the central action, even if that is the quasi-action of self-examination or meditation on the past. But except for its pro forma use of the journey-narrative form, *Ship of Fools* is static. The passengers leave one place and arrive at another by way of a sequence of episodes that essentially tell us the same things over and over from first one point of view and then another.[12] The physical journey does not serve as a compelling metaphor for psychological or spiritual movement because at its end the characters are essentially the same as they were when they embarked. And in its virtually unrelieved tone of spite and world-weariness, *Ship of Fools* offers little of the richness or variation we expect in a successful novel. It yields no illumination.

To be sure, the time-setting of the novel, 1931, does not allow an examination of the realpolitik that worked itself out in Germany (which her brief stay in Berlin would not have qualified her to write about anyway) or the onset of armed combat, but rather the root causes of what has sometimes been called the Good War. She locates these in an excessive nationalism, or jingoism, that characterizes all the German characters aboard the ship and in prejudice, or race superiority. Her approach to the coming of World War II is essentially a moral one. Like Marianne Moore in "In Distrust of Merits" (a poem that has been both roundly criticized and praised), she locates the guilt of war in the human heart rather than in a specific society.[13] Yet her broadening of the moral issue ends in making all the German passengers on the ship either anti-Semites or Jews, an overgeneralization that reflects not only the very misrepresentation that fuels hatred of an identity-group but also her personal dislike of Germans, an intemperate aversion she developed after arriving in Berlin. In both *Ship of Fools* and "The Leaning Tower" she characterizes Germans as a race as smugly judgmental, stuffy, and superior, even calling them "pig-snouted" (*Ship* 12). Language like this leaves it unclear whether she is criticizing bigotry or furthering it.

Another problem with Porter's urge to broaden the moral guilt of the war while keeping it centered in Germany is that her insistence that we are all, all of us, marred by prejudices and anti-Semitism differs only slightly from other forms of spiritual ugliness and makes her ship of fools a vessel carrying little *but* malignity, as if all humankind are bigots. Over and over, as she shifts from one narrative perspective to another, we see hidden or expressed misogyny, hidden or expressed hostility toward blacks or the Spanish, hidden or expressed religious dislikes, hidden or expressed repugnance toward the handicapped or deformed. At the moral level, there is simply too little human variety for a group this size.

This is where the presence of the one Texan among the passengers, William Denny, comes into play. Although Jenny Brown, one of the four passengers on the ship representing Porter herself, seems to have spent at least part of her life in Texas (one of her best memories is of a day of swimming in Corpus Christi Bay), only Denny is explicitly labeled a Texan. And he is a viciously unpleasant one. Upon his first appearance he is seen as a "tall shambling dark young fellow" who embarked from "some port in Texas" (18). At his second appearance the crudeness hinted at in "shambling" is confirmed and amplified as we learn of both his persistent desire for prostituted sex and his virulent prejudices:

The tall shambling young Texan, whose name was William Denny, came in and sat in a corner of the bar and watched [two ladies of the trade] with a wary, knowing eye . . . they never once glanced at Denny, who felt it as a personal slight. He rapped sharply on the bar as if calling the barman, still staring at them, a mean cold little smile starting in his face. Chili Queens. He knew their kind. He had not lived most of his life in Brownsville, Texas, for nothing. . . . In the small town on the border where his father was a prominent citizen, mayor for many years and rich from local real estate, the lower classes consisted of Mexicans and Negroes, that is, greasers and niggers. (24)

This kind of crude ethnic labeling will characterize Denny's thoughts and speech throughout. He is a sharp contrast to Adam, the ideal lover of "Pale Horse, Pale Rider," as fresh as Eden itself.

Why does Porter make the two Texans who appear in her fictions of war so extreme? Why does she bring them in at all?

If we reconceive *Ship of Fools* as a novel about prejudice rather than a novel about the world's approach to war, the presence of so caricatured a figure is more readily explained. Denny exemplifies prejudice. He is eaten up by it. Yet many other characters in the novel also demonstrate the ugliness of prejudice—for instance, the "whinnying" Lizzi and the "pig-snouted" Rieber. Simply as to numbers, Denny would seem to be as great a redundancy as the repetitiveness of his racist language. A tenth of the way through the book we know him quite well without needing to be shown over and over.

For Porter, though, Denny was essential. He is the vehicle of her deepest personal resentments. Although her accounts of her work on the novel in letters and interviews implied an intellectualized working-out of an aesthetic problem, we know that throughout the twenty-something years she worked on the book she was continuing to wrestle with her conflicting feelings toward Texas. Her mind never stopped turning back to her childhood and early adult years there. Her father's death in January 1942 provoked a particularly intense bout of such wrestling. In part, Denny represents her first husband, John Koontz, limned in hostile caricature with all his violence and his determination to have sex even if he has to force it. The reiteration of Denny's base faults expresses the deep resentments of that marriage that never left her. She must have felt great vengeful glee in attributing to this Catholic ex-husband an intemperate anti-Catholicism when she has Denny say, "If there's one religion on this earth that I despise, it's those

Catholics. I don't like anything about 'em. Where I come from, only the lowest kind of people, greasers and wops and polacks, are Catholics" (96).

Since the targets of his distaste were fairly common where he came from, though not perhaps the intensity of his fixation, Denny's prejudices are also offered as being representative of Texas more generally. He looks forward to "getting back to Brownsville once more, where a man knew who was who and what was what, and niggers, crazy Swedes,[14] Jews, greasers, bone-headed micks, polacks, wops, Guineas and damn Yankees knew their place and stayed in it" (334).

Denny also likes violence. When the passengers in steerage kill one of their own he exults in true Texas idiom, "Well, I be dog! They got him! Well, I be dog!" (328). Joined with his bigotry, his taste for violence makes him emblematic of one of the aspects of Texas history and culture that most impelled Porter's disaffection, at least in its public dimension. In "'Noon Wine': The Sources" and elsewhere, she made it clear that she not only abhorred the societal and personal violence of her life in Texas but also disapproved of the rampant racism toward blacks and Mexicans she saw there. At the time the essay was published, 1956, she was still wrestling her behemoth and trying hard to believe, as she told people at the University of Texas, the book would "appear early next year."

By the time the long novel was finally completed, Porter's own racial attitudes had so hardened that her generally deft handling of narrative point of view became unsteady. Except for William Denny's omni-hostilities, prejudice appears in the novel mainly in three forms: anti-Semitism, distaste toward Germans, and misogyny. It can well be argued that the first two reflected Porter's own prejudices, though she probably did not believe she was expressing personal anti-Semitism but only the German anti-Semitism that had fueled the war. Such hostilities are so pervasive, however, that every character is smeared with the muck and it becomes impossible to use narrative point of view as a key to her own attitudes. As if she were a brawler fighting one or two main bullies, while nevertheless thinking she could spare a hand to take a swipe at another target now and then, she also sneers at the one Texan on the ship as if he represents the whole, distasteful state.

Porter's settled dislike of Germans in her adult years is puzzling. It may have been an expression of a deep-seated envy from childhood because her best friend in Kyle, Erna Schlemmer, who was from Germany, could enjoy luxuries and travel unavailable to herself. If so, that envy was deeply buried; she never expressed any overt resentment of Erna—quite the contrary. But by the time she had been in Berlin only a few weeks, in late 1931, she was referring to Germans in derogatory terms that carry over into both *Ship of Fools* and "The Leaning

Tower." Her dislike would become more deeply entrenched as time went on. She recognized on the streets of Berlin the devastation that the Great War had cost the German people, and wrote about their suffering sympathetically both in a letter to Gene Pressly on December 21, 1931, and in notes to herself dated that same week. She wrote of emaciated and shivering beggars on the streets, some of them blind or crippled, singing carols in hope of attracting alms. Young men so thin their teeth showed against their cheeks, she wrote, stood on street corners wearing signs asking for work. "All around her," Unrue writes, "she saw the cruelties and irrationality of chauvinism and the baleful aftereffects of the World War and the 1918 Armistice" (*Life* 133). Perhaps, though unintended as such, that is the severest judgment that can be pronounced on *Ship of Fools:* that despite having seen for herself the effects on Germany still left from World War I, she omitted them from her account of the roots of the second plunge into world war. Given the rigid limitation of the book to the ocean crossing, it was of course a necessary omission. But by neglecting the explanation provided by history and focusing only on individual failings, and by tarnishing the whole with the virulence of her dislike of Germans, she produced a novel that implicitly claims to explain while it neglects the most tangible, traceable explanation.

~

Much of the thinking about war and the nature of the German people in *Ship of Fools* was already stale when the novel came before the public in 1962, having appeared twenty-one years earlier in the 1941 novella "The Leaning Tower." This is not surprising, since Porter's work on the two overlapped. She told Wescott in a letter of September 13, 1940, that she was working on them in alternation, using "The Leaning Tower" as a relief from the laborious novel. As a form, the novella was far more congenial to her, more compact, with fewer characters and a more focused theme. Rather than trying to show the ultimate causes of war in the human heart more or less universally, she attempted in "The Leaning Tower" to demonstrate Germany's reason for going to war again. Rather than an allegorical ship, its Berlin setting is very real and obviously pertinent. And rather than operating solely on the moral level, as *Ship of Fools* does, it fully if sparely addresses the historic factors involved in the drive toward war. It is both a tighter work and a more fully realized one.

The story opens on December 27, 1931, six days after Charles Upton has arrived in Berlin. The date of Porter's own arrival had been three months earlier. It seems clear, then, that she wanted to compress the interval between Upton's first sight of the city and the events of the story, thus accentuating his sense of unfamiliarity and increasing the impact of each new impression or encounter.

She could have accomplished this in any number of other ways, of course, but by placing the action so near the end of the year she was able to evoke a compelling atmosphere of wintry cold and dark, symbolic of Germany's living death between the wars. Opening the story on December 27 also allowed her to use New Year's Eve for the climactic episode while maintaining a compressed overall time frame.

Upton is another Texan, but he in no way resembles William Denny of *Ship of Fools*. He is more like a Katherine Anne Porter rendered male. An aspiring but uncertain artist living on a shoestring, as she was—a shoestring being supplied by his father in Texas, as she could only have wished—Upton struggles against depression, as she did, while looking for affordable, acceptable lodgings. His impressions of the city also replicate hers as, at every turn, he encounters Berliners who strike him as sneeringly supercilious or miserably poor or both. After rejecting several dismal lodgings, he is shown into a stuffily overdecorated room in the house of a woman named Rosa Reichl, who lives in penurious gentility. As he stands pondering whether to take it, he carelessly picks up a plaster model of the Leaning Tower of Pisa, which shatters in his hand—a mishap that had in fact befallen Eugene Pressly when he was helping Porter look for a room.[15] It quickly becomes obvious that though only a cheap souvenir, the little tower was a keepsake to which the landlady attached great sentimental value. As if to compensate, he agrees to take the room for three months even though he finds its shabby-genteel air oppressively gloomy. Moving in at once, he finds himself, as did Porter, all but paralyzed by misery, and when he does try to work he is continually distracted by the officiousness of his landlady, who bustles in and out, misarranging his drawings.

Soon he meets the other boarders: a Polish pianist named Tadeusz Mey, modeled on Porter's conspiratorial lover in Mexico, J. H. Retinger; an aspiring mathematician from the north of Germany, Herr Bussen, who speaks a clumsy Plattdeutsch and is looked down upon by the others; and a student from Heidelberg, Hans von Gehring, who is in Berlin for treatment of an infected *mensur* scar (the greatly coveted dueling scar that signified traditional Prussian militarism). Together, the four go on a New Year's Eve excursion to a cabaret, where they celebrate by getting drunk. In a long conversation about the nations and ethnic groups of Europe, it becomes evident that the two Germans are Nordic supremacists. Joining Otto Bussen in denigrating every European nationality except their own, Hans proclaims that "the true great old Germanic type is lean and tall and fair as gods" (*CS* 481). The conversation grows increasingly tense until Hans, who has insisted that "power" is "the only thing of any value or importance" in the world, at last comes to the point: "We Germans were beaten in the last war, thanks to your great country, but we shall win in the next" (*CS* 486). With a chill of foreboding, Charles decides that he "trusted none of them" and had better not let himself get as drunk as they do.

Nevertheless, he does. Emboldened by drink as he watches a girl doing some kind of dance apparently intended as a rumba, and knowing that is the one dance he can do really well, he demonstrates by first seizing the maracas from the band member who obviously finds them culturally alien, then taking the girl in his arms and trying to dance with her, though her version of the rumba is more like "a combination of the black bottom and the hoochy-coochy such as he had seen, sneaking off furtively with other boys, in carnival sideshows during his innocent boyhood in Texas" (*CS* 489). Her only interest in him is an unfounded hope that he can get her into the movies in Hollywood. She fends him off every time he tries to hold her close, but when Hans cuts in, kisses his cheek over and over. It is clear that the two young men are using the girl as a counter in a contest of masculinities, and Upton finds himself feeling a "sharp hatred" toward the militant Hans. With an exclamation of "Hell, what of it?" he regains his self-control, and when Tadeusz, the Pole, echoes that sentiment the three of them—Charles Upton, Otto, and Tadeusz—sit drunkenly vowing their friendship while Tadeusz goes off into a long reverie about his childhood in Cracow when at Easter his family "ate only pork in contempt of the Jews" (490). At midnight the cabaret-goers sing together with interlocked arms, enveloped by a brief illusion of good-fellowship. But Upton has recognized a barely suppressed hatred and a potential for violence all around him.

After staggering back to his room, he goes to bed with a feeling of something "threatening, uneasy, hanging over his head or stirring angrily, dangerously, at his back" (*CS* 495). What he feels is the peril of the next war inchoately gathering itself together out of the ethnocentrism and diffuse hostilities glimpsed at the cabaret. Looking around with eyes that "swam in his head," he sees nothing "familiar, nothing that was his." He does notice, however, that the souvenir Leaning Tower has reappeared, this time safely ensconced behind glass in a display cabinet: "It was there, all right, and it was mended pretty obviously, it would never be the same. But for Rosa, poor old woman, he supposed it was better than nothing. It stood for something she had, or thought she had, once. Even all patched up as it was, and worthless to begin with, it meant something to her. . . . Leaning, suspended, perpetually ready to fall but never falling quite, the venturesome little object—a mistake in the first place, a whimsical pain in the neck, really . . . yet had some kind of meaning in Charles' mind. Well, what?"

(494-95). What it signifies is of course the moral brittleness of German society, joined to its prideful claims to cultural richness. Rosa's cheap replica of a tower set on poor foundations, bought during a long-ago trip to Italy, is a shrine to a dead past, as irrelevant to her present situation as the German past of Bach and Beethoven is to Germany's present social ugliness. Just as the tower leans toward its fall, Germany leans toward war and its own moral and cultural ruin.

The tower's fragility may also be emblematic of Germany's vulnerability to the wiles of an unprincipled strongman who exhorts its starving people to wrap their sense of racial superiority about them and fight their way out of their misery. If so, that meaning is deeply buried. And if it implies that the German war machine will crumble in the hands of Americans, that, too, is buried in silence and left undeveloped. Characteristically, Porter refrained from making her symbolism too overt.

During the period when she was actively working on "The Leaning Tower," her friend and faithful correspondent Glenway Wescott was working on his own short novel of the approach of war, *The Pilgrim Hawk*. The letters they exchanged during this period clearly show how heavily the coming war weighed on their minds. On March 23, 1939, Wescott wrote, "I haven't any idea what steps to take personally when the war begins, if . . ." His significant and poignant breaking off of the sentence conveys a sense of personal helplessness in the grips of world events much like that expressed by Charles Upton in the last sentence of "The Leaning Tower"—the knowledge that "no crying jag or any other kind of jag would ever, in this world, do anything at all for him" (*CS* 495). On August 31, 1939, Wescott reported "fiddling with the radio" to get news of "where we are at in our endeavor against that horrible great man H." Six days later Porter mentioned her anxiety about "all the uproar of millions of men being marched here and there" and the "billions of dollars being spent" on arms. "Twice in one lifetime is too much." To express the "extraordinary premonition of disaster" she was feeling, she again drew on an image of marching feet, making it now "the steady sound" of the "iron hooves" of evil.[16] All through 1940 and 1941 she and Wescott continued to write in mutual encouragement about their two novellas—their "war work," as Wescott put it, punning on the familiar phrase for civilian mobilization—and, always intertwined, their concern about the war. On January 9, 1942, with her "Leaning Tower" now published in journal form but still awaiting book publication, Porter remarked in a letter to Wescott that the month-old U.S. involvement in the war was already "a thriving young monster."

∾

Why do Texas and Texans appear in all three of Porter's fictional works about war, when they are not essential to any of them?

We have seen that William Denny in *Ship of Fools* bears a huge autobiographical weight in his personal brutishness and as a voice of the prevalent racism Porter saw in Texas. In this latter aspect, he serves her goal of demonstrating a worldwide ill will contributing to the coming of the war. Adam, in "Pale Horse, Pale Rider," is quite the opposite, a beautiful, quietly humorous young man who for all his garb of military violence serves as a tender caregiver to Miranda when she contracts the flu. His finely tailored uniform is an allusion to the well-fitting grays in which wealthy young officers of the Confederacy went to war, but rather than inflict violence and pain, he provides comfort, and in doing so he lays down his life for her. The fact that he, too, is a Texan may indicate that Porter's imagination turned, for her beau ideal, to the image of her tall, slim father. Regardless of whether we accept that frequently stated view, in the story itself his Texas origins provide a quality of familiarity with or destined empathy toward their brief time together.

Porter sometimes said that Adam was based on a real man she was in love with in Denver, whom she called the great love of her life. But like so many of her other statements about herself, this is based on only a small kernel of truth amplified and dramatized. In a letter of January 21, 1933, she told her father that when she was "so desperately sick" with the flu a "young boy twenty one years old" had taken care of her for three days—someone, she said, she "did not know at all, who happened to be living in the same house" (*SL* 90). So much for her great love. It was after she had reconstructed the situation in "Pale Horse, Pale Rider" that she felt a need to insist on the version that elevates this nameless twenty-one-year-old to the status of true love. Her letter to her father makes no mention of his being from Texas.

Charles Upton of "The Leaning Tower" is somewhere between these extremes, neither a brutish villain nor an idealization. Like Adam, he is a victim of war, or rather of impending war; the "something . . . threatening . . . stirring angrily, dangerously, at his back" cannot be eluded, and nothing "would ever, in this world" fend off that evil. His momentary feeling of solidarity with Berliners is only a passing illusion. At the same time, Upton manifests in the "flicker of sharp hatred" for Hans that passes through him as the two contend for the attentions of the cabaret dancer his potential for becoming a cog in the American machine of patriotic German-hating. It was no more necessary here than in Porter's other war fictions that he be a Texan; he could equally well have been an aspiring artist from Iowa. But bringing him closer to her own past allowed Porter to identify with her creation emotionally and ascribe to him her own feelings about Berlin and art and dreariness, and her own war anxiety. By making him a Texan like herself, she could move her imagination into him.

The Texan characters in Porter's war fiction are not by any means duplicates of each other. She does not generalize about them as her prejudiced passengers on the *Vera* do about groups they dislike. In fact, she differentiates among the three in much the same way that she varies her evocations of her Texas past. In some passages of "'Noon Wine': The Sources," when she recalls the abundant natural world of her childhood, her associations are idyllically positive. In "Pale Horse, Pale Rider," where the Texan is an idealized sweetheart, she dreams of a Texas where (in moving quasi-biblical language) the farm well bubbles "with living water." Hatefulness and death intrude from outside in the form of a stereotyped Boche villain or an apocalyptic pale horseman. But when she evokes the social or historical life of Texas, as she does with the guns leaning in the corners of closets, the associations are negative. And there are no pictures of Texas countryside in *Ship of Fools* or "The Leaning Tower," only social references.

The connection of Texas and Texans with Porter's writing about war may seem tenuous, but when seen through the lens of Porter's biography it makes perfect sense. To her, personal fulfillment and success were achievable only through travel and attaining a measure of internationalism. She went to Mexico and to Europe for positive reasons, to experience cultural richness and achieve a wider perspective. These were, so to speak, the pull factors. But there was also a powerful push factor—her desire to escape Texas. She had long felt that the prospect of achieving her career goals was hopeless so long as she remained there. Having left, she did to a great extent reach those goals. But she was never able to let go of her ties to Texas or her resentment of the hurts she had experienced there. Her wider cosmopolitanism was a richer context within which to think about her origins.

Writing about war served Porter in much the same way as her travel experiences. It multiplied and amplified the ways in which she could think about the violence of her historic heritage. War and the inescapability of war's approach provided her a powerfully felt subject in its own right and at the same time an added way to think about her essential subject: Texas and her sense of her own life there as a drama of doomed innocence.

9

Two Almost-Last Straws

I chose a perfect old stone house and barn sitting on a hill, renovated it splendidly, and left it forever, all in one fine June morning. In this snapshot style, I have also possessed beautiful old Texas ranch houses; a lovely little Georgian house in Alexandria, Virginia; an eighteenth-century Spanish-French house in Louisiana. . . . Indeed, I have lived for a few hours in any number of the most lovely houses in the world.

—Katherine Anne Porter, "A House of My Own" (1941)

In 1939 and 1958 two events occurred that drove Porter's ambivalence about Texas nearly to estrangement. Both must be told along with a great deal of contextual material, including what I consider to be very pertinent to both: her long wish for a house of her own. As her poem "Anniversary in a Country Cemetery" tells us, she regarded herself as essentially homeless throughout her adult life, and when she visited her mother's grave in 1936 (the "anniversary" referred to in the poem, which may actually have been drafted on that occasion) she briefly thought of herself as being "home again." The following year, 1937, when she went back to Texas to celebrate her father's eightieth birthday at the Old Settlers Reunion in San Marcos, she became caught up in nostalgic emotion and began to wonder if she might make her home in Texas. Of course, she did not do so. But her wish for a home, combined with her nostalgia for a childhood bliss she never actually experienced and her wish to be embraced by "her own people," as she was at the reunion, added to the feeling of rejection she experienced after the episodes in 1939 and 1958.

As if the mellowness she felt at the Old Settlers Reunion were not enough, Porter's feelings toward Texas were further softened by a four-month stay in Houston, largely at her sister Gay's house, at the beginning of 1938 when she was waiting for her divorce from Pressly so she could marry the ardent Albert Erskine. This relatively happy time compounded her vulnerability to hurt when she was passed over for the Texas Institute of Letters (TIL) award in 1939. Being left as runner-up after she had thought *Pale Horse, Pale Rider* was a "certain winner" (*KAP* 315) struck her as another fundamental rejection by Texas and Texans. The year was an emotional roller coaster for Porter in other ways as well, from the high of publishing her most artistically triumphant book to the low of yet another marital failure and the disaster of another world war. Germany invaded Poland on September 1, 1939.

It was a big year for the fledgling Texas Institute of Letters, too. The organization had been founded only in 1936 for the promotion and recognition of literature in Texas. The TIL prize, being awarded for the first time in 1939, was designed to recognize the year's best book written by a writer born in Texas or who had lived in Texas for at least two years or to the writer of a book substantially concerned with Texas. Porter had every reason to regard herself as the leading candidate on multiple grounds—as a native Texan, as author of a book about Texas (even if not very recognizably so), and because of the superb literary quality of the book. But when she returned to Louisiana in the fall after her summer stay at Olivet Writers' Conference, she learned that the prize had gone to folklorist J. Frank Dobie for *Apache Gold and Yaqui Silver*. Dobie himself felt awkward about it; it was his organization, after all. But the award committee had expressed itself. Dobie's book was the winner for its "indigenous nature" (*KAP* 315). This, too, is problematic. There would seem to be no good reason why a book of the rough-and-ready western stretches of the state would be more "indigenous" than one about central Texas and its ties to the South. But that was exactly the image of Texas Dobie was seeking to displace in favor of an image of Texas as the West. The award, then, had broadly political ramifications.

What it represented to Porter, though, was simply rejection of her efforts to launch a reciprocal love affair with Texas. This was the last straw—or would have been if the camel had not struggled back up nineteen years later to have another straw laid on its back.

The summary I have given is at any rate the standard story. Porter's most frequently cited biographer, Joan Givner, reports as fact that Dobie's selection for the prize meant "the reconciliation with her native state, achieved after a long estrangement, was suddenly destroyed" and she was "convinced once again that Texas was no place for her" (*KAP* 315). Her more recent biographer, Darlene Unrue, likewise states that she was "badly disappointed" at being "snubbed" by the TIL (*Life* 178). Neither cites any source for this information.[1] Folklorist Sylvia Grider characterizes the story of the prize not given, or not given to Porter, as "a kind of academic oral tradition" often told "with much embellishment," on the order of an urban legend (234). Grider's comment prompts the question, was Porter really so disappointed as reports have had it and if so, how do we know?

So far as I have been able to find, Porter never openly stated that she felt offended by being left in the position of runner-up for a prize whose purposes perfectly fit herself and her finest book. How could she? It would have been graceless in the extreme. And in any event, at least in her fiction, she was more often one to make her points indirectly. With that in mind, I believe we can take her remark to William Humphrey, in a letter of October 8, 1950, that it was only in the "last fewest years" that Texas had seen fit to show the slightest interest in her, as having been made with the TIL prize decision in mind. Similarly, the following statement, made in 1958, strikes me as a disguised indication that she had been quite miffed by it:

> Texas has no serious writers. I am the first serious writer Texas has produced. That is, up to now. There are two young writers who are very promising. William Humphrey has written a good book. "Home is the sailor" . . . How does it go? "Home from the sea And the hunger home from the hill . . ."
>
> I thought William Goyen had a really brilliant and strange talent. When his first works came out I thought he had a first rate talent. But he seems to have—gone off. But maybe he will come back and produce more good work. . . . I am the first and only serious writer that Texas has produced. These young people may turn out to be first rate. The woods are swarming with writers. In all this ferment, we're bound to get more good ones. But so far I am the only one. If you can show me others, I'll be glad to see them. . . .
>
> What is more "regional" than "Noon Wine"? Than "Old Mortality"? . . . But I don't know any first rate person who is a regional writer. (*Conv.* 33–34)

Conspicuously absent from this passage was J. Frank Dobie. But we are well justified in believing that Dobie was intended in the reference to the "regional writer" who is not "first rate" and that he is flatly dismissed from consideration by the phrase "first and *only* serious writer" (emphasis added). Givner notes, too, that Porter also at one point dismissed Dobie as a "mere chronicler" ("Problems of Personal Identity" 49). It does appear that she never got over the sting of having been beaten out by an unworthy rival.

Most critics and historians of Texas literature now agree that the 1939 TIL prize did not recognize the best Texas book of the year. Dobie's selection for the award has been variously attributed to sexism, a weakness for shoot-'em-up westerns, and gratitude for his membership in the young organization. James Ward Lee points to another reason, however: the locus of each writer's following. Though preeminent in Texas letters, Lee writes, Dobie had little national reputation, while Porter was prominent in national letters but rarely even thought of, at that time, as a Texas writer ("Porter and Dobie" 73–75).[2] For that very reason, he argues, the award was appropriate, especially considering that it was the inaugural year of the prize. I would counter that by choosing Dobie's book over Porter's masterwork, the institute defined itself as provincial from the get-go (as Texans say).

James Lee's statement about Porter's national reputation and Dobie's solely regional one has been questioned by Steve Davis, who points out that Dobie's 1930 book *Coronado's Children* was reviewed in such eastern newspapers as the *New York Times* and was chosen by the Literary Guild in February 1931 as its featured selection (81). As to Dobie's and Porter's 1939 books competing for the prize, he continues, the *New York Times* gave *Apache Gold and Yaqui Silver* a lengthy review on March 16, 1939, but only about half as long a review of *Pale Horse, Pale Rider* (by the same reviewer) on March 30. Column inches in a pre-eminent outlet are certainly a possible measure of relative standing, but as a matter of fact they do not, in this instance, support a conclusion that Dobie's national reputation surpassed Porter's. The short review of *Pale Horse, Pale Rider* on March 30 cited by Davis was not the only one. A second *New York Times* review followed only three days later, this time a four-column spread with photograph. Moreover, the language of the reviews clearly placed Porter on a higher literary plane. Ralph Thompson summarized Dobie's book in a way that showed he found it lively and enjoyable, but he referred to its material as "yarns" and said that the author was "not disturbed by differences between probable and possible." His review was dotted with regional markers, and he ended with the loaded observation that Dobie seemed to have "found ample paying ore" of his own in writing two books about hidden treasures. In contrast, Thompson said of Porter's work (which he paired with an only slightly longer review of T. S. Eliot's *The Family Reunion*) that it showed "unmistakable quality" and was "simple in pattern, substantial, honestly moving." The second review of *Pale Horse, Pale Rider,* by Edith Walton, compared Porter to Kay Boyle and Virginia Woolf, pronounced two of the three stories in the volume "flawless," and said that the collection as a whole "justif[ied] all that has been claimed for her." The quality of Porter's volume of novellas was recognized at the time, and time has confirmed Walton's estimate. The institute clearly erred in its judgment, and its award of its first book prize to Dobie almost—but not quite—sealed Porter's disaffection from Texas.

～

Capitalizing on the reception of *Pale Horse, Pale Rider,* Porter signed a new contract the following year, 1940, with Harcourt, Brace. It provided additional advances for the long-moribund Cotton Mather book, the novel then being called "No Safe Harbour," "The Man in the Tree," and "The Leaning Tower." Only "The Leaning Tower," out of the four, was ever completed in the form then envisioned. Its completion and publication that same year might have been expected to lift her spirits, but the other commitments she had entered into predictably began to cause her anxiety and depression.

As already mentioned, she went to the writers' and artists' refuge Yaddo that summer. While there, she experienced a resurgence of her long wish for a house of her own and scouted the area, with Elizabeth Ames driving. In January 1941, ten miles from Saratoga Springs, she saw an old Colonial house that she immediately declared to be "hers." Short of funds because she had spent her advances from Harcourt, Brace on clothes, dental work, and a share of her father's nursing care, she took on extra speaking engagements to make the down payment but still fell short and had to take out a loan. How she would pay for the extensive renovations the house needed was a question she seems to have avoided facing, but it was one that would become more and more pressing as the needed repairs and remodeling, once begun, grew more and more extensive. In the meantime, she further delayed completing the work for which she was contracted.

The summer of 1941 brought Eudora Welty to Yaddo. Immediately taking her up as a protégée and friend, Porter bought a car that Welty drove as they toured the area buying furniture for South Hill, as she had named her house. She was to write the introduction for Welty's first volume of stories, *A Curtain of Green,* and in a kind of reciprocity gave an honored and grateful Welty the first sixty pages of "No Safe Harbour" to read. But the only piece of work Porter actually finished that summer other than the introduction to Welty's book was the wryly humorous essay "A House of My Own," published in *Vogue.* She launched into an extensive correspondence with her nephew Paul and enjoyed recommending books he should read, but other projects lagged. Desperate for money, she signed more contracts and accepted more advances.

In January 1942 her father died, but though she grieved hard she did not go to Texas for the funeral. She was tense and depressed about her work, about the war, about infringements on Americans' civil rights. That spring, while she was in Reno to divorce Erskine, she was visited by an FBI agent investigating Josephine Herbst, who had applied for a government job. It appears that under the spell of his good looks and abundant drinks, she spoke freely about Josie's political views.[3] Five years later, perhaps partly out of regret for this betrayal and for having collaborated with the kind of government surveillance she deplored, Porter would bravely take a stand in print and on radio against McCarthy-inspired communist witch-hunting. "On Communism in Hollywood" ends with a resounding

12. Katherine Anne Porter in a meadow in front of her house, called South Hill, at Ballston Spa, New York, in June or July 1941. All her life she wished for a home of her own, but South Hill was the only house she ever owned. Katherine Anne Porter Papers, Special Collections, University of Maryland Libraries.

assertion that the activities of Anti-American Activities Committee were "the most un-American thing I know" (*CE* 208). Both then and during the later John Birch Society days, her views differed from those of many, or most, Texans.

She finally moved into her house in September 1942 but quickly found herself lonely. Winter comes early and comes hard in upstate New York. She had supposed her friends would visit, but South Hill was remote, that year's winter was unusually hard, and few made the trek. At times she was snowbound. Only a year after moving in she moved out again, assisted financially in doing so by Barbara Harrison, Monroe Wheeler, and Glenway Wescott. In the hope that she might finish work she had under contract, these staunch supporters put her up at a quiet inn at Cold Spring, New York, but her stay there did not prove to be another Water Wheel Tavern. She was unable to work.

In early 1944 Porter was freed from her frustratingly unproductive stay at the inn by an appointment as Fellow of Regional American Literature at the Library of Congress. She took rooms at the home of Marcella Comés Winslow and on May 15 celebrated her fifty-fourth birthday with a party. That was how she met Charles Shannon. He was among several servicemen from nearby Fort Belvoir who were invited. Naturally, her period of unproductivity was prolonged by their affair. Also, she was ill and hospitalized during this time.

December brought a new opportunity, however, and one that might have set her on firm financial footing long term—an offer to work in the movie industry as a writer and "advisor" at MGM. She went the following month and remained in California almost three years, until September 1947, working stints of a few

13. Katherine Anne Porter at fifty-four, in the garden of Marcella Comés Winslow's house, 3106 P Street, Georgetown, Washington, D.C. Photo taken on July 9, 1944, possibly by Sgt. Charles Shannon. Katherine Anne Porter Papers, Special Collections, University of Maryland Libraries.

months each at various studios at very high pay. Unfortunately, she did not hold onto much of the money that was coming in and, even worse, did very little writing. Two happy events of that period came in 1946—the sudden appearance of buyers for South Hill and the arrival of her still-admiring nephew Paul, newly discharged from the army. Yet even before she sold South Hill—her wish for a home having followed her to the West Coast—she bought on impulse eighty acres of mountainous land, though she had no means of paying the $10,000 price.

Hollywood brought Porter a closer friendship with photographer George Platt Lynes, whom she had known in Paris. Toward the end of 1947, in desperate financial straits, she moved into his house, where she posed for a series of highly dramatized photographs, some of which were published in glossy magazines. Lynes was one of several gay men with whom Porter maintained real friendships without abating her aversion to homosexuals as a class, perhaps because they were impervious to her charms. An interesting example is a young man she had met in New York who had been proclaiming his love for her ever since. In August 1946, when he came to visit her in California with what she thought were romantic intentions, he made it clear that what he loved was her writing, not her carnal self. She was irate, and in a letter to Josie Herbst on January 30, 1947, denounced him as perverted.

Since the beginning of World War II or somewhat before, she had become increasingly fixated on Nazism and fascism, including domestic fascism. She very much wanted to get back to "No Safe Harbour" but continued to spend her time in speaking engagements in order to get by financially. After spending the spring semester of 1947 at Stanford, she left the West Coast and once again became a "little Texas girl in New York." At first she moved into her niece Ann's small apartment, but when speaking fees allowed her to, she rented larger quarters of her own in order to write in solitude—but then, in another instance of self-destructiveness, invited Ann to move in!

At last, in 1950, she was able to publish three excerpts from the novel. She also published some essays and book reviews that year, one of them a review of Texan William Goyen's first novel, *The House of Breath.* The handsome Goyen had told her his book was written with her "great work" as his "guiding principle" (*Letters* 159). Soon the two were involved in an intensely turbulent affair despite the fact that he was bisexual—an evil in Porter's mind for which she repeatedly berated him in letters. Goyen was then thirty-five to Porter's sixty-two. She also became acquainted, about this time, with another good-looking young writer from Texas, William Humphrey. This protégé's devotion was purely literary. It is not hard to see that both relationships would have contributed to the roiling mix of her feelings toward Texas.

While continuing to delay completion of her novel by dissipating her time in speaking engagements and amorous melodramatics,[4] she made an agreement with Harcourt, Brace for a collection of her essays. To ensure that she would complete the necessary preparations, the publisher put her on salary as an editor, with the requirement that she actually spend time at the office. *The Days Before* appeared in 1952. Before it came out, however, Porter went to Paris with the American delegation to the International Congress for Cultural Freedom, unaware that it was being funded by the CIA. She then spent a month on the coast of Brittany, supposedly to write the preface for the volume of essays. After some serious thinking, she concluded that she could not complete any of the other work for which she had obligated herself, and so informed Harcourt, Brace when she returned to New York.

In September 1953 she went to the University of Michigan for what was supposed to be a full academic year but continued to give talks elsewhere. In December, worn out by the hectic pace, she had to be hospitalized. She collapsed again in March with chest pains, the third such episode in three years, yet tried to squelch the news because she had applied for a Fulbright and didn't want to lose out because of rumors about her health. Her most treasured keepsake of the year in Ann Arbor was a long, long string of pearls.

The Fulbright came through, and she sailed for Brussels on September 17, 1954, but arrived sick with bronchitis and had to be put to bed before going on to her assignment in Liège. In December she went to London to read "The Circus" for the BBC, then on to Paris to buy clothes and to Rome for Christmas. When she returned to Belgium, she had to spend another three weeks in a Brussels hospital. Doctors thought she could recover and complete her Fulbright year, but she knew she could not. She returned to the United States at the end of February 1955, taking with her a linen winding sheet she had bought for her final disposal.

We have already seen how, in the mid-1950s, Porter attempted to settle into work on *Ship of Fools* under the oversight of Seymour Lawrence, sometimes coaxing, sometimes pressuring. When she broke off work on the novel to go take up her writer-in-residence appointment at the University of Virginia in the fall of 1958, she found Charlottesville delightful. There were polo games on Sundays— her "favorite of all games to watch," she told her agent, Cyrilly Abels. And the man chairing the English department was from Texas! On this occasion, she took that as a positive, probably because she could link it with the fond memories she had recently elaborated on in "'Noon Wine': The Sources." He was "born within twenty miles" of herself, she enthused, and they remembered "nearly exactly the same things" (*SL* 557–58). The university's expectations for teaching were very flexible in return for her $500 monthly stipend, plus living quarters. She could have used the unstructured time to finish *Ship of Fools*. Instead, she chose to enjoy herself and go on speaking tours, including a stop at the University of Texas in October. This proved to be the second of the two "last straws."

At three different times during her fully adult years Porter made visits to Texas that evoked momentary thoughts of returning to make her home there. The first was her 1937 observance of her father's eightieth birthday at the Old Settlers Reunion in San Marcos. The 1958 speaking engagement in Austin was the second. Bubblingly pleased to have been invited, she chose to regard it as a kind of homecoming, to the point that she described it to her niece Ann in much the same language she had used for the Old Settlers Reunion more than twenty years earlier. In doing so, she was misleading herself.

Her relations with the university were already problematic. In June 1939, before the awarding of the TIL prize, the university's librarian, Donald Coney, had written to Porter soliciting her donation of the manuscript of "Noon Wine" to the library's special collection. It would have been better if he had stopped there, but he went on to state that the manuscript would go into the Texas collection. Porter, who never wished to be regarded as a regional writer, found this last proviso irksome. Even so, she sent the manuscript—not of "Noon Wine" but of "Old Mortality." Richard Holland, who worked in the University of Texas library system for many years and thus has an insider's view, believes that she did so because she was thinking about her "literary legacy" but that her anticipation of the TIL prize might also have been persuasive (80). A souring denouement to this exchange about manuscripts came fourteen years later when another librarian wrote to Porter without mentioning the earlier gift. Her response, dated June 10, 1953, might have been written in acid. She said that she assumed the manuscript had been lost, but if they found it and didn't want it she would like to have it back.[5]

Holland does not mention that there was apparently another approach between 1939 and 1953, for which documentation is less direct but no less convincing. On August 14, 1948, writing to her nephew Paul, Porter put the acid tone of the 1953 letter to shame. She told Paul that the "Library of Texas" had asked her to donate another manuscript, then mocked them in the kind of exaggerated regional dialect she habitually brought out for her heaviest sarcasm—"pore lil ole thaings." She also called the library staff bastards.

The groundwork for resentment had long been laid, then, and it produced a major misunderstanding during the party given at the end of her 1958 visit. She came away believing the university was going to name a new research library in her honor. Of course, that was not true. This misunderstanding, which went on simmering for some time, was truly the last straw, or at any rate one that broke the back of any goodwill her well-paid lecture and cordial reception might have produced. Mark Busby calls the two episodes, the non-prize in 1939 and the misunderstanding in 1958, "major estranging event[s]" that sealed her hostility toward Texas (137). That is almost true.

The university provost at the time was Harry Ransom, former chair of the Department of English. The year he scheduled Porter as a speaker was in Richard Holland's words his "great year of coming out as a national and international literary power" (83). Ransom's high aspirations for the university included building a distinguished collection of literary manuscripts, as well as holding events that would attract attention and donors. Porter's visit was expected to serve both purposes. Invited, technically, by William Handy, a protégé Ransom had named Director of the Texas Program in Criticism, she was offered, and accepted, a

$600 honorarium for a lecture on a topic of her choice. She was to follow T. S. Eliot in the series—distinguished company indeed.

It was during this trip to Austin that Winston Bode conducted the interview published in the *Texas Observer,* not only one of the most revealing and thought-provoking of Porter's many published interviews but also one that is exceptional in its emphasis on her Texas roots. Before, during, and after the lecture, an event she treated as "a kind of beautiful family gathering" (*Life* 242), she spent much of her time reminiscing about her early life as a Texan. She had said that her talk would be her "first attempt to 'account for a story.'" Its title was in fact "Noon Wine, the Sources": much the same material as had been published two years before in *Yale Review.*

As usual, her emphasis was on her appearance at least as much as the content of her talk. Her instructions as to setup for the hall had specified "a rose-color or amber spotlight" on her face, and she was festively dressed. Holland remembers her as a "literary spectacle . . . decked out in evening dress, opera-length gloves, and lorgnette" (84–85). It's the lorgnette that strikes one as seriously over-the-top and begins to raise questions about her mental stability. At the closing party in her honor, someone apparently misspoke or Porter misheard. She left Austin with the happy but quite incorrect illusion that the university was going to name its new research library—all of it—in her honor, in return for the donation of her papers. One result, prepared for by her long years of feeling homeless, was that she began to think of finding a house near the campus and making it her home.

Holland conjectures that the misunderstanding began when someone at the party broached "the idea of her literary papers finding a home on the UT campus." As he explains, however, that would have been only the germ. Two weeks after Porter's lecture, on November 7, 1958, Harry Ransom wrote her a letter including three "carefully worded" sentences: "I know Texas. I think you know it too. Therefore I believe you will understand the sincerity and conviction with which the Administration has voted to establish in the new library Center the Katherine Anne Porter Library." Porter replied with evident satisfaction, "Your decision to establish in the Library Center a library in my name is the kind of honor I never imagined for myself, not being much concerned with honors, but now it is bestowed, I am enraptured with it" (Holland 88–89). She seems to have taken it for what is known in Texas as a done deal.

Other correspondence following her lecture should probably have awakened both university officials and Porter herself to the likelihood of friction in their working relations. In navigating the publication of a fifty-four-page excerpt from

14. Porter with a rapt circle of admirers during her visit to Austin in 1958. The photo, taken on October 22, 1958, appeared in the *Daily Texan* on the following day. Dolph Briscoe Historical Center, University of Texas.

Ship of Fools in the debut issue of the ambitious journal the *Texas Quarterly,* the editorial board's proposal to move one comma evoked her large "NO!" (Holland 88). Nevertheless, in her December 26, 1958, reply to the offer of a visiting professorship for the fall of 1959, Porter mentioned several thousand books, an enormous quantity of papers, a "trunkful" of photographs—all, presumably, to come to the library—and made a passing reference to her literary estate. On January 1, 1959, she asked for guidance on what she might tell people in the interim until the cornerstone was laid, and on the same day wrote a note to Frank Lyell, a professor with whom she had become acquainted during her visit, of her pleasure in "having the Library of the new Center named for me in full" (Holland 90). Records at the Center for American History in Austin show that both Lyell and Mody Boatright, chair of the English department, alerted Ransom that she seemed to think "the whole shebang" was to be named for her and perhaps he should write to her in clarification (Holland 91). Instead, he again mentioned to her in a note six months later something that he called the "Porter Library." As late as 1962 the plan was referred to in publicity for the release of *Ship of Fools*. No clarification was ever made.

It is hard to place the entire blame for the misunderstanding on Porter's wishful thinking. The university's communications were of a nature that allowed such thinking to go on. When her correspondence did not elicit firm arrangements and the truth came to light that they only meant to name a room in the library for her, she was further embittered against the entire state of Texas. In Givner's words, the "library fiasco" ended what had "seemed at the time to have been completely harmonious" (*KAP* 427). Her flirtation with the possibility of a late-life return to Texas ended—to be revived briefly, however, another twenty years later.

The sequence of misunderstandings related to the supposed library was a far more complex and prolonged source of estrangement than the award of the Texas Institute of Letters prize to J. Frank Dobie in 1939. The two were similar, however, in that they confirmed her thinking of Texas as a literary backwater lacking in discernment and taking no interest in her achievements. Both events would have confirmed her long-established impression that Texas society not only did not encourage female creativity but actively opposed it—indeed, to adapt Givner's words about Dobie to slightly different ends, a society "flauntingly and exaggeratedly masculine."[6] When celebrated critic and sometime friend Malcolm Cowley said once that her letters were her masterpieces, she took it both as a reiteration of her father's insistence that if she wanted to write she should write letters and as confirmation of her suspicion that male literati were no more ready to recognize women's writing than Texas was.

~

Back in Virginia in January 1959 after her momentous visit to the University of Texas, Porter became involved in yet another love affair, this time with an attractive young naval officer named Jordan Pecile whom she had met briefly some years before when he was a student. He was now twenty-eight; she was sixty-eight. They arranged various trysts in nearby inns, the first on Valentine's Day in Williamsburg. True to custom, she wrote him adoring love letters, some of which, however, veer off into anger and make distinctly unpleasant reading. On April 22, for example, she complained that his lovemaking was overly rough and accused him of gouging her breasts with his thumbs. It is hard to know whether at this point in life, with over half a century's experience of sex, she still felt so alarmed by intercourse that she overstated any roughness involved or whether she actually experienced what she said she did. If so, there is sad irony in the fact that this affair in which the disparity of ages was the greatest of any of her romances, forty years, had returned her to much the same situation as her first sexual experience: physical abuse.

It was not, however, her first exposure to violence since her escape from Texas forty years before. She had led a hard-drinking, promiscuous life and on a number of occasions suffered physical injuries as a result, some of them caused by men, some not. In December 1929 she either was raped at a party or willingly engaged in sex that got rough, and suffered broken ribs. In 1949 she gave Glenway Wescott (as he records in his diary) a "hair-raising account of the damage" Charles Shannon had caused her; whether this meant she had claimed entirely emotional damage or also physical damage is not clear. In 1960 and 1962 she would suffer falls leaving her with a long, open cut in one instance and six broken ribs in the other, with alcohol involved both times. This is only a partial list but sufficient to show what a high frequency of violence her life included in the setting of home or hotel, partly related to drinking and to her troubled relations with men.

Perhaps no one realized so well as Wescott how her insatiable hunger for being wooed and her obsession with feminine glamour, her feelings of victimhood and her aggression, were bound up together into a sense of being imperiled by her gender in a powerfully masculine world.[7] In many ways, tensions and anxieties about her sex and gender roles fired her best work, but they also ate away at her stability. And their roots were in her Texas childhood, in her longing for a man to give her the total love she never felt from her father, and in the abusive love she experienced in her first marriage.

While still in Virginia, in 1959, Porter learned that she was to receive a Ford Foundation grant-in-aid of $13,000. She had been saying how nice it was to be back in the South, but now that she had some resources, she decided to go elsewhere. She had earlier told her niece Ann that she would like to live either in a world capital or deep in the country (letter of February 15, 1957). She chose a world capital, Washington, D.C., and took a two-year lease on a house on Q Street NW, near Marcella Winslow's. The one major task of this last stage of her career was to finish *Ship of Fools*.

First, there was a speaking engagement to get out of the way. She had been scheduled to give the Ewing Lectures at UCLA, a pair of lectures on a topic of her choice, in May—that is, on Washington and Lee's time—and had chosen Mark Twain, a favorite of her father's. The fee was an unusually attractive $2,500. A week before the scheduled date she begged off, citing laryngitis, and rescheduled the lectures for October. To Seymour Lawrence's emphatic dismay, this meant she had to fly to Los Angeles shortly after moving into the Q Street house. Fully aware that she was pushing him very close to the limit, she went into hysterics and refused to see him when he dropped by the day before she was to leave. Part of her agreement with UCLA was that they could publish the lectures, but even after repeated requests, they never got them. In fact, the only traces among her papers are some rough drafts labeled "Notes for Mark Twain

Lectures." In thirty-six disjointed pages, these essentially consist of a series of tries at an opening plus pages of transcribed passages from Twain's own work, occasionally with varying versions of bits of commentary ranging from a few sentences to a few paragraphs in length. She must have found it stressful indeed to present two lectures before a distinguished audience out of such material. When she returned to Washington, she was ill and unable to resume work.

Once she recovered, Washington offered too many social distractions, and for all Lawrence's insistent pleadings, things went on much as before: her goal kept slipping over the horizon. But now Porter herself was becoming embarrassed. She had told J. Frank Dobie in October 1956 that the novel would be published the following spring.[8] Then on July 21, 1957, she had written Kay Boyle that she had only about twenty thousand words to go. More recently she had made careless statements at parties that the book was in fact finished. But still she couldn't get it done.

One of the more positive aspects of her move to Q Street was that there was another tenant already occupying the basement.[9] Rhea Johnson, an employee of the U.S. State Department, proved to be a congenial admirer who quickly assumed a role as informal assistant, daily cocktail companion, frequent dinner guest, and regular escort when she did not want to attend events alone. Like the department chair at Virginia, he was a Texan—a fact that she again took as a positive. Among her "baskets and bales" of papers Johnson located the long-buried drafts of "The Fig Tree" and "Holiday," both set in Texas, which she was able to place well in *Harper's* and *Atlantic Monthly* in 1960. This is how it happened that two years after the alienating fiasco in Austin, two of her finest and most-read stories expressed a deep affection for Texas.

Sexual Politics and Ship of Fools

Although of an age to be a grandmother, Miss Porter somehow still commands the aura of the Southern belle.

—Mary McGrory, *Washington Star,* April 12, 1953

In 1964 a new phrase, "women's liberation" (or simply "women's lib"), entered the American lexicon. Propelled by two major publishing events—the English translation of Simone de Beauvoir's *The Second Sex* in 1953 and Betty Friedan's *The Feminine Mystique* in 1963—reinforced by the launching of *Ms.* magazine in 1972, the movement labeled by these widely circulated terms quickly stimulated both discomfort and defensiveness about customary social practices. Debates over the status and appropriate roles of women, and even their appropriate underwear, erupted into the public's attention and at times seemed to take it over.

Unlike what is known as first-wave feminism, which had finally succeeded in gaining woman suffrage after decades of effort, second-wave feminism focused less on individual rights than on issues of polity that sometimes struck the public as being excessively taken up with hostility toward men. It focused on freeing women from roles and assumptions, often unconscious ones, that limited their choices in life; on the concept of equal pay for equal work; and on the reform of language in order to avoid gendered terms that might skew concepts of suitable occupations and values. Women's liberation never achieved its political goal of an Equal Rights Amendment to the Constitution, but it was a serious and in the main a successful social movement.

It would be reasonable to assume that Katherine Anne Porter was a strong supporter of "women's liberation." In her youth she had been an outspoken or, as she told Donald Elder in a letter of February 6, 1942, a "roaring" advocate for woman suffrage and access to careers, especially her own. She was sufficiently emphatic in her support of the cause that her brother wrote a letter in 1909 chastising her for her "unwomanly" arguments for equality and the ballot.[1] The letter that had prompted this rebuke, assuming there was one, has not survived. It would be interesting to see the wording Paul found so objectionable. We do, however, have the wording of a review she published some sixteen years later, showing that at that early stage in her career she still retained her zeal for the cause. Appearing in the *New York Herald Tribune Books* for November 8, 1925, it was actually a review of a pair of books on the subject of gender—*Lysistrata, or Woman's Future and Future Woman* (1924) by Anthony M. Ludovici and, responding to it, *Hypatia, or Woman and Knowledge* (1925) by "Mrs. Bertrand Russell," to whom Porter pointedly accorded her own name, Dora Russell, rather than the "Mrs. Bertrand" as shown.

The review was titled "Dora, the Dodo, and Utopia," with the word "dodo" obviously referring to Mr. Ludovici. In witty language often edging into ridicule and sarcasm, Porter discredited his heavy-handed expression of masculine superiority. She summarized the argument of his book this way:

Briefly, there was a time, says the author, taking refuge in pre-historic aeons, when men were lords of life and women were their cheerful, obedient dependents. On these terms love was ecstasy, health was perfect, there was no provoking feminist agitation or scientific tampering with the psyche. Of economic and political problems he says nothing, so we are happily to presume that they had not been invented. The decline of this natural supremacy of men over women, due to the unaccountable discontent of the women themselves, whom nothing can please, has brought man low and the world to its present unhealthful state.

Acknowledging that the reader may find this "mere childish nonsense, not worth repeating," she facetiously insists that the booklet is "a literary curiosity of genuine value and should be preserved as part of the records of our times" (29). A record of social woolly-headedness, she might have said. But Mr. Ludovici wrote "without reckoning on Mrs. Dora Russell," who, it seems, is a doughty woman indeed, "a direct descendant of that first pre-historic virago who turned a realistic eye upon her surroundings and perceived that a man standing between her and the world represented not so much defense, protection, entertainment and nourishment as a mere shutting out of light and air." The phrase "realistic eye," as much as anything else, demonstrates Porter's endorsement of that reasonable virago's perception—as well as the "neat job" Dora Russell did in "demolish[ing]" Mr. Ludovici.[2]

Except for its sarcasm, "Dora, the Dodo, and Utopia" is not an isolated example; Porter voiced opinions we would readily label feminist in other reviews during the 1920s, as well as in letters both then and later. On April 12, 1929, she vented her irritation about inequality in a letter to Kathleen Millay that reminds one of Virginia Woolf's *A Room of One's Own,* published that same year, in its insistence that women writers had as much right to set their own schedules and working conditions as men did. Equality of the sexes as artists was Porter's primary feminist interest after the right to vote was gained. On July 15, 1929, she upbraided Matthew Josephson for remarks he had published in *transition* belittling a male writer by accusing him of "feminine hysteria." His terminology, she told him, betrayed a deplorable prejudice against women. In 1933 she speculated to Josie Herbst that a male power grab might explain her inability to get Herbst's latest book to review for the *New Republic.*[3] Once again, it seemed, the "gempmum" were trying to keep "us" down. Such complaints were not unusual in the letters Porter and Herbst exchanged, especially complaints about the unequal allocation of domestic work, hampering women's artistic productivity. In 1944 Porter complained bitterly to Robert Penn Warren about male editors and authors who could not or would not take a woman writer seriously (*SL* 295). As late as 1958 she expatiated at some length to Edward Schwartz on men's "antagonism" to women and lifelong urge to belittle them: "When I think well and am intelligent, the critics say I have a man's mind. When I am silly or not at my best, they admit indulgently that I am very feminine" (*SL* 549). One cannot imagine a clearer statement of the matter.

Even without the feminist implications of much of Porter's fiction, then, which are considerable, we might assume she would have welcomed the 1960s resurgence of feminism. Quite the opposite was true. She heartily disliked and even mocked it. An interview published in the *Baltimore Evening Sun* on March 25, 1970, quoted Porter as laughing when asked if she was ready to join the women's liberation movement and saying, "Certainly not . . . I don't agree with them. I told them, 'I will not sit down with you and hear you tell me men have abused you'" (*Conv.* 155). It was as if she was so committed a first-wave feminist and so gratified by its achievements that she could not see any ongoing need for more.[4] Yet Cleanth Brooks and Tillie Olsen, both of whom knew her well, recognized her commitment to equal gender rights. Olsen said that she "found in her what we now call by the name of feminism," and Brooks wrote in *A Shaping Joy* that she had "a wide streak of the feminist."[5] He would have been surprised to know that she wrote in the margin of her autographed copy, "I resent this tag."

Robert Brinkmeyer, whose tracing of Porter's career I generally find excessively schematic, is right on target in stating that a "hardening" of her thinking in her last few decades "led her into extreme and often contradictory positions" (203, 192). We can see this in her response to second-wave feminism as well as in her thinking about race and even personal likes and dislikes. Her copy of Simone de Beauvoir's *The Second Sex* is heavily marked up with protests against its arguments on grounds of being unrealistic or contrary to common sense, and she notoriously dismissed Betty Friedan's influential work by saying that *The Feminine Mystique* made her think, "Oh, Betty, why don't you go and mix a good cocktail for your husband and yourself and forget about this business" (*Conv.* 156). But there was more to it than the reactionary dottiness this flippant comment implies. Porter was not the only adherent of what Nina Baym calls "liberal feminist individualism" who objected to the more collective vision of second-wave feminist (*Feminism* xi). Her interest was in individual rights, and she took offense when she felt the new movement's sexual politics as a threat to that principle. Individualism was a concept she was not willing to reconsider, whereas second-wave feminism advocated a social agenda that painted groups or classes with a rather broad brush.

Along with distancing herself from the sexual politics of her mature years, Porter increasingly insisted on being regarded as "feminine." Her uses of this word and the word "lady," often in combination, are keys to understanding her late-in-life sexual politics. Certainly the word "lady" was a privileged term according to the teachings about gender and propriety inculcated in Porter as a child. As we know, these strictures, reinforced by her father's misgivings about a lady's writing for money, placed her under great pressure to conform, and she rebelled from her early teenage years on. But in this instance rebelling did not mean something so simple as a flat rejection. Instead, her complicated rebellion against these familial expectations entailed a profound inner discord, a conflict she never resolved. Even in middle age she paid tribute to her grandmother's ideas (in "Portrait: Old South") although at other moments she recognized them as outmoded and hampering.

In sketching her grandmother she outlined a set of personal qualities we can take as defining an ideal Southern lady:

> Grandmother was by nature lavish, she loved leisure and calm, she loved luxury, she loved dress and adornment, she loved to sit and talk with friends or listen to music; she did not in the least like pinching or saving and mending and making things do. . . .
>
> Grandmother had been an unusually attractive young woman, and she carried herself with the graceful confidence of a natural charmer to her last day. Her mirror did not deceive her, she saw that she was old. Her youthful confidence became matriarchal authority. . . . Her bountiful hos-

pitality represented only one of her victories of intelligence and feeling over the stubborn difficulties of life. (*CE* 163)

This image of the lady, feminine but strong, is reflected in many of Porter's own photographs in her later years, where she appears poised, confident, tastefully dressed, and surrounded by beautiful objects—still "a charmer."

The word "charmer," with its potentially snide overtones, may well give us pause. In "Old Mortality" Porter writes satirically about an aging belle who is also "a noted charmer," who refused to progress to the status of lady. Cousin Molly Parrington "dyed her hair, and made jokes about it. She had a way of collecting the men around her in a corner, where she told them stories" (*CS* 177–78). Then, too, "you really could not say that Molly had ever been discreet," and she lied about her age—as, of course, did Porter. And there is at least one photograph among Porter's papers in which we see her as just such a woman, decked out in strapless gown and evening gloves, trying to be still a "charmer" at seventy or eighty and succeeding, if not at that, at least in appearing feminine.

When Jane Flanders sent Porter a working draft of her 1976 article "Katherine Anne Porter and the Ordeal of Southern Womanhood," Porter wrote in the margin, "I am not anything ending in -ist. Say female, feminine, even womanly—I am *not* a member of a political or social party, but *very* feminine." Charm, or allure, for the other sex was part of what she apparently meant by femininity. Like Cousin Molly Parrington, she continued to "gather men around her" even into her old age. Her conception of a feminine persona was only partly that of the dignified lady; it also included the role of slightly sleazy, sexy old dame. Rhea Johnson told Givner in 1977 that at the Q Street house Porter made advances toward him the first time she went to his apartment for cocktails (*KAP* 433). This would have been in late 1959. Marcella Winslow, who had known Porter well during her affair with Charles Shannon, wrote her daughter in March 1960 telling her that Porter was back in Washington and was "having a real raging affair" with her forty-nine-year-old eye doctor: "Utterly incredible but there it is—she is so sure of her charm" (quoted in *KAP* 432). The word "charm" keeps popping up—an important word when we think about Porter but one that carries slippery meanings.

We have seen in the "Old Order" stories and "Old Mortality" Porter's thinking about the development and nature of the female child in the South. "Old Mortality" also conveys her awareness of the brittle nature of the belle's charm and the doom that awaits her. The doomed belle reappears in the Miranda of "Pale Horse, Pale Rider." But at times Porter wrote about a more startling kind of female character. The unnamed woman in the short story "Rope" is such a character—a woman who is aggressive toward her man but needs him in order to fulfill a deep-seated urge toward femininity. Other tough females appear in "Magic," "Theft," and "The Cracked Looking-Glass," but it is primarily the woman character in "Rope" who shows such a hard edge combined with remnants of femininity—the combination that takes over the spectrum of women characters in *Ship of Fools* except for a small group of docile *frauen* at the opposite extreme.

～

It would be tempting to suppose Porter's hostility to the women's liberation movement contributed to shaping the abrasiveness of the female characters in *Ship of Fools,* but chronology makes that implausible. The term "women's liberation" came into use about 1964; the novel was published in 1962. Moreover, she had been working on it for many years. The angers of these strong dames must have been in her imagination long before women's lib. During the last seven years of her work on the novel, her relationship with her editor, Seymour Lawrence, sometimes assumed a trace of sexual warfare itself, as did her relations with other men. Lawrence was savvy enough to keep mostly under wraps the irritation he must often have felt. Certainly he did not want to get totally at odds with her as William Jovanovich had. But her continual evasions and reversals must have been sorely frustrating.

Porter's desire for a house of her own also remained strong and would prove to be an issue between herself and Lawrence. When she moved to the Q Street house in 1959, she initially declared that she loved it, but by early 1960 she had changed her mind. It had hordes of cockroaches, and her plants somehow failed to thrive. Moreover, she had a vitriolic exchange with Jordan Pecile in which she told him (in a letter dated January 1, his birthday) that she wanted him to stop writing to her, that she did not need or want him, and that his complaints of having felt used while she was in Virginia had no merit. Any such upset with a lover put her off her work. In addition, she kept going off on trips that kept her more or less solvent but impeded the completion of her book, which would have served her financial interests better in the long run.

In the summer of 1960 she went for a one-month visit to Mexico City for the U.S. State Department, taking her niece Ann with her (on Ann's dime). At the end of the two weeks, having run into some old friends from the 1920s, she stayed on for two more weeks. When she returned to Washington, she again let her social life run away with her. In late December she wrote Lawrence that she expected to finish the "god-damned book" soon, but less than a month later informed him she had accepted speaking engagements on campuses in California and Ohio and hoped he would not write or call (*Life* 247).

Over a year earlier, on August 18, 1959, she had written her old friend Erna Schlemmer Johns, whom she rediscovered when she lectured in Austin, that what she needed was quiet and solitude. In May 1961 she got just that. To isolate her from distractions, Lawrence arranged another quiet retreat, this time at the Yankee Clipper Inn on Cape Ann, Massachusetts. Astute as he was and knowing Porter as he did, he arranged for her to have dinner companions to relieve the solitude of the typewriter and desk—and provided a stock of good wine for John Malcolm Brinnin and Bill Read to bring when they turned up in the evenings for dinner. Under these circumstances, Porter was finally able to finish *Ship of Fools*. Her papers at the University of Maryland include a note to herself dated June 15, 1961, exactly one month after her seventy-first birthday, indicating that the book had finished its voyage at last and would not weigh her down any more. Some last touching-up was still needed, but she returned to the inn in August and finished it. She dated the manuscript "Yaddo, August 1941/Pigeon Cove, August 1961"—a substantial underestimate. In an interview published in the *New York Times* on the day the novel appeared—April 1, 1962—she said that she began it in 1940, in Louisiana, but had made notes for it "for years" before that (*Conv.* 72). In another interview published that same day she stated more accurately that it had begun with a log kept during her voyage to Europe in 1931, but she actually began writing it in June 1940 at Yaddo (*Conv.* 75). The truth was, she had begun it as a novella in 1936 at the Water Wheel Tavern, if not before.

Exulting in her long-delayed victory over the sea monster, Porter wrote to Erna Johns on August 31, 1961, before leaving the Yankee Clipper Inn, that she had finally gotten what she earlier said she needed, quiet and solitude, and had made good use of it. She then reeled off a list of the distractions the inn did not have—no this, no that, a litany of absences strikingly like the passage in "Pale Horse, Pale Rider" where Miranda, newly returned from near death, gives her friends a shopping list for what she needs for her departure from the hospital: "One lipstick, medium, one ounce flask Bois d'Hiver perfume, one pair of gray suède gauntlets without straps, two pairs gray sheer stockings without clocks." William Nance (a Jesuit priest) had taken this passage as evidence of the author's pattern of "rejection" in a book about her that Porter heartily disliked. Now, in her letter to Erna, she unthinkingly confirmed that very pattern.

Her personal inclination was always for abundance—of friends and company and parties, of food and pretty clothes, of elegant furnishings, perhaps most of all of conversation. The great problem with this was that for her writing she needed its opposite—not total seclusion and not day after day, because then she fell into depression, but for at least a major part of every day. Glenway Wescott, whose own struggle with writer's block so closely mirrored hers and who pondered her plight with great insight, wrote in his journal that "in the city overstimulation would kill her, . . . in the country she bored herself to death." It reminds one of Porter's statement that she would like to live either in a world capital or out in the country but makes a different point, which she did not recognize herself: that she needed "both ways of life in fairly frequent alternation," not all one or all the other. Wescott believed he had learned that his own "tremendous talk" had a "grave ill effect" on his writing and that when he pursued "involvements in life and others' lives generally" he depleted his creative energy. But he thought, and we must agree, that Porter had not learned that lesson (*Continual Lessons* 225).

It has been conjectured that one reason Porter was so dependent on quiet and withdrawal in order to write was that she had a limited attention span. That may be true. More precisely, I believe, she needed a more or less stark, uncluttered work environment in order to achieve the focus necessary for achieving her spare style, itself so reliant on powers of exclusion. She may actually have needed silence in order to "hear" the cadences of her prose. Whatever the reason, Seymour Lawrence understood her needs and exerted himself almost beyond reason to supply them. The Yankee Clipper Inn was not the first quiet retreat he had set up for her, but in 1961, almost at the point of giving up, he was successful.

With the publication of *Ship of Fools,* Katherine Anne Porter's life's work was essentially finished. After years of pinching pennies and borrowing her way through life, she was rich—at first from the book and then from the movie. The first thing she wanted was a house of her own. In her 1941 essay "A House of My Own" she had written about her long wish for a home, her purchase of the isolated old house in upstate New York, and her efforts to get it renovated so that she could live in it. Reflecting on the significance of home and homelessness in her life, she wrote that she had never had "permanency of any sort, except the permanency of hope" (*CE* 175).[6] South Hill, of course, did not prove permanent either. Now she hoped to fulfill her long wish, but it was again deferred, this time by safeguards that Seymour Lawrence, working with Washington attorney Barrett Prettyman, had placed on her royalties. Trying to prevent her from spending her money all at once, they doled it out to her in monthly sums. Glenway advised her to reconcile herself to these terms and live accordingly, but she resented all the masculine interference. Finally convinced that she had to forego buying a house for the time being, she instead bought a startlingly large emerald ring and then went off to Europe for a year, raiding shops wherever she went and gathering booty that she sent back to her nephew Paul to put into storage.

She never did buy a house, though toward the end of 1963 she made one last try. She signed a contract and put money down but then backed out, with the result that she had to pay legal fees to get out of it and landed in a hospital in New Jersey to recover from nervous exhaustion. The following spring she leased a large house in Silver Spring where she lived for four years, very much the elegant lady, the grande dame. Mary Titus writes that she had long since become "a professional southerner, performing southernness for her readers and friends" as if on a stage, and as she aged she increasingly "took on the role of aristocratic Southern Lady of Letters." It was a role that, as Titus sees, "offered a revised past to cover over her unwanted origins" and "completely negated any charges that her independence and commitment to a literary career were unwomanly" (178–81, 187).

After a fall down the long staircase of the house in 1968, she moved to a townhouse in College Park, Maryland. In 1970, at the age of eighty, she enjoyed the publication of her *Collected Essays and Occasional Writings,* but was greatly displeased when she discovered that Seymour Lawrence had added, without her permission, an acknowledgment thanking various literary friends for "their help and guidance in the preparation of this volume." Seeing in it an imputation that she was not capable of managing her own authorship, she made a practice of writing disavowals in any copies she signed, fuming that the acknowledgment was a "piece of impudence" committed by the "morally irresponsible" Lawrence. One of these disavowals ends, "Damn their eyes, one and all!" (*KAP* 490–91). She was becoming more and more intemperate.

One name not on the officious list was that of Barrett Prettyman. Prettyman was of course her attorney, not a literary advisor, but he was a personal advisor as well, and the volume bore an eloquent dedication to him:

> To E. Barrett Prettyman, Jr.
> Faithful friend, able and
> fearless counselor, gifted writer,
> and joyful company, who has guided me
> through a rain-forest in these
> past rather terrible years.
> Yet we can laugh together
> and we know what to laugh at.

In a sense, Prettyman was her last great love. Until she turned on him, too, and fired him, he visited her regularly and she wrote him romantic-sounding notes that led Givner to believe their relationship was more ardent than it was, or indeed physically ardent—an imputation Prettyman greatly resented. Unrue wisely refers to it as a "fantasy romance" (*Life* 269).

Soon after the *Collected Essays* appeared, Porter suffered a broken hip. Both then and later, as one medical problem followed another, her nephew Paul was nearby to help and advise her, and often to extricate her from trouble when her temper erupted, as it sometimes did at him as well.

∽

In the previous chapter we looked at *Ship of Fools* as a piece of war writing. Here, I want to think about its treatment of relations between men and women and especially the conflicts and anxieties of women in their mature years. Gender and gender conflicts are as prominent a theme in the novel as prejudice against Jews and the approach of World War II. But my route toward this topic will be somewhat circuitous, by way of "Rope," published in 1928, and "St. Augustine and the Bullfight," published in 1955.

"Rope" is a highly compressed story with vivid scenes of domestic hostility almost certainly based on Porter's summer in Connecticut with Ernest Stock. It consists of a single argument between the story's only two characters, a man and woman, plus a brief coda. Never given names, the two characters seem to represent embittered versions of Male and Female. In a further stripping down to essence, even such expository tags as "he said" and "she said" are eliminated. The story is told almost entirely through indirect dialogue.

In the country for the summer, the two find themselves dismayed by unexpected inconveniences and by each other. Their discontent erupts into a quarrel on a hot day when the man returns from a long walk to the nearest store without the coffee she specifically asked for. For purposes even he cannot divine, though, he has purchased some rope. The coil of rope remains a sinister presence throughout. Despite the near-absence of exposition, passing references to other disagreements show that their exchanging of verbal barbs is a long-established, dreary pattern. This time, they seem to reach a narrow ledge verging on a drop-off into actual physical violence, but pull back. Promising to go exchange the rope for what they actually need, he sets off again, but instead of taking his coil of rope back to the store he conceals it under a bush. At the end, when he returns from this second walk to the store, now bringing coffee, he is again carrying in one hand the offensive rope.

Lopez sees this as a sign of "his *machismo* defiantly reaffirmed" (103). I disagree. As I read the male in "Rope," he does not possess the kind of excess masculinity that would justify that term. Fully expecting a resumption of the earlier quarrel, he clings to the rope (rather than, say, leaving it hidden) as reassurance that he is not going to let her get the best of him. But now she greets him with a great show of affectionate baby talk, as if they had never quarreled at all. Just as he has resumed a tenuous masculinity by carrying his rope, so has she resumed, for the moment, a traditional femininity, having dutifully and even pleasantly cooked dinner. The abruptness of the transformation empties their earlier verbal sparring of any real significance. If the relationship can so readily go back and forth, neither emotional extreme means anything. They may at any time, without reason or warning, find themselves standing again on that verge.

Wescott wrote in his diary in 1940 that Porter had a "lifelong mild foreboding" (67). Perhaps it was more like a lifelong conviction of impending disaster, a fixation on death, a lifelong self-destructiveness. But Wescott was not usually one to underestimate her explosive disposition. At another point in the diary he exclaimed, "What a devil she is!" and recalled an incident when she and Christopher Isherwood actually came to blows over a literary question. When pressed into any kind of corner, she could strike out as readily as the female character in "Rope," whose unsparing portrayal seems to manifest the self-doubt or even self-hatred that Porter felt intermittently throughout her life.

If the primary reference of "Rope" is to her summer with Ernest Stock in Connecticut, Texas hangs over the story as well, in its references to burning sun and oppressive heat. Knowing what her first marriage was like, we can well believe that it also reflects her life there with John Koontz.

The other work whose bearing on *Ship of Fools* I want to point out, the narrative essay "St. Augustine and the Bullfight," is very different from "Rope" in tone, technique, and ultimate intent. Porter's endeavor in this puzzling yet masterful work is much like Miranda's at the end of "Old Mortality": to know the truth of what happens to her. More specifically, she works toward knowing the truth about her own response to violence. That effort is couched in terms of distinguishing between (as already mentioned) "adventure," what one does or what happens, and "experience," the remembered and interpreted history of one's adventures.

In "Old Mortality," we recall, Miranda's determination to "know the truth about what happens to me" are not the final words. The story does not end there, but rather in the narrator's, Porter's, encompassing voice, adding a disquieting comment that reflects her greater knowledge of what is possible in this world: that Miranda's promise to herself is made "in her hopefulness, her ignorance." These last five words transform the vision at the end of the story from one of aspiration to one of tragedy. "St. Augustine and the Bullfight" offers a verbal parallel, not so much pointing to a connection with "Old Mortality" as commenting on it: "So I intend to write . . . on a fateful thing that happened to me when I was young and did not know much about the world or about myself" (*CE* 94). The younger, remembered self is placed into a position very much like Miranda's at the end of "Old Mortality," with the narrative voice in both cases implying that she, the narrating self, has gained understanding since she was that age and believed she could know the truth. Only by having learned more would she be able to judge her earlier state of mind to have been an ignorant one. "St. Augustine and the Bullfight" shows that the project of understanding what has happened to her is long, difficult, and only occasionally successful.

Thomas Walsh, in his informed and thoughtful commentary on "St. Augustine and the Bullfight," mentions another parallel in Miranda's statement of purpose at the end of "Old Mortality." The phrase "happened to me" implies passivity and in this way evokes Laura in "Flowering Judas," to whom things happen. Porter loaded her own paralysis of not knowing but fearing onto Laura, who knows but cannot understand the political events that occur around her and impinge on her life in dangerous ways. Later, as Walsh points out, Porter said that Mary Doherty was the model for the character who "didn't know what was happening to her" (*Illusion* 202), but really there were two models, Mary Doherty and herself. In the narrative essay about the bullfights and her reflections on what happened, Porter owns her previous ignorance. Having claimed, in the news commentaries she wrote while in Mexico, knowledge of what was happening, she now, in "St. Augustine and the Bullfight," reaches understanding. Her arrival at "experience" comes long after the "adventure" of attending the bullfight, and she reaches it by a very indirect path.

Walsh reads "St. Augustine" primarily as a story about the transformative power of art. He bases this reading on a phrase in the story essay that reveals both Porter's commitment to formal structure and, by a small clue, a connection with her earlier concern with the Southern belle as victim. "My own habit of writing fiction," she states, "has provided a wholesome exercise to my natural, incurable tendency to try to wangle the sprawling mess of our existence in this bloody world into some kind of shape" (*CE* 93). Again, Walsh says, the trail of blood leads back to Amy, the belle doomed to inauthenticity or to death, as symbolized by blood. In "Pale Horse, Pale Rider" the awakening belle's doom is a living death. In "The Old Order," the child Miranda, with all her liveliness and curiosity, gives promise of evading this doom, but only if she follows in Great-Aunt Eliza's footsteps and resists belle-dom. In all these stories, Miranda can begin to shape her own life only through reflection and imagination, by turning adventure into experience.

The association of the belle with victimhood and with blood is so firmly established that Porter can dare to carry its essence into "St. Augustine at the Bullfight" in the form of that most masculine of animals, the bull. It, too, is a doomed creature to which things happen at the initiative of men. As the animal enters the ring, a goad with fluttering green ribbons is "stabbed into his shoulder," with the result that an "interesting design in thin rivulets of blood" colors his hide (*CE* 99). He becomes a re-sexed avatar of the filly in "Old Mortality," who runs a race not through her own volition but that of her owner and jockey, and pays with "two thick red rivulets" of blood "stiffening" her chin (199).

If the belle appears in "St. Augustine and the Bullfight" in doubly displaced guise, the Southern lady appears more literally, in the form of Hattie Weston, a fine horsewoman. Graceful and bold riding, we recall, is one of the attributes of the belle held up for Miranda's and Maria's emulation. Hattie Weston is just such a rider. She gives a display of horsewomanship before the bullfights begin on the day a reluctant "Porter" is compelled to go witness them for the first time by an egoistic male of her acquaintance. Hattie Weston was in fact an American who lived in Mexico during the revolution and, as Porter's story-essay indicates, made her living by raising horses. The actual Weston had a friend named John Shelley, the source of the character Porter calls simply "Shelley" (*Illusion* 200). As Walsh observes, Porter devotes more prose to this image of the ladylike rider than she does to the bullfighters—a fact that indicates her priorities in a possibly intentional contrast to those of Ernest Hemingway in *Death in the Afternoon* (*Illusion* 203).

The figure of Hattie Weston does not replicate the sylphlike belles in "Old Mortality." Not that she is obese like Great-Aunt Keziah, whose husband considers her too heavy to ride his horses, but she is a solid, "buxom" woman of middle age. In any event, she doesn't need anyone's permission; she is riding her own horse, and she does so magnificently: "And there she went, the most elegant woman in the saddle I have ever seen, graceful and composed in her perfect style, with her wonderful, lightly dancing, learned horse, black and glossy as shoe polish, perfectly under control—no, not under control at all, you might have thought, but just dancing and showing off his paces by himself for his own pleasure" (*CE* 97). Hattie Weston is so "superb on horseback" that her control over her mount never appears strained or compelled; it is so subtle, so restrained that the viewer can momentarily imagine the horse is performing for its own delight and she merely happens to be seated in the saddle. Her kind of control as a horsewoman is offered as a direct contrast to the control over animals being exerted by the bullfighting males who enter the ring after her. The narrator, we might say

"Porter," has been so pleased and "calmed" by the rider's performance that she is caught "off guard" when the bull is "stabbed" in the shoulder as it enters.

From its beginning the essay emphasizes Porter's reluctance to attend the bullfight. She says she had repeatedly refused Shelley's insistent invitations because "all forms of cruelty offend me bitterly." With Hattie Weston's exit from the ring her worst expectations are at once confirmed. She has tried to maintain a sophisticated detachment when observing the first bull's bleeding from the goad, sarcastically pronouncing it "highly aesthetic," but it then "rushed at the waiting horse, blindfolded in one eye and standing at the proper angle for the convenience of his horns, the picador making only the smallest pretense of staving him off, and disemboweled the horse with one sweep of his head. The horse trod in his own guts" (*CE* 99). At this point she covers her eyes, but Shelley forces her hands away and, as if her "feelings were the sign of a grave flaw of character," insists that she "face it!" When she does, she is captivated by the very cruelty she had previously so abominated: "When the time came to kill the splendid black and white bull, I who had pitied him when he first came into the ring stood straining on tiptoe to see everything, yet almost blinded with excitement, and crying out when the crowd roared, and kissing Shelley on the cheekbone when he shook my elbow and shouted in the voice of one justified, 'Didn't I tell you? Didn't I?'" (101). If that were all, it would be a simple initiation story—squeamish female accepts direction by assertive male and comes to realize that violence is a core meaning of life. She would be simply replicating the reaction of Miranda to the horse race, screaming and shouting as Miss Lucy comes in to win. But just as Miranda realizes the cost of the spectacle when she sees that Miss Lucy is bleeding from her nostrils, so the narrator of "St. Augustine and the Bullfight" has more to learn.

She has made the point that "no matter whatever else this world seemed to promise me, never once did it promise to be simple." But the moment when Shelley forces her to look at the killing elicits more than merely the judgment that the world is not simple. After being certain that "he had been wrong before to nag me into this, and I was altogether wrong to have let him persuade me," she realizes at that moment—or *thinks* she realizes—that he was right after all. "And I did look," she writes, "and I did face it." But then the telling phrase: "though not for years and years" (*CE* 99). Facing "it" does not mean, after all, looking at the blood and the trodden-in guts but facing honestly the significance of that moment and her own reactions.

Once again, then, understanding comes only through retrospective reflection. Between the day of that first bullfight (when her revulsion turned to ecstatic enthusiasm) and the moment of clear vision after years of reflection, she attended "perhaps a hundred bullfights," though "never again" with Shelley, the man who had insisted she see her first one. She and he were "not comfortable together after that day"; there was "bloodguilt" between them. They "shared an evil secret, a hateful revelation. He hated what he had revealed in me to himself, and I hated what he had revealed to me about myself" (*CE* 100).

What Shelley revealed was that she was fully as capable of enjoying vicarious cruelty as anyone else: "I loved the spectacle of the bullfights, I was drunk on it." At first she avoided facing the fact that her newfound taste for bullfighting was no different from what motivated the rest of the crowd; she tried to believe her sensibilities were more refined and it was the art of the bullfighting she cared about. When she finally admitted to herself that it was not art but "the death in it" that she cared for, that she, too, had a taste for violence, she was "bitterly ashamed of this evil" in herself. Yet even this is not the end of her process of reflection. After years of reveling in the bullfights before coming to see the "evil" in herself that caused her to enjoy an animal's torment and death (*CE* 100), she then spent years of reveling in the distinctiveness of her guilt, much as she had previously reveled in the supposed distinctiveness of her taste for bullfighting.

That is how St. Augustine enters the essay. During those intervening years she read St. Augustine and came across his story of the unspoiled youth who comes to Rome deploring the gladiatorial contests but then, when he sees the slaughter, becomes "more bloodthirsty" than all the rest. Having tried to believe herself a different and special "fallen angel," she now sees her likeness to St. Augustine's youth and knows that even her sense of shame for having loved the bullfights was not distinctive. It is a lesson in commonality with flawed humanity.

"St. Augustine and the Bullfight" tells us that the true lady is a woman who controls herself and rides her base passions, like her horse, with grace and without undue exhibition. It implies, too, that the lady is a woman who has wide experiences and learns from them. Otherwise, these experiences are only meaningless adventures. The lady is also someone who knows her place. "What was I doing there?" the character identified as Porter herself asked as again and again she went to bullfights in Mexico and "consented not just willingly but with rapture" (*CE* 100) to the spectacle of killing.[7] But by thinking and writing about her infatuation with bullfighting, she sees that indeed she did not belong in either the actual or the emotional "place" where she had found adventure. She had betrayed her principles.

By the act of writing, she was reclaiming them. Through this act she was illustrating the distinction between "adventure" and "experience," as she labels them in the essay, as well as the importance of memory and reflection. Adventure is what happens, what immediately engages us. Experience is adventure interpreted, adventure that has yielded up its meaning through the long process of reflection. And the setting reminds us that Porter came to herself, as an artist and as a thinker, by crossing the border from Texas to Mexico.

〜

Ship of Fools appeared seven years after Porter's subtle pondering of the figure of the competent lady and the lady seized by blood-lust in "St. Augustine." The pondering of the nature and status of the adult woman given us in *Ship of Fools,* however, is carried on in ways that are scarcely subtle at all. Porter's gender concerns here are with the problem of maintaining or failing to maintain the elusive combination of dignity, charm, and moral authority that together define the lady and with the issue of women's equality or inequality with men. These themes, together with the apparent inevitability of conflict between the sexes, are presented with a drearily unvarying reiteration and lack of nuance. In Mary Titus's words, "the complexity and contradiction that accompanied gender representations in her short fiction are largely missing" (200). This does not mean that she herself was any less conflicted about gender than before but that her treatment of gender and gender conflict in this longest and most laboriously produced of all her works follows the pattern that characterizes every other aspect of the novel: repetition rather than development. In the whole extensive cast of characters, there is no Hattie Weston to embody the ideal of the balanced, authoritative, yet feminine woman.

One of the paradoxes of *Ship of Fools* is that even as it seemingly represents a move away from Porter's autobiographical Miranda stories, it is still deeply autobiographical. There is no trace of what we think of as her characteristic material—her Texas childhood, her Southern heritage—but its general outlines as well as many details draw directly on her own 1931 voyage to Europe. The long diary-letter she wrote to Caroline Gordon during the voyage (available in Isabel Bayley's volume of selected letters) is a clearly traceable source. But the novel differs significantly from the journal-letter in that it retains none of the letter's friendly observations about fellow passengers, even Germans. It is thoroughly acerbic toward every single one.

Both in the novel itself and in subsequent interviews Porter said that she, too, was a passenger on the ship. In the most general sense, this simply means that she is part of the human race, all "fools" on the ship of life as it makes its symbolic journey. That is, she again recognizes that she shares the common lot of humankind. But we can also take her statement to mean, more specifically, that she is on the ship in the form of one or another of the characters. Mary Titus identifies Jenny Brown as that "self-portrait"—a forty-one-year-old painter (the age Porter was in 1931) who manifests "all the inner afflictions and outer adversities that had impeded" Porter in her professional life (198). Darlene Unrue identifies not one but three characters as representing aspects of Porter: Jenny Brown, the "lonely, childless" Mrs. Treadwell, and Frau Rittersdorf, who keeps a notebook where she records "sharp comments" about the other passengers (*Life* 256). I would add a fourth, the glamorous, troubled exile referred to as La Condesa.

Other characters are also autobiographical in that they have had experiences similar to hers or bear traces of people she knew. Jenny's lover, David Scott, is a soured version of Eugene Pressly. The crude Texan, William Denny, may represent John Koontz. And as Unrue cleverly observes, the overweight bulldog Bébé jokingly represents Porter's perennially obese younger sister, always called Baby, who was a breeder of bulldogs (*Life* 257). It is hard to imagine that Baby would have found the joke very endearing.

Jenny Brown is probably the fullest self-portrait of the four. Besides the similarities of age and the fact that she is an artist, she is traveling with a man to whom she is not married, as Porter was on the *Werra*. She is also, like Porter, moody, swinging between high highs and very low lows, incorrigibly flirtatious, and often paralyzed by doubt of her own competence as an artist. In Jenny's relationship with David we see Porter's great need to be loved as well as the volatility evident in letters to her various husbands and lovers. Too, like Porter's protesting the execution of Sacco and Vanzetti, Jenny has picketed and been taken to jail "several times," but remembers the experience as "just a lark" because "somebody always came from a mysterious Headquarters with plenty of money, so it was out on bail for everybody and back to the line" (164). Throughout the voyage, Jenny and David quarrel and plot ways to hurt or humiliate each other, only to fall in love afresh. Perhaps most telling of all, Jenny easily falls into depression when she is alone. She seeks out "the sound of voices and the nearness of others" as a diversion from her low spirits, yet realizes that "nearness" impedes her painting or her equally important thinking about her art (87). One wonders how completely Porter was aware that these traits of Jenny's are transparent self-revelations. Such an awareness of what she was doing with this character would have required her to draw on reserves of detachment and unflinching self analysis that she may not have possessed.

As to the other three self-portraits, Frau Rittersdorf, the notebook keeper, is an insecure woman incessantly concerned about both her appearance and her image more generally. She is at times malicious and deceptive, a manipulator, and has a history of failed relationships with men. Mary Treadwell, a tastefully attractive woman leaving Mexico after what she refers to as a "visit" there, is deeply fearful of sex but wants and needs admirers. She is preoccupied with death, as Porter was, and characteristically deals with troubling situations by escaping. What she thinks of herself on her forty-sixth birthday seems also apt as a comment on her novelist-creator: that middle-aged women are likely to "marry men too young for them and get just what they deserve" and that "Lesbians lurk in the offing, waiting for loneliness and fear to do their work" (253). Certainly Porter married men too young for her; whether she got what she deserved in doing so is up for question. And Mrs. Treadwell's anxiety about lurking lesbians is an expression of Porter's own keen dislike of both lesbians and gay men.[8] Last, La Condesa: elegant, mysterious, impecunious but the owner (or supposed owner) of fine jewelry and clothes, and she is aging, unwell, and sexually aggressive.

Notably, none of these characters is sketched as a true lady, let alone a Southern lady. Every one of them—indeed, every passenger on this ship of truth (*Vera*)—is deeply flawed and viewed with criticism if not contempt. The women characters most concerned to maintain ladylike decorum—the widowed Frau Schmitt and three repressed wives, Frau Hutten, Frau Baumgartner, and the Swiss Frau Lutz, who is always worried that her marriageable-age daughter will compromise herself—are subservient and convinced that society or perhaps God compels them to regard themselves as lesser beings than their men. Anti-feminist though she avowedly was during the period of sexual politics in the 1960s and 1970s, Porter refused to accept the traditional idea of female subservience. Her portraits of these three married women are heavily ironic. Yet she gives no model of constructive relations between the sexes. *Ship of Fools,* in fact, offers no internal standard by which to judge any character other than tones of language. When every opinion and every personality is presented as being intolerably flawed, it is difficult to identify any as gauges of an author's intentions.

Porter's aims relating to the position of women and relations between the sexes are further complicated by the fact that her work on the novel had gone on for years before she began to mock second-wave feminism. True, she worked on the novel more consistently in later years, after what Brinkmeyer calls a "hardening of her conservatism" set in, but the long history of its writing encompassed changes in her opinions, leaving us uncertain how to read the women characters' sense of inequality. We can appeal to Porter's own behavior and her letters, both early and late, but there is still the contrary evidence of her express demurral from 1960s-era feminism.

If the women in the novel are either torn by doubts or subdued into adopting male supremacist views as their own, the men are consistently presented as what were usually called, in the 1960s, male chauvinists. William Denny, the crude Texan, is the extreme example. Having lusted after one of the Cuban dancers, Pastora, through most of the voyage without being willing to pay her price, he "consol[es] himself by spitting through his teeth and repeating under his breath short nasty names for women—all women, the whole dirty mess of them" (313). During a *walpurgisnacht* when the dancers pretend to organize a party honoring the captain, Denny gets even drunker than usual and decides to avenge himself. Yelling "Come out here, you whore" and banging on what he believes to be her cabin door, he shouts "descriptions of the Gothic excesses he intended to commit upon Pastora's person, of which rape would be the merest preliminary" (464). The rather prissy language in which this is expressed does not reflect Denny's characteristic vocabulary, of course, but that of Mrs. Treadwell, at whose door he has mistakenly arrived. When she jerks it open, momentarily throwing him off balance, he recovers sufficiently to "surg[e] forward," grab at her bodice, and give a painful "twist to her breast," glad to punish any female body standing before him (464).

Though less brutish than Denny, the other men among the passengers reflect similar opinions of the inferiority of women. Indeed, every relationship between men and women seen in the novel is characterized by condescension, hostility, and verbal abuse if not physical violence. Herr Schmitt, one of the Germans aboard, thinks of women as "merely children of a larger growth" who "needed a taste of the rod now and then to keep them in order" (298). When his wife apologizes for having expressed an opinion of her own that proves contrary to his and says she didn't mean it, his indignation only increases: "You did not mean it? . . . You were then only talking frivolously? Like a woman?" (297). Freytag, a Swede, also shows violent inclinations, thinking at one point, "The one sure way to bring upon yourself the inescapable devotion of a dog was to beat him regularly. Certain kinds of women were not so different" (261).

The spirit of misogyny also inhabits the ship's steward and the captain. Maintaining an "utter contempt for the female sex," the steward operates according to the old stereotype that women are beyond understanding and therefore treats female passengers with a "false front of indulgent good humor" (331)—a manner still familiar to many women. The captain, an anti-Semitic German convinced of his own superiority, gossips to the passengers seated at his table that La Condesa is probably "one of those idle rich great ladies who like excitement" and "make mischief . . . without in the least understanding what they do." In fact, he adds, the entire female sex lacks "the least understanding," at any rate in politics (107). Since we know that Porter considered herself rather astute politically, we have in this case, at least, a touchstone allowing us to feel confident that her sketch was satiric. Later, when several of the ladies tell the captain he should have the crew return some woodcarving tools confiscated from one of the men in steerage, he denies their wish "in a voice of blistering courtesy," thinking superciliously about their "unbalanced female emotions, their shallow, unteachable minds" (176). In the face of Frau Schmitt's fatuous admiration, he reflects that "women were almost first among those who must be kept in their place" (248). Almost, but not quite; he has a longstanding policy of never allowing a Jew to sit at his table, to which he does reluctantly admit women.

David Scott maintains a similar attitude of condescension toward Jenny's aspirations and productions as an artist. His thinking about women is particularly marked by double standards. For example, he cannot conceive that Jenny has any right to privacy, while at the same time "his own boundaries and reserves were inviolable"—to the point that he plots revenge whenever she presumes to step on them (340). But his feelings toward her are more complicated than just this. He is possessive and jealous, once coming between Jenny and a casual dance partner, "seiz[ing]" her by the elbow and "snatch[ing] her away" (132). As his gestures show, he regards her as property. David's convoluted feelings toward Jenny and toward women in general appear to be rooted in an obscurely twisted sexual nature. He is "glad to be able to say," or rather think, that after unrestrained bouts with prostitutes he is always "sick of the thought of sex for a good while." Feeling "superior to his acts and to his partners in them," he can respect himself again only when his "purifying contempt" separates him from the "vileness" of the women (281). He expresses similarly convoluted reactions by frequently recoiling against Jenny, especially at times when he feels he has her on the defensive.

The one male character who actually surprises us with his misogyny is the ship's doctor, sometimes held up as the one admirable person aboard, particularly in his kindness to the troubled La Condesa. But as the voyage goes on his attentions to her take on an erotic quality despite his resistance to such unprofessional urges. His hidden attitudes are revealed when the two have a long conversation about their sexual innocence or lack of it as children and La Condesa admits, "I loathe women . . . I hate being one. It is a shameful condition. I cannot be reconciled to it" (202). Not only does the doctor know that "in his heart . . . he quite agreed with her," but in seeking to soothe her he stumbles into an egregious display of condescension, telling her it "may be a misfortune to be a woman" but there is nothing actually "shameful" in it (202–3). He is both repulsed and threatened when she replies with envy of men's sexual freedom and opens her arms to him. Retreating, he tells her she is "talking like any foolish woman!" (203)—Herr Schmitt's views again.

One of the principles of second-wave feminism was that women who have lived under masculine control often internalize the terms of their own repression. Porter's female characters repeatedly demonstrate the truth of that principle. Frau Schmitt has been conditioned by her husband to think she is "always wrong" (248) and "a wife's first duty was to be in complete agreement with her husband at all times." When she has the effrontery to contradict him in public she falls into a panic that she has "ruined his life" (295). Other women on the *Vera* express much the same attitude. At times Porter ties such submissive attitudes to repressed sexuality. Frau Rittendorf gets a perverse "thrill" when she muses that "the crown of womanhood was suffering for the sake of love" (155). Even Jenny Brown is capable of switching abruptly from "her most difficult and perverse mood" to "abject tenderness," telling David in one such moment that she is glad to go to Spain as he wishes rather than to France but not really meaning it (148). Frau Hutten, the wife of a stereotypical stuffy professor, cites him in almost parrot-like fashion when she admits, "I wished to continue with my teaching after marriage . . . but my husband would not hear of it for a moment. The husband supports the family, he told me, and the wife makes a happy home for them both. That is her sacred mission, he said, and she must be prevented at all costs from abandoning it" (156).

The Huttens are an interesting and far from pleasant illustration of the kind of gender hierarchy regarded by all the German characters as being at the essence of the national virtue. Returning to Germany, her husband's career as a professor in Mexico at an end, Frau Hutten takes pride in having coped with all the "stupid details" of daily life and having "interposed herself, literally, bodily, between her husband and the seamy, grimy, mean, sordid, tiresome side of life that he simply could not endure." She had protected "the superiority of his mind, the importance of his profession" at the cost of giving up her own. Satisfied that she could think of herself as "the ideal German wife," she had "carried everything, his books, paper parcels, suitcases, string bags," so consistently that "no one had ever seen the professor carry even the smallest parcel in his hand" (291).

The Huttens are childless but have long doted on their bulldog Bébé, pouring great excesses of pampering and baby talk onto the animal. When they return to their cabin to find the dog missing, Frau Hutten knows full well that it was her husband who left the door ajar, allowing their four-legged baby to wander off (and in fact be thrown over the rail by the Cuban twins Ric and Rac). Momentarily forgetting her subservience, she tells him it was his fault. But when Bébé is rescued, at the cost of a man's life, and they weep together in relief, she resumes her place: "Forgive my weakness, forgive me, I need your help. You are goodness itself." Though she still knows quite well that it was he who failed to close the door securely, she tells him, "I am certain I left the door open" (322). Herr Professor Hutten is so pleased by her servility that he becomes aroused and falls on her "as if she were a bride" in one of the most distasteful sex scenes in all literature, in which they "grappled together like frogs" (323). Afterward he calls her "my little wife" and she replies "my husband," he "forbid[s]" her to cry any more about the dog's close call, and male-supremacist order is restored.

The sequence of anti-woman diatribes and actions reaches its climax in the scene when the drunken William Denny beats on Mrs. Treadwell's door by mistake and twists her breast. Although she insists she is not Pastora, he tells her she can't fool him. At that, the hostility hidden beneath Mrs. Treadwell's ladylike demeanor wells up. She is no stranger to male violence, having once married to a man "so jealous he beat me until I bled at the nose" (208). Her disgust at the drunken Denny now joins with her long-buried resentment. She pushes him down "with more force than she knew she had" and watches in "amazement" as her would-be abuser falls to the floor and hits his head. She at first thinks the fall may have broken his neck, but when he proves to be still breathing she unleashes a lifetime of pent-up fury and hits Denny repeatedly, first with her fist and then with her high-heeled shoe. Holding it by the sole, she "beat him in the face and head with the heel, breathlessly, rising on her knees and coming nearer, her lips drawn back and her teeth set. She beat him with such furious pleasure a sharp pain started up in her right wrist and shot to her shoulder and neck. The sharp metal-capped high heels at every blow broke the skin in small half moons that slowly turned scarlet, and as they multiplied on his forehead, cheeks, chin, lips, Mrs. Treadwell grew cold with fright at what she was doing, yet could not for her life stop" (465). In effect, Mrs. Treadwell acts out the female side of a horrifying scene related earlier in the book, before the ship sailed, perhaps as an extreme version of what was to come. Based on a brief "flash" that Jenny Brown once saw from a bus window on the road from Mexico City to Taxco, which she has subsequently relived in dreams, the scene becomes a deeply pessimistic parable of male-female relations:

As the bus rolled by, Jenny saw a man and a woman . . . locked in a death battle. They swayed and staggered together in a strange embrace, as if they supported each other; but in the man's raised hand was a long knife, and

the woman's breast and stomach were pierced. The blood ran down her
body and over her thighs, her skirts were sticking to her legs with her own
blood. She was beating him on the head with a jagged stone, and his features were veiled in rivulets of blood. . . . Their flesh swayed together and
clung, their left arms were wound about each other's bodies as if in love.
Their weapons were raised again, but their heads lowered little by little,
until the woman's head rested upon his breast and his head was on her
shoulder, and holding thus, they both struck again. (144)

Jenny could not possibly have seen so much detail in a brief glimpse, but the am-
plification of the scene can easily be explained as reflecting her dreams. On the
other hand, knowing the intensity of Porter's own relationships with men and
how readily they changed to mutual destructiveness, we can well believe it represents her ultimate conception of relations between the sexes. We can conjec-
ture that the ugliness of Mrs. Treadwell's beating Denny with her shoe heel may
have given Porter a hidden satisfaction if, consciously or not, Mrs. Treadwell then
represents herself and Denny represents John Koontz. The female gives as good
as she got.

Porter never resolved the conflict caused by her adherence to mutually inconsistent convictions about the nature of women and their roles in society. She ad-
hered to the idea of the lady but at the same time persisted in a determination to
live her own life freely and unconventionally. She was haunted by the repeated
ugliness of her relations with men but continued her compulsive pursuit of one
entanglement after another, sometimes cracking jokes about how many there had
been. She regarded her own mental acuteness and artistic capability as the equal
of any man's and expected to pursue her writing career and reap its rewards on
an equal playing field. Even so, she did not applaud the renewal of the feminist
movement in the United States. In a letter to Jordan Pecile dated July 3, 1961,
that illustrates her habitual warding off of the label "feminist," she wrote that
T. S. Eliot "made a reputation, actually! on Thoreau's famous opening line—or
on the first page, anyway, of Walden 'Most men lead lives of quiet desperation.'
(At the risk of being called a feminist, I would say, that goes for women, too,
doubled in spades)" (SL 588). Why she thought it was a risk remains the puzzle.

In Ship of Fools, published the year after Porter wrote this letter to Pecile, she
has one of her self portraits, La Condesa, admit to a dislike of being female and
a wish for the freedom, especially sexual freedom, accorded to men. Yet that
same year, in an interview about the book, Porter insisted she had "never felt that
the fact of being a woman put me at a disadvantage, or that it's difficult being a

woman in a 'man's world'" (*Conv.* 77). Perhaps this only shows, once again, her inconsistency.

She was conscious of her physical beauty from her early teen years on and remained flirtatious until very nearly the end of her life. At the same time, while still living in Texas, she espoused equality of the sexes and, as we have seen, argued with her brother for women's right to vote. Also disagreeing with her father on the issue, she opposed his restrictive expectations by assuming an independence necessary for the pursuit of her art and adopting an "emerging persona" as a woman who refused to be subjugated (DeMouy 7). She did newspaper work in Texas and elsewhere, had friends in New York who actively protested for feminist causes, and while in post-revolutionary Mexico during the 1920s encountered and supported feminist ideas. Her papers saved from those years include an announcement of a program of the "Femenist [*sic*] Council for Economical Emancipation for Women" and a roughly jotted list of Mexican political leaders, among whom she approvingly labeled Felipe Carillo Puerto the "only intelligent pro-feminist in Mexico."

It is puzzling, then, that in her later life she made no common cause with feminists. She dismissed Betty Friedan's then electrifying book *The Feminine Mystique,* which deplored the necessity for women to rely on such demeaning ingrained habits as using their sexual attractiveness to get what they wanted rather than pursue their goals directly. Women, she thought, ought to do exactly what Friedan said they should not—make themselves charming and please their men. That is what she did herself. She made herself charming in high heels and glamorous clothes, and she pleased a great many men. After a lifetime of attentiveness to politics and the political struggles of the oppressed, she failed to understand the need for sexual politics. Nevertheless, she demonstrated in *Ship of Fools* that she understood the wellsprings of sexual violence and even, in the horrifying scene of Mrs. Treadwell's beating of the Texan William Denny, that she may have relished the idea, so long as it was female violence against a man.

11

Never Reconciled

I suffered a lapse of faith in Texas.
 —Stephen Harrigan, "What Texas Means to Me"

With Saint Francis let us praise our sweet sister Death, who sometimes
comes late but never fails us.
 —Katherine Anne Porter to Glenway Wescott, January 5, 1960

One of the two happiest events of Porter's last few years was her return to the
Catholic Church. She had developed friendships among the nuns of the College
of Notre Dame of Maryland, in Baltimore, and they gently led her back. As long
as she was able, she went to special services in the college chapel and received
communion. The other happiest event was a final return to Texas, two decades
after her lecture at the University of Texas that launched the misunderstanding
over the supposed Porter Library.

In May 1976, Howard Payne University in Brownwood held a symposium in
her honor. Roger Brooks, the president of Howard Payne and the host of the conference, later stated that the surge of emotion she felt there constituted "a reconciliation that brought happiness and peace to what was a really tumultuous career" (111). My purposes in this concluding chapter are to explain why I do not
believe Brooks's statement is correct and, having approached various aspects of
Porter's ambivalence toward Texas in the preceding chapters, to address the question directly, by way of summary.

It is often noted that an impetus toward estrangement from Texas may have
come from losses and conflicts within Porter's family and the discouraging environment in which she conceived an ambition to become a writer. Don Graham speaks of "family dynamics" driving her "wish to escape" and explains that
"when Porter began writing in the early 1920s there was no advantage attached
to being a 'Texas' writer" ("Katherine Anne Porter's Journey" 4, 7–11; "A Southern Writer" 59–60). Mark Busby, in an essay subtitled "Ambivalence Deep as the
Bone," points to several factors that have been discussed here: family, an urge
toward independence, the social geography of Texas (citing Pilkington on rims
and borders), and offenses given by the Texas Institute of Letters and the University of Texas. He also posits the somewhat less convincing theory that Texans
in general are inherently ambivalent (135). Willene Hendrick, who visited In-

dian Creek when her husband was writing his 1965 biography and coauthored the revised version, cites Porter's "sense of rejection in Indian Creek and in Texas by 'her people'" (12). Except for the fact that she could not have felt rejected at the time she left Indian Creek, it is a persuasive answer. Such a sense of rejection would—and did—naturally launch a pattern of response and re-response that, like crazing in a windshield, keeps proliferating. A process of that kind can be seen, for example, in Porter's having "turned that rejection, with its intense emotions and insights, into remarkable artistry" (W. Hendrick 12). Another, less positive example of proliferation relates to the Texas Institute of Letters prize in 1939, when the selection of J. Frank Dobie's book over hers apparently reinforced and compounded her earlier resentments.

The problem I see with all these assessments except Graham's sketch of the literary context in the 1920s is the narrowness of their focus on biography. Their attention to historic and cultural dimensions contributing to Porter's ambivalence is, in general, scant and inadequately detailed. I have proposed here that these public dimensions (which I sometimes designate by the broad term "history") are essential to any explanation of the dynamic at play and that the violence of Texas's past as well as of Porter's early adult years spent there had a particularly strong bearing on her disaffection.

In seeking to establish my own version of the various dimensions of Porter's ambivalence toward Texas, let me begin with the words of another successful Texas writer noted for both fiction and nonfiction. At the opening of his essay "What Texas Means to Me," Stephen Harrigan identifies a tension within himself that is strikingly parallel with hers:

> Lying in a feather bed, in the guest room of a friend's two hundred-year-old house in western Massachusetts, I suffered a lapse of faith in Texas. I'm not sure what brought this crisis on. Perhaps it was simply the act of waking up, looking out the window at the syrup buckets hanging from the maple trunks, at the banked snow glistening in the sharp air, and realizing that Texas would never be like that.
>
> I could stand to live here, I thought. . . .
>
> But it was not just Massachusetts. The hard truth was that I was getting tired of Texas and was now able to imagine myself living in all sorts of places. (166–67)

Much of Harrigan's work is set in Texas and explores Texas life (and even Texas caves). Not quite a native Texan but almost, he now resides in Austin. He knows the state well. But in the essay from which I have quoted he finds himself yearning otherwhere. He does not renounce Texas for the sake of the beauty of Massachusetts, nor does he experience a loss of all affection for Texas, only a "lapse" of faith. What has lapsed can be reclaimed. After the lapse, however, his imagining of his life is no longer bounded by the borders of one state; it extends to "all sorts of places."

It was somewhat the same with Porter. Once she managed a temporary escape from the expulsive factors that were driving her away—primarily her abusive marriage but also conflicts with her birth family, what Graham calls the "corseted straightjacket of gender" in Texas ("Katherine Anne Porter's Journey" 10), and the general cultural atmosphere—her imagination expanded. Even while she kept writing about Texas, at times in idealizing terms, she variously claimed an instant sense of belonging in Pennsylvania, Virginia, Tennessee, upstate New York (where she bought the only house she ever owned), presumably California since she bought land there, and France. She imagined building a house in each of these places and also in Mexico, where she fantasized a beautiful but modest home in harmony with the natural world in Amecameca.

Yet even though she thought of the South in idealized retrospective terms much like those of the Agrarians (Warren, Tate, Gordon, Brooks, et al.) and wrote paeans to a Texas greatly enhanced in memory, she nevertheless declared more than once that she could not bear to live in Texas or, at times, anywhere in the South. Even in the lyrical "'Noon Wine': The Sources" she introduced into the Texas of memory, like the snake in Eden, violence and the tools of violence.

After leaving Texas at the age of twenty-eight, Katherine Anne Porter lived sixty-two more years in a great many other places, returning only for visits of at most a few months. She never again had a permanent residence in the state. In a letter of May 28, 1951, to fellow Texan William Goyen, she insisted that she had made the right decision in casting herself out from Texas the first time and the right decision again when, after her first visit to her mother's grave, she left again. Even so, she felt passing impulses to return to Texas as a home during three visits that engendered short-lived feelings of nostalgic affection: the Old Settlers Reunion in San Marcos in 1937, her lecture visit to the University of Texas in 1958, and the symposium held in her honor at Howard Payne University in Brownwood in May 1976.

The story of the symposium is difficult to reconstruct. It can confidently be said that even those in attendance would not be able to resurrect accurately all that went on and went into it and why. Naturally enough, each observer was influenced by the particularities and predilections of her or his own vantage point.

15. Katherine Anne Porter holding a piñata for her eighty-second birthday celebration. Many of her keepsakes were of Mexican origin. Katherine Anne Porter Papers, Special Collections, University of Maryland Libraries.

We find, then, conflicting accounts of the event, no one of them complete. Perhaps we can best think of the symposium as a tragicomedy in which heroes and villains kept changing places depending on who was watching and from where.

At eighty-six, Porter was truly frail. She had a long history of drinking to excess, and her intemperate outbursts toward close friends or associates such as Seymour Lawrence and Barrett Prettyman over the previous three years indicated an increasingly erratic mental state. Her behavior during even the brief time she was at the symposium bounced between extremes in a way indicating irrationality. In succeeding months she would begin to suffer debilitating strokes.

President Brooks knew her reputation for unreliability and fractiousness. One has to believe that he weighed these problems against an expectation of the publicity benefits that might accrue to Howard Payne, perhaps even a rise in status among other small institutions, and decided the risk was worth taking. In an account of the event delivered by Brooks as a luncheon address in 1999, a transcript of which is printed as "Hosting Miss Porter," he explains the idea for the conference by saying he had enjoyed a long friendship with her by mail, apparently since the 1960s, which was deepened in 1985 when he sent her a rubbing of her mother's gravestone soon after moving to Brownwood (112). The headstone rubbing was the best gift he could possibly have chosen if he hoped to elicit her gratitude and renew her old yearnings for home, and thus spark an inclination to visit Howard Payne. President Brooks then issued his invitation, and Porter responded warmly. In Givner's words, "She yearned, as always, for a reconciliation with her native state, and the return to her birthplace at this point in her life promised a deeply satisfying completion of a pattern" (*KAP* 501).

Only two weeks before the carefully planned gathering, however, Porter sent Brooks a telegram saying that her doctor had forbidden her to make the trip. He wrote back that he had arranged for his personal physician to "attend [her] on every public occasion" and stay close at hand throughout her visit, and with that she reversed herself and said that she would come after all. Contrary to the predictions of a variety of Brooks's Texas friends, she did (113–14). Two members of the English department were designated to meet her at the airport, and one stayed in the hotel room adjoining hers, in case of need.

During her few days in Brownwood Porter was alternately happy and furious, so emotionally unpredictable that it was touch and go whether she would attend the closing dinner. After worrying endlessly about her appearance, she was greatly distressed by the untimely publication of an unflattering picture of her in the local newspaper, which she happened to see on the day of the dinner. Calling it "damnable" and "cruel," she announced to her faculty caregiver that she would not go, or if she did, would not speak (Rodenberger 125). Roger Brooks does not mention this incident. He does mention that she wished to avoid Joan Givner or any other potential biographer, that there were continuing medical worries about her, and that she ignored the conservative Baptist nature of the institution and served champagne at the farewell dinner she hosted the following day.

Besides her upset over the unflattering photograph, there were other rough moments as well. One occurred when Porter possibly hyperventilated during the graduation ceremony after she impulsively decided to hand out the diplomas. Another occurred when she visited the cemetery and held a (presumably one-sided) conversation with her long-dead mother. It was her second visit to her mother's grave. She recited the poem she had drafted there on the first visit (in 1936), "Anniversary in a Country Cemetery." She also made it clear that she wanted to be buried there. Despite the few difficult moments, she greatly enjoyed her return not merely to Texas but to her very origins. Once again, as with her visit to the University of Texas, she felt her few days at Howard Payne University in Brown County to be a kind of homecoming.

I have indicated that Brooks's account of the visit differs in various particu-

16. Katherine Anne Porter, age eighty-six, laying roses on the grave of her mother at Indian Creek Cemetery during her final visit to Texas, spring 1976. The original photograph in the University of Maryland archives shows clearly that the roses were pink. Katherine Anne Porter Papers, Special Collections, University of Maryland Libraries.

lars from those of Joan Givner, Darlene Unrue, and Lou Rodenberger. Both he and Rodenberger are at pains to correct Givner's statement that her hosts provided pink rather than yellow roses for her to place on her mother's grave. More important, Brooks misreports Givner's assessment of the significance of the visit, saying that she called it "the most important pilgrimage of her [Porter's] career" (110). Even on the face of it, such a statement would seem preposterous. This is not to say the visit was unimportant, but an attentive reading of Givner's few pages about the symposium in her biography shows that she actually called it the most important *of three excursions that Porter made in the one year 1976*—a very different order of magnitude.

Under the warm glow of being idolized by Texans—which was what she always most wanted—Porter said that she felt that she had returned to her only home. In addition, she made an impulsive offer of furniture and other effects to create a Katherine Anne Porter room at the Howard Payne Library. Unfortunately these objects were apparently already bequeathed to the University of Maryland,[1] and the offer generated considerable uproar later when Brooks set out for Washington to gather them up. Only with difficulty and on the intervention of both Paul Porter and Barrett Prettyman was he persuaded that they did not belong to him and that Katherine Anne was not competent to make such a promise. Preparations for filing for guardianship for her were in fact already in preparation.

Brooks did visit with Porter while he was in Washington, however, and accepted two small gifts signifying her warm regard for him. Afterward she did occasionally speak of going back to Texas to live. But she was past making such decisions. At any rate, both her nephew and her longtime attorney certainly believed she was, and there is considerable evidence that they were correct. Nor does it seem that by that time in her life, at age eighty-six, she was mentally capable of arriving at the true reconciliation with Texas that Brooks claims as the great result of the visit. A momentary reconciliation, yes, and one that gave her much comfort at the time, but her outbursts at old friends and sudden reversals over the previous years afford no reason to believe that a momentary reconciliation would have lasted or that it reflected any considered thought about the past.

At numerous points throughout this study I have consulted Porter's letters for direct (though that does not necessarily mean reliable) statements of her opinions or feelings. In the case of a fiction writer of such subtlety, letters can be enormously valuable, especially if one wishes to understand how the creative intelligence was affected by, and worked with, real-life contexts and relationships. In Porter's case, however, probably more than in most cases, the value of such documentary evidence is qualified by the problem of a lack of candor or, in harsher words, by her habitual lying. She offers, then, a special challenge of methodology in archival research. One must always work back and forth between her letters (or other documentary material) and both her fictional and her nonfictional (or supposedly nonfictional) works, reading the one in light of the other. That is what I propose to do once again here in closing. I have selected three letters written in her later years (after the age of sixty) that offer reflections on her home state, and along with these I will take a brief last look at *Ship of Fools,* published when she was seventy-two. Together, these display both the persistence of her ambivalence toward Texas and, I hope, some clarification of the nature of that ambivalence.

First Letter

In 1951, in the throes of her turbulent love affair with William Goyen, Porter wrote him an irritated note complaining of his prolonged absence (he was in Texas, she was in New York and Washington) and accusing him of having other amorous interests there, perhaps homosexual ones. She had met Goyen in 1947 and had conceived an ardent passion for him in early 1951 at Yaddo. Perhaps it was the combination of his good looks with his sophisticated artistry and his Texas origins that she found so exciting. Like Adam of "Pale Horse, Pale Rider," he embodied a polar opposite to the crudeness and insensibility to art that she often associated with Texas men.[2] The more usual Texas man, in her greatly jaundiced view, was represented by her first husband, John Henry Koontz, and by the gross caricature she drew of him in *Ship of Fools,* William Denny—a man of no breeding, notably given to violence. One of Porter's self-portraits in the novel, Frau Rittersdorf, thinks of Denny as "that dreadful American . . . with his mean sneer and evil eyes" (271). Besides being a racist, a demeanor of women, and a blusterer, Denny has no taste and no sense of social correctness. He considers that "champagne, even the best, tasted like thin vinegar with bubbles in it," and during the ship's stop at Tenerife he sits down with David and Jenny at a wine shop "as if he had been invited" (278, 280). This, then, in Porter's characterization begun in the mid-1930s or before but not completed until 1961, is the representative Texan: crude, ignorant, mean-looking, a bully—and quite the opposite of William Goyen.

In her letter to Goyen, one of many in a bitter series, she rejected his claim that he could work better in Houston than in New York, calling Houston a rotten place unredeemed by the fact of being in the South. Having thus rejected the reason he offered for being in Texas at the time, she could only conclude that he was lying. My point is this: that even in passing—because her purpose was not a critique of Texas but of Goyen's honor and his sexual orientation—she could not resist making a slap at Houston. She mentioned its heat and humidity, which she said could not possibly be an improvement over New York's in the summer, and went on to insist that it was simply not true that he could find artistic colleagues there even remotely comparable to those on the East Coast.

Her comments on Houston—a city about which she would naturally have had conflicting feelings, having had both good times and bad times there—are echoed in *Ship of Fools* in a passage where the self-important captain of the *Vera* ponders the United States. Apparently on no basis other than hearsay, he regards it as a "barbarous nation" always in a "total anarchic uproar" (426). At once he reminds himself that it is "a place he had never seen, for no ship of his carried him into any port more interesting than Houston, Texas, with its artificial canal in a meadow in a part of the country far removed from any marks of civilization" (427). This is one of the few times in the novel when Porter lapses in her shifting narrative point of view. Having seen only the Houston Ship Channel (completed in 1914, before Porter left Texas), the captain would not have anything in America to compare it with and would not have known—except again on hearsay—that other parts of the country had more "marks of civilization." Yet on whatever basis, he believes the only part of Texas he has seen to be inferior to the rest of the country. Once again, the passage has the ring of a slap she couldn't resist making, since it has no function in the novel whatever.

Second Letter

In 1952, the year after the letter to Goyen, Porter made a similar swat-in-passing at Texas in a reply to a fan letter requesting biographical information. After making her customary claim to being "the very first serious writer that Texas ever produced," she explained that precisely because she was a serious artist she had gotten as far away from Texas as she could and had only been back once. Certainly her claim about subsequent returns was not true in a literal sense; she had been back a number of times. As hyperbole, though, it is close enough. And she went on to explain why a serious artist would want to get away: because Texas was an intellectually unaware ("unconscious-in-the-head") state (Porter to unidentified Corporal Adams, January 10, 1952). Much as she did in her angry letter to Goyen, she again labeled Texas a place of artistic stagnation, generally insensitive to art or literature.

This is not at all surprising, of course. Critics and biographers have repeatedly said that Porter left Texas because it repressed her as an artist. The trouble comes when such statements are made as if they provide the sole explanation. To be sure, Porter tended to present her views on Texas in that way herself. She singled out one thing at a time and kept some things hidden. She might denounce her family for neglect or emotional abuse or might on another occasion point to the conditions that inevitably resulted from her mother's or her grandmother's death, or she might (and repeatedly did) cite her father's discouragement of her writing, when he suggested that she simply write letters to friends. She might imply that she felt her identity as a Southerner imperiled by the ambiguous regional identity of Texas: "I have been told that I wasn't a Southerner, that anyone born in Texas is a South-westerner. But I can't help it. Some of my people came from Virginia, some from Pennsylvania, but we are all from Tennessee, Georgia, and Carolinas, Kentucky, Louisiana. What does it take to be a Southerner?" (*Conv.* 45). At times in her letters she said she had to get away from Texas to escape that brute Koontz or attributed her departure to her family's indignation that she would stoop to divorce. None of these was the sole explanation. They need to be combined. And she never publicly commented at all on the physical abuse she suffered in that marriage or on her views of Texas history, except for the presence of slavery and lynching and the Texas Rangers' abuse of racial others. She left these explanations—which are also partial ones—to be inferred through careful reading. This is especially difficult in the case of "The Man in the Tree," since it was left unfinished but nevertheless gives the most emphatic expression of her response to racial violence.

Third Letter

On January 21, 1963, when Porter was not quite seventy-three, she wrote to Rita Johns, the daughter-in-law of her friend Erna Schlemmer Johns. She had learned, she said, that Rita was living in Berlin, where her husband was serving as a military officer. She herself had found Berlin (as could be seen in "The Leaning Tower") to be "gloomy and oppressive to the spirit" and had "never [been] easy there for a moment." As we know, the Texan in "The Leaning Tower" who is the story's narrative eyes, ears, and voice reacts to Berlin in much the same way, finding it gloomy and "mysteriously oppressive" (*CS* 436). He senses an alarming incipient violence in the place. In her letter to Rita Johns, Porter continued that it was not just the cold and the wintry dark she disliked in Berlin but the fact of being there when she was, in 1931, "a truly horrible moment in history" when Hitler was coming to power. Some Germans were still resisting the mob spirit and whispering against him, she said, but those who resisted were soon dead or in concentration camps.

She implies in this letter that her memories of her few months in Berlin are of having been "staggered" at the time and of subsequently looking back at those memories through a knowledge of what they were leading up to. History and public events mattered to Porter. They colored her sense of place.

It struck her as odd, she told Rita, that Erna was also in Germany because when they were girls together in Kyle, Erna always came home from Germany saying that she hated it. She herself, she said, had hated Texas fully as much as Erna hated Germany, but she conceded that her attitudes had softened since then. She had to grow up and get old, she wrote, in order to go back to Texas and see it differently, and when she did, she found herself adoring the state capitol building and appreciating the beauty of the Texas countryside. She had indeed made the same comment about the capitol building to others after her lecture in Austin. Did this mean that Porter was already "reconciled," even before her late-in-life trip to Brownwood? No. She might enjoy the scenery in the hill country and certain public artifacts, but she still knew that "the life" there had made her "miserable." She might have softened sporadically in her feelings toward Texas, but she was never reconciled. The ambivalence remained. That deep ambivalence, which so many have observed and which for many reasons she was never able to resolve, was finally Porter's greatest burden in being Texan.

By the time her last book, *The Never-Ending Wrong,* appeared in 1977, the same year she was put under legal guardianship, Porter had suffered two strokes. From then until her death, additional strokes ravaged her mind and paralyzed the right side of her body. For a while she stayed in her apartment with round-the-clock nursing, but she drove nurses away as fast as her nephew could hire them. She conceived all sorts of resentments and theories of persecution that estranged her from old friends, and she took to giving away whatever took her fancy to even the most casual of visitors. In March 1980 she was moved to a nursing home where, on her ninetieth birthday, she briefly let go of her anger to make a joke. Referring to her useless right hand as "baby," she tucked it in under the covers. In Unrue's words, that hand, representing her writing, was "finally the only 'child' she had" (*Life* 295).

Porter told an interviewer in 1962 that she'd had "a good run for my money—a free field in the things that matter" (*Conv.* 77). Few of us can say as much. And she might not have said it if she had known what the end would be like. But she lived a long life into which she crowded an enormous range of experiences and a highly developed conception of art. Her literary achievement, though not expansive, was of an extraordinary level of excellence. She died on September 18, 1980, at the age of ninety years and four months. At her request, her ashes were returned to Indian Creek, the place where she began, and were laid to rest next to her mother.

Notes

Chapter 1

1. For example, in an interview by Winston Bode, "Miss Porter on Writers and Writing," first published in the *Texas Observer* in 1958, now readily available in *Conv.,* 30–38.

2. At this time Porter was in ill health but struggling to resume work on the "Old Order" material. Porter to Josephine Herbst, July 27, 1932.

3. Information about Indian attacks (as well as lynchings) comes from Newton and Newton, *Racial and Religious Violence in America.*

4. When white settlers did pursue the raiders, usually to get back their stolen horses, they also wanted to get revenge, and sometimes, like the Indians, they took scalps. See, for example, the history of Somervell County (about sixty miles northeast of Brown County) by Nunn, *Somervell,* 36–37; see also Newton and Newton, *Racial and Religious Violence in America.*

5. Porter to George Sessions Perry, February 5, 1943.

6. Regional linguists confirm Vliet's assessment, though with far greater complexity. See, for example, Carver, *American Regional Dialects,* 225–32.

7. See Bakhtin, *The Dialogic Imagination,* on "heteroglossia."

8. Cormac McCarthy also liberally incorporates Spanish into his English-language novels. Neither a native of the borderlands nor a native speaker of Spanish, he began his life in the South and wrote about the South before moving both his residence and his writerly interest to far western Texas. He is frequently discussed in terms of border issues and border theory.

9. Aware that facts about her early years were less well-known than the rest, Porter wrote to Joan Givner on April 12, 1978, asking her to come visit so they could talk about it; Givner, private collection.

10. American history was not often taught in school classrooms until about the

mid-nineteenth century. Its frequency as a school subject approximately doubled between 1850 and 1900. It did not become standard classroom fare until the twentieth century. Since Porter's elementary school years ended in 1901 or 1902 and she had only one year of schooling after that, it is possible that she may never have encountered either Texas or American history in a school setting.

11. The title "Mother of Texas" was bestowed on Jane Long because it was said that she bore the first white baby in Texas—a reason that overlooks the many non-white babies that preceded hers. Historians now say that she did not bear the first white baby in Texas anyway. My teachers also emphasized that in the absence of her husband and his men, she fired a cannon and killed numerous Indians, as if that were obviously a good thing. To be sure, the deed was done in defense under attack, and it did show her willingness to take an active role usually performed by men.

12. I am drawing here primarily on Foster, *Spanish Expeditions into Texas, 1689–1768,* 1–27.

13. Austin's first colony came to be known as the Old Three Hundred because his initial grant from the Spanish, ratified by Mexico, allowed him to settle three hundred families. Due to a few awards of double grants, the number of families was actually 294. A convenient, compact guide to Texas history published by the Texas Historical Association, *The Handbook of Texas,* is available online at http://www.tshaonline.org/handbook/online (accessed June 6, 2012).

14. One of the ironies involved in Texas racism toward Mexicans (that is, people of Mexican descent, whether born south of the Rio Grande or north of it) is pointed out by Stewart and De León: even though Mexicans were widely believed by Anglos to be lazy, they were also seen as foreigners (in what had been their own land) who *actively* pursued "disloyalty and subversion" (*Not Room Enough,* 87).

15. See Zamora, Orozco, and Rocha, *Mexican Americans in Texas History.* Crook's strongly visual accounts of both the Goliad and the San Jacinto massacres in *Promised Lands* is even-handed in its horror and revulsion, but by admitting atrocities on the Texians' side at all and by refusing to demonize Mexicans it is an intensely revisionist work of fiction.

16. A slave rebellion or rumors of one had occurred as early as 1835. By 1860 slaves represented one-third of the population of central Texas. In Brazos County, the "northernmost reach" of Austin's land grant, there were more than a thousand slaves out of a population of twenty-five hundred (Carrigan, *The Making of a Lynching Culture,* 19, 50; Nevels, *Lynching to Belong,* 15).

17. Wooster, "Civil War," *Handbook of Texas.*

18. For a lively diary and letters written by the son of one of those hanged in Gainesville, see Clark, *Civil War Recollections of James Lemuel Clark.*

19. See "Lynching in America: Statistics, Information, Images," http://www.law.umkc.edu/faculty/projects/ftrials/shipp/lynchstats.html (accessed June 6, 2012).

Chapter 2

1. The Spanish influenza of 1918–19 was unusual in that it targeted young adults and progressed to pneumonia so rapidly that some patients died within forty-eight hours of the onset of cough and body aches; Crosby, *Epidemic and Peace, 1918,* 5, 322, 8. The epidemic killed three hundred thousand in the United States alone.

2. Porter also celebrated the citrus fruits grown in Texas in her late "Notes on the Texas I Remember" in the *Atlantic Monthly* in 1975: "I remember the fruits of my childhood, the orchards, red grapefruit, oranges, peaches." This can't be correct. Citrus fruits do not grow in central Texas, where she spent her childhood, or not in any abundance. On the other hand, she may have been recalling a later time, unknown to any of her biographers, when she lived in the Rio Grande Valley, where citrus fruits do grow. More likely the oranges and grapefruit found their way into the Texas she remembered simply because her father later had citrus orchards on an acreage where he spent the last years of his life, in deep South Texas. Paul Porter, son of Katherine Anne's brother Paul, has noted on the back of a picture among Porter's papers that his father bought the acreage but Harrison never took care of the trees. Or maybe they are just evidence of confusion. She was eighty-five when the piece appeared, and there are other patently incorrect statements in it, such as "I left Texas and the South almost for good and forever when I was nineteen years old. I haven't gone back except once for fifty-five years."

3. Unrue, "A Newly Discovered Children's Story," 189–90. The story reprinted in this article, titled "How Baby Talked to the Fairies," appeared in the *Dallas Morning News* on March 18, 1917. Unrue's critical reading may overstate the extent to which the story "foretell[s] the mature canon."

4. Darlene Unrue, in her biography of Porter, accepts the phrase "familiar country" and states as fact that "in childhood she often had crossed the border" (*Life,* 70) apparently on the sole basis of Porter's own claims.

5. See De León, *They Called Them Greasers,* 80–81. Stewart and De León write in *Not Room Enough* that even though San Antonio was "as much an economic center as there was in the Mexican region" of Texas, business and trade there were controlled more by Anglos than by Texas Mexicans (37).

Chapter 3

1. In the review, identified by Ruth M. Alvarez and Thomas F. Walsh (*Uncol.,* 28), Porter called Blasco Ibañez's book "scandal-mongering." For a detailed and knowledgeable account of Porter's time in Mexico, see, in addition to the introduction to *Uncol., Illusion* and *S/T,* 68–91.

2. Porter's longtime friend Cleanth Brooks and his wife heard her say "several

times" that she had been a card-carrying member in Mexico but had been "thrown out because she failed to keep party discipline." Another friend, Frances Cheney, stated positively that she was a party member in Mexico, though presumably her only evidence was Porter's own statements. Brooks to the author, May 27, 1992; Cheney, telephone interview by the author, April 24, 1993.

3. "The Fiesta of Guadalupe" is listed in the Hilt and Alvarez annotated bibliography as having been published only in 1970 in Porter's *CE*. However, Alvarez has subsequently documented its earlier appearance; see *Uncol.*, 32.

4. Walsh resolves his dilemma by deciding that Porter must have "rejected Christian dogma and probably religion itself" before she came to Mexico (*Illusion*, 18).

5. Porter to Josephine Herbst, July 21, 1932.

6. None of the letters cited in this paragraph appears in Isabel Bayley's selection, which tends to omit anything that Bayley judged contrary to her avowed aim of displaying Porter's "goodness of heart" (*SL*, 2).

7. My thanks to Professor Worth Robert Miller for sharing his research.

8. Webb's history of the Texas Rangers and other works, though now often deplored, would be widely applauded in the state, and he would be accorded the status of a literary father of Texas.

9. A picture showing Porter as Marie in *Poor Old Jim*, a comedy, can be found in Jones, *Renegades, Showmen, and Angels*, 133. Her hair is dark in this one, too.

10. The authoritative source on Porter and Mexican art is the doctoral dissertation of Alvarez, "Katherine Anne Porter and Mexican Art."

11. One of these was "Holiday," set on a German farm in south-central or southeastern Texas and based on a month-long retreat from her marriage to John Koontz that Porter made in 1912 on a farm at Spring Branch, Texas. This was almost certainly (as Unrue reports; *Life*, 48) the Spring Branch then located on the western edge of Houston, now very much a part of the city. The Hillendahl family, into which her sister Baby would soon marry, owned the last working farm in the community. I continue to wonder, however, whether the Spring Branch she chose as a refuge might have been the tiny community by that name located between San Marcos and Kyle, since its location would seem to have made it a reasonable place for her to go. Porter wrote "Holiday" while working on several stories of Mexico, some with characters modeled on Diego Rivera. Not published until long afterward, it is now regarded as one of her best, largely because of its palpable human sympathies but largely too because of its powerfully realized sense of place.

12. Curiously enough, Retinger was a former lover of Jane Anderson, Kitty Crawford's war reporter friend. Anderson is sometimes said to have had an affair, too, with Joseph Conrad, who described her in a 1916 letter to Richard Curle as "quite yum-yum." After World War II she would be indicted on espionage charges along with Ezra Pound.

13. See *Illusion,* 27–28 and *Life,* 84–85.

14. For an authoritative explication of the sources of "Flowering Judas" and its themes of "betrayal and disillusionment," see *Illusion.*

15. Braggioni's language of "gaping trenches" obviously reflects the iconography of World War I, over a decade in the past when Porter published "Flowering Judas." Like the even further retrospectives of *Ship of Fools* (1962), this detail illustrates the slow working of memory and meditation through which she turned her experiences into fiction, or to use the terms she would invoke in "St. Augustine and the Bullfight," turned "adventure" into "experience," or meaning.

16. Her statement about "self-delusion" was made in introductory remarks to the story as reprinted in *This Is My Best,* edited by White Burnett (1942), 539–40.

17. See Unrue, *"This Strange, Old World,"* 106.

18. One of the most disingenuous of Porter's many disingenuous moments was when she referred to Crane as "that crazy American poet who once lent me his house" and told Hank Lopez she didn't remember his name (*Refugee,* 63).

19. Porter to Dorothy Day, July 20, 1930, and to Delafield Day, February 17, 1931.

Chapter 4

1. The journal-letter to Gordon is printed in *SL,* 46–60. The letter to Mary Doherty, at the University of Maryland with the bulk of Porter's papers, is dated October 21, 1932.

2. Eleanor Clark, indignant at what she thought was Lopez's sensationalizing of the evening with Göhring, wrote correctly in her review of *Refugee* that it was easy to make too much of this.

3. Unrue observes astutely that Porter visited country cemeteries in Texas only a few months before she wrote most of "Old Mortality" and commented on the headstone doggerel she saw there. Her father wrote the verses for Mary Alice's grave:

Dearest loved one
We have laid thee
In the Peaceful
Grave's embrace
But thy memory
Will we cherish
Till we see thy
Heavenly face.

Mary Alice almost certainly wrote the lines on her father's (Porter's maternal grandfather's) headstone:

Servant of God well done
Rest from thy loved employ
The battle fought
The victory won
Enter thy master's joy.

Porter was apparently too embarrassed by her parents' indulgence in such doggerel to explain, when she told friends that she had found it interesting to see so much poetry in old cemeteries during her visit to Texas, that her mother and father had authored some of it. See *Life,* 8, 163–64.

4. See *S/T,* 119, 285. Herbst's letter to Porter (September 1930) and Warren's to Bill Wilkins (April 1, 1977) are at the Beinecke Library, Yale University.

5. Porter traces these and other conflicts I have mentioned in an unfinished draft titled "Pull Dick—Pull Devil" located among the KAP papers at the University of Maryland, College Park. The draft should not be confused with a book review for which she used the same title.

6. The "weep weep" sound in "The Fig Tree" was actually heard by Porter in Bermuda in the year she wrote the story, 1929.

7. Callie apparently did tell when she and her brother had the actual experience on which the fictional episode is based and got her brother a hard whipping (*KAP,* 71).

8. In "The Old Order," the Grandmother and Nannie discuss the weakness that must have led to Harry's wife's having died "when her third was born" (*CS,* 339). Harry is the fictional representation of Harrison Boone Porter, Katherine Anne's father. Her mother, Mary Alice Porter, actually died soon after the birth of her fifth, but one child had died and of the four living (counting the infant), Callie, or Katherine Anne, was the third. The story's reference to the wife's having died after her third can be read as a disguised form of Porter's statement to Lopez about her mother's death. She is making the same claim indirectly in the story of Miranda.

Chapter 5

1. Although there has been considerable controversy on this point and the names have been blacked out in the pertinent official records, it appears that Porter would later, in 1942, betray Herbst to the FBI.

2. Porter to Josephine Herbst, August 15, 1937; see *SL,* 149–52.

3. Porter would formulate this connection yet distinction between remembering and understanding more fully in "St. Augustine and the Bullfight."

4. My account of the Thompson episode draws on both Givner (*KAP,* 73–77) and Unrue (a single paragraph, *Life,* 30–31). Givner has it that Gay went with their

father, Unrue that Harry Ray, soon to become Paul, went. Both mention that Eugene Thompson was an offensive tease; both say the Thompsons' house was very small; both report that they had two sons (Unrue adds that the sons were twelve and nine years old); and both say that the Thompsons had a hired man named William Helton or Mr. Helton. Besides Givner, Unrue cites "'Noon Wine': The Sources"—that is, taking it as fact—and the same letter from Porter to Gay that Givner cites (October 8, 1956). Unrue does not make any reference to the letter dated June 14, 1978, that Givner reports having received from a family descendant named Mabel Kirkpatrick, nor does she emphasize, as Givner does, Porter's chagrin at being kin to such lower-class people.

5. Porter may have picked up the detail about the pebbles in the creek bottom when she visited her birthplace in the spring of 1936, shortly before completing "Noon Wine."

6. My thanks to Beth Alvarez for locating the reference to "Pink" Hodges.

7. Porter read her Cather well. Only six pages later in *My Ántonia* we find another source she used, this time in her short story "He." Mr. Shimerda's son Marek, "the crazy boy," can accompany his mother and sister to the barn where the (now frozen) body lies "because he did not feel the cold." In "He," the parents give their daughter "the extra blanket off His cot" because He, the mentally disabled son, "never seemed to mind the cold" (*CS,* 50). Porter's close reading of Cather is also evident in her essay "Reflections on Willa Cather" (*CE,* 29–39).

8. Thomas F. Walsh uses the phrase "illusion of Eden" in reference to Mexico, but it is also a good phrase for describing Porter's intermittent idealizing of Texas.

9. Contrast Unrue, *Truth and Vision in Katherine Anne Porter's Fiction,* 219: "The grand theme of her work has been all along the search for truth."

Chapter 6

1. Steven Trout points out, in discussing race relations after World War I, that the North was "no racial paradise, either" (*On the Battlefield of Memory,* 91).

2. O'Connor, *The Habit of Being: Letters,* 276.

3. Years later he would recall that she had worn a simple white gown and no jewelry but "her earlobes were rouged!" Porter, "Remembering Aunt Katherine," 25. Paul would become one of the most important persons in her life.

4. During the 1938 Olivet conference Porter met, among other interesting people, Robert Frost.

5. Thomas Austenfeld, in his chapter on Porter in *American Women Writers and the Nazis,* refers to her "politics of emotion" and surprisingly asserts that her fiction set in Germany shows that "instinctual judgment and emotional response may

constitute specifically female tools of political analysis" (34). In addition, Austenfeld writes as though what is puzzling to her fictional character is necessarily puzzling to the author as well, a fallacious reading from art to life.

6. Laura was avowedly modeled on Porter's friend and sometime housemate in Mexico, Mary Doherty, but we can also see Laura as another "Miranda," a fictional representation of Porter herself.

7. A letter to Eugene Pressly dated December 15, 1936, indicates that she added the dates at the end of the writing process, apparently in response to some comment of his asking for greater clarity in her intentions. While sarcastically rejecting the notion that her intentions in the story were not already perfectly clear, she acknowledged that the addition of the dates pulled the work together.

8. Marilyn M. Sibley, "No-Tsu-Oh," *Handbook of Texas.*

9. Graham, "A Southern Writer in Texas," 67.

10. Ciuba explores the parallel further: "After the Civil War the South cultivated the Lost Cause through a recommitment to the bedrock teachings and values of its religious past. And after World War I the South defended itself against the liberalism of the North through a biblical fundamentalism that opposed evolution, drastically limited the social gospel, and scrutinized the orthodoxy of college faculty" (*Desire, Violence, and Divinity in Modern Southern Fiction,* 123).

Chapter 7

1. Decades ago the term "aunt" or "auntie" was used by whites toward blacks as a condescending honorific when they meant to indicate goodwill or recall caregiving in infancy. At the same time, it inescapably hints of blood relationship.

2. See the well-argued essay by Sarah Robertson, "Accessing Blood-Knowledge in Katherine Anne Porter's *The Old Order.*"

3. The satanic presence in "Noon Wine" is well explored by Tom Walsh in "The 'Noon Wine' Devils" and "Deep Similarities in 'Noon Wine.'"

4. This and other information about racial violence are provided by Newton and Newton in *Racial and Religious Violence in America;* details of the "bungled attack" are on p. 349.

5. Carrigan, *The Making of a Lynching Culture,* 12–13; Nevels, *Lynching to Belong,* 2.

6. Jacqueline Goldsby gives the number as 3,220 during the years 1882–1930 (*A Spectacular Secret,* 15). Trudier Harris estimates that 4,951 lynchings were carried out in the United States between 1882 and 1927, of which 3,513 were of blacks. Out of this 3,513, 76 were of women (*Exorcizing Blackness,* 7). Most lynchings were in the South, but they also occurred in the Midwest, the Northeast, and the West.

7. See Unrue, "Katherine Anne Porter's Birthdays."

8. See Unrue, "A Newly Discovered Children's Story."

9. In a way, lynching never entirely ended but only changed forms. Trudier Harris-Lopez mentions in this regard the burning to death of a black man in Elk Creek, Virginia, in August 1997 and the dragging to death of James Byrd behind a pickup truck in Jasper, Texas, in June 1998.

10. Much of this section is adapted from S/T, primarily from chapter 6, "Among the Agrarians."

11. Porter to Josephine Herbst, December 29, 1930.

12. Porter to Josephine Herbst, July 12, 1930.

13. Remarks summarized here are from Porter's letters to Gay Porter Holloway at the University of Maryland, May–July 1964 and February 1965.

14. The fears attributed to Maria about the effects of her daughter's seeing the lynched body would have been well-founded. Sherrilyn A. Ifill, in *On the Courthouse Lawn* (144–46), writes about the "indelible picture etched" on a child's mind (she is referring to a black child) by seeing "victims' bodies or . . . part of the lynching" and cites psychological studies indicating the likelihood of "sleep disturbances, flashbacks, and emotional detachment" as "routinely reported symptoms of children who have been exposed to acts of violence" (146). Ifill is also particularly informative on the role of lynchings as messages of warning to the black community. Note that her book centrally concerns twentieth-century lynchings not in Texas but on the eastern shore of Maryland. She quotes historian Frank Shay as observing that in the first half of the twentieth century lynching was "as American as apple pie." It occurred throughout the country (though mostly in the South) and frequently involved burning.

15. In addition to the echoes of Cather's *Sapphira and the Slave Girl*, there is an echo of Miranda's "Oh, I want to *see*" (in "The Grave") in the manuscript's fixation on the child's seeing or not seeing the body. As if in a note to self, Porter wrote by hand, "She has seen it. Nightmares." There is even a faint echo of one of the most famous lines in all of Southern literature, Quentin Compson's tormented cry at the end of Faulkner's *Absalom, Absalom!* when he insists that he doesn't hate the South. In addition, there is a forerunner of Porter's " 'Noon Wine': The Sources," where she writes of an author's re-experiencing of material. Maria likewise thinks that everything she does is at least a double or triple task—thought about, then done, then endlessly repeated in remembering. Since we must suppose this draft was written before the essay on the sources of "Noon Wine," it would seem that Porter first produced the sentence here and liked it well enough to want to use it in publication. Besides being keenly attuned to the reality of lynching in Texas, then, the "Man in the Tree" fragments are curiously allusive generally, more so than is usual in Porter's writing.

16. I know of no evidence that Porter ever witnessed a lynching.

17. In this paragraph and the following two I am drawing on my own S/T, 137–39.

Chapter 8

1. This important letter from Porter to John Herrmann is at the Harry Ransom Humanities Research Center, University of Texas, Austin.

2. Many historians regard World War I and World War II as two different phases of one great war.

3. Among Porter's papers at the University of Maryland is the carbon copy of a letter to Malcolm Cowley dated October 3, 1931, from Berlin. Years later she wrote in at the bottom of the page, "I wrote 'The Leaning Tower' and re-wrote 'The Cracked Looking Glass' here between October 1, 1931 and January 21, 1932." She almost certainly did make notes for the story while living at Rosa Reichl's stone boarding-house on Bambergerstrasse, but it is not true that she "wrote" it there. Clear evidence of her having completed it in 1940 is provided by her correspondence with Glenway Wescott, while he was struggling to complete his own short novel of World War II, *The Pilgrim Hawk,* as well as in Wescott's diary.

4. Apparently having liked the image at the center of the phrase, which made its appearance in her essay "The Wooden Umbrella," published in 1947, Porter lengthened it, made it less focused, and thereby spoiled its effect in her 1950 essay on Ezra Pound, "'It Is Hard to Stand in the Middle'": "[Pound's letters are] the truest document I have seen of that falling world between 1850 and 1950. We have been falling for a century or more."

5. The United States purchased the Philippines from Spain for $20 million in 1898, at the end of the Spanish-American War, despite the fact that the Filipinos had rebelled against their colonizer and established their own republic. President McKinley declared them unfit to govern themselves. In response to this, as he saw it, disgusting war, Mark Twain launched the American Anti-Imperialism Society.

6. See Willa Cather's accurate depiction of public concern with the war in her Pulitzer Prize–winning novel of 1921, *One of Ours.*

7. If Porter read Siegfried Sassoon in 1918, as Unrue asserts (*Life,* 61), that would indicate antiwar leanings. However, it would be surprising, since she would have had to become aware of his first characteristic war poems very soon after their 1917 publication in England.

8. Porter's long awareness of the fate of socialists in wartime is indicated in a letter to her husband Albert Erskine dated October 18, 1940: "I'd rather see Roosevelt win than Willkie, but I'd like best to see Norman Thomas in. What do you want to bet that when and if we go to war, Mr. Thomas is going to jail? Mr. Debs, Socialist candidate, did the last time, and maybe that is one tradition that won't be broken."

9. Denise Levertov would raise the same concern in relation to the Vietnam War (known in Vietnam as the American War) in her poem "An Interim," a parable of such manipulations of meaning as "it became necessary to destroy the town to save it."

10. The popular World War I song "There's a Long, Long Trail a-Winding," written by two Yale seniors, Stoddard King and Alonzo Elliot, was first published in 1914 in London and first recorded in 1916.

11. See Kennedy, *Over Here,* 99–106.

12. Issues of structure have been at the center of critical debates over the merit of *Ship of Fools.* Robert Brinkmeyer is alone among Porter scholars and critics, to my knowledge, in calling attention to Porter's own emphasis on the structure of repetition in the novel. Darlene Unrue, in her 1985 book *Truth and Vision in Katherine Anne Porter's Fiction,* makes it clear that she believes the journey or quest structure succeeds (170). In the Barbara Thompson interview for the *Paris Review* in 1965, Porter used a musical metaphor of harmonies or chords to characterize the book's form. Likening a novel to a symphony, "where instrument after instrument has to come in at its own time," she told Thompson that the challenge of writing *Ship of Fools* "was all a matter of deciding which should come first, in order to keep the harmonious moving forward [*sic*]" (*Conv.,* 98). Her analogy minimizes the forward movement in formally constructed music; it is not just a matter of harmony or repeated motifs but of evolving and developing ones. At the same time, she claimed for her novel a degree of "moving forward" that most readers have not found in it.

13. In 1945 Porter argued the other side of the question of universal guilt in an exchange with Josephine Herbst. Herbst admonished her on May 5, 1945, that she should not issue blanket declarations affixing national blame entirely on the Germans. In saying that all were guilty, Herbst wrote, she was referring to the greed and uncaringness of all people. This letter is located at the Beinecke Library, Yale University. Herbst's voice seems to have found its way into *Ship of Fools,* though without significantly abating its anti-German cast.

14. The reference to Swedes harkens back to "Noon Wine."

15. See *KAP,* 320; also *S/T,* 113.

16. The image of marching feet was an obvious one for the time. Writing about the same time as Porter, for publication in his 1942 volume *Parts of a World,* the great symbolist Wallace Stevens, rarely thought of as a war poet, used the metaphor of marching feet in "Dry Loaf" to express a nightmare vision of events the world seemed doomed to repeat. Gwendolyn Brooks also used the image, including Porter's descriptive word "iron," in one of her "Gay Chaps at the Bar" sonnets, which appeared in the 1944 volume *A Street in Bronzeville.* The language of marching was in the air.

Chapter 9

1. Richard Holland also uses the word "snub" in his essay "Katherine Anne Porter and the University of Texas," 78.

2. Steven L. Davis puts it slightly differently in his book on Dobie: "No one considered her 'a Texas writer' at the time" and she "rarely acknowledged her birthplace" (*J. Frank Dobie*, 135). The latter is not quite so clear, however. Certainly she was inconsistent in her accounts of her personal origins, but she acknowledged her birthplace quite openly in interviews published in the *New York Post* in 1937 and the *New York Times Book Review* in 1940.

3. Many words in Herbst's FBI file are blacked out and the informant is unnamed, but Herbst's biographer Elinor Langer argues persuasively that it was Porter.

4. We should be clear: Porter needed speaking tours to support herself. However, discipline in spending could have reduced that need and afforded her more time and tranquility to produce work that, with her reputation by then, would have paid her well.

5. Letters in this sequence, including Ransom's letter of November 7, 1958, and Porter's of November 16, 1958, mentioned later in the chapter, are located in the Center for American History, Harry Ransom Papers, University of Texas, Austin. They are catalogued and summarized by Sally Dee Wade in "A Texas Bibliography."

6. Quoted by Lee in "Porter and Dobie," 69.

7. See, for example, Wescott, *Continual Lessons*, 302, 317, 327, 380.

8. Porter's letter to Dobie dated October 3, 1956, is located in the Dobie Collection at the University of Texas, Austin.

9. Unrue says that she knew the other tenant was there when she signed the lease; Givner says that she did not.

Chapter 10

1. The letter from Paul Porter Sr., dated March 23, 1909, addressed to Mrs. K. R. Koontz, is found among Porter's papers at the University of Maryland.

2. Unrue, *"This Strange, Old World,"* 28, 29.

3. Porter to Josephine Herbst, November 11, 1933.

4. Certainly we can say without hesitation that Porter would have opposed third-wave feminism, with its validation of the equal rights of lesbian, bisexual, and transgendered persons.

5. Olsen, talk at a centennial conference on Porter at Georgia State University, November 10, 1990; Brooks, *A Shaping Joy*, 208.

6. Mary Titus writes perceptively that "homelessness, homesickness, and exile are all words that appear again and again in Porter's writing, published and private," and her letters are "filled with descriptions of houses" (*The Ambivalent Art of Katherine Anne Porter*, 74).

7. Ciuba sagely compares the "barely suppressed sadism" of the spectators in

"St. Augustine and the Bullfight" to that of the crowd that so horrifies Miranda in "The Circus" (*Desire, Violence, and Divinity in Modern Southern Fiction*, 71).

8. In a letter to her niece Ann dated January 21, 1958, Porter described a "charming" man from Weatherford, Texas, who designed and made expensive clothes for her in California as being "queer as a feathered rabbit."

Chapter 11

1. Unrue states that the objects were already bequeathed (*Life*, 292); Brooks says they were not ("Hosting Miss Porter," 117).

2. For a fuller summary of Porter's and Goyen's troubled and troubling letters, see *S/T*, 177–83.

Bibliography

Alvarez, Ruth M. "Katherine Anne Porter and Mexican Art." Ph.D. diss., University of Maryland, 1990.

Alvarez, Ruth M., and Thomas F. Walsh, eds. *Uncollected Early Prose of Katherine Anne Porter.* Austin: University of Texas Press, 1993.

Anzaldúa, Gloria. *Borderlands/La Frontera: The New Mestiza.* San Francisco: Aunt Lute Books, 1987.

Austenfeld, Thomas Carl. *American Women Writers and the Nazis: Ethics and Politics in Boyle, Porter, Stafford, and Hellman.* Charlottesville: University Press of Virginia, 2001.

Bakhtin, Mikhail. *The Dialogic Imagination: Four Essays.* Trans. Caryl Emerson and Michael Holquist. Austin: University of Texas Press, 1981.

Barkley, Mary Starr. *A History of Central Texas.* Austin: Austin Printing, 1970.

Baym, Nina. *Feminism and American Literary History.* New Brunswick, NJ: Rutgers University Press, 1992.

———. "The Myth of the Myth of Southern Womanhood." In *Feminism and American Literary History.* New Brunswick, NJ: Rutgers University Press, 1992.

Bode, Winston. "Miss Porter on Writers and Writing." *Texas Observer,* October 31, 1958, pp. 6–7.

Brantley, Will. *Feminine Sense in Southern Memoir: Smith, Glasgow, Welty, Hellman, Porter, and Hurston.* Jackson: University Press of Mississippi, 1993.

Brinkmeyer, Robert H., Jr. *Katherine Anne Porter's Artistic Development: Primitivism, Traditionalism, and Totalitarianism.* Baton Rouge: Louisiana State University Press, 1993.

Brooks, Cleanth. *A Shaping Joy: Studies in the Writer's Craft.* New York: Harcourt Brace Jovanovich, 1971.

———. "Southern Literature: The Wellsprings of Its Vitality." In *A Shaping Joy: Studies in the Writer's Craft.* New York: Harcourt Brace Jovanovich, 1971.

Brooks, Roger. "Hosting Miss Porter." In Busby and Heaberlin, *From Texas to the World and Back,* 110–21.

Brundage, W. Fitzhugh. *Under Sentence of Death: Lynching in the South.* Chapel Hill: University of North Carolina Press, 1997.

Busby, Mark. "Katherine Anne Porter and Texas: Ambivalence Deep as the Bone." In Busby and Heaberlin, *From Texas to the World and Back,* 133–48.

Busby, Mark, and Dick Heaberlin, eds. *From Texas to the World and Back: Essays on the Journeys of Katherine Anne Porter.* Fort Worth: Texas Christian University Press, 2001.

Carrigan, William D. *The Making of a Lynching Culture: Violence and Vigilantism in Central Texas, 1836–1916.* Urbana: University of Illinois Press, 2004.

Carver, Craig M. *American Regional Dialects: A Word Geography.* Ann Arbor: University of Michigan Press, 1987.

Cather, Willa. *My Ántonia.* 1918. Scholarly Edition, edited by Charles Mignon with Kari Ronning, with historical essay and explanatory notes by James Woodress. Lincoln: University of Nebraska Press, 1994.

Ciuba, Gary M. *Desire, Violence, and Divinity in Modern Southern Fiction.* Baton Rouge: Louisiana State University Press, 2007.

Clark, Eleanor. "The Friendships of a Lifetime." Review of Enrique Hank Lopez, *Conversations with Katherine Anne Porter: Refugee from Indian Creek. Washington Post Book World,* July 26, 1981.

Clark, L. D., ed. *Civil War Recollections of James Lemuel Clark Including Previously Unpublished Material on the Great Hanging at Gainesville, Texas in October, 1862.* College Station: Texas A&M University Press, 1984.

Clifford, Craig Edward. *In the Deep Heart's Core: Reflections on Life, Letters, and Texas.* College Station: Texas A&M University Press, 1985.

Crook, Elizabeth. *Promised Lands: A Novel of the Texas Rebellion.* Dallas: Southern Methodist University Press, 1994.

Crosby, Alfred W., Jr. *Epidemic and Peace, 1918.* Westport, CT: Greenwood Press, 1976.

Davis, Steven L. *J. Frank Dobie: A Liberated Mind.* Austin: University of Texas Press, 2009.

De León, Arnoldo. *They Called Them Greasers: Anglo Attitudes toward Mexicans in Texas, 1821–1900.* Austin: University of Texas Press, 1983.

DeMouy, Jane Krause. *Katherine Anne Porter's Women: The Eye of Her Fiction.* Austin: University of Texas Press, 1983.

Flanders, Jane. "Katherine Anne Porter and the Ordeal of Southern Womanhood." *Southern Literary Journal* 9 (1976): 47–60.

———. Letter to Katherine Anne Porter, September 4, 1976. University of Maryland, College Park.

Foster, William C. *Spanish Expeditions into Texas, 1689–1768.* Austin: University of Texas Press, 1995.

Gallegly, Joseph. *Footlights on the Border: The Galveston and Houston Stage before 1900.* New York: Mouton, 1962.

Gibbons, Reginald. *William Goyen: A Study of the Short Fiction.* Boston: Twayne, 1991.

Givner, Joan, *Katherine Anne Porter: A Life.* Rev. ed. 1982. Athens: University of Georgia Press, 1991.

———, ed. *Katherine Anne Porter: Conversations.* Jackson: University Press of Mississippi, 1987.

———. "Problems of Personal Identity in Texas' 'First Writer.'" In Machann and Clark, *Katherine Anne Porter and Texas,* 41–57.

Goldsby, Jacqueline. *A Spectacular Secret: Lynching in American Life and Literature.* Chicago: University of Chicago Press, 2006.

Gould, Lewis L. *Progressives and Prohibitionists: Texas Democrats in the Wilson Era.* Austin: University of Texas Press, 1973.

Goyen, William. *Selected Letters from a Writer's Life.* Ed. Robert Phillips. Austin: University of Texas Press, 1995.

Graham, Don. *Giant Country: Essays on Texas.* Fort Worth: Texas Christian University Press, 1998.

———. "Katherine Anne Porter's Journey from Texas to the World." In Busby and Heaberlin, *From Texas to the World and Back,* 1–19.

———. "Nine Ball, Corner Pocket." In Jameson, *Notes from Texas,* 46–61.

———. "A Southern Writer in Texas: Porter and the Texas Literary Tradition." In Machann and Clark, *Katherine Anne Porter and Texas,* 58–71.

———. *Texas: A Literary Portrait.* San Antonio: Corona, 1985.

Green, James R. *Grass-Roots Socialism: Radical Movements in the Southwest, 1895–1943.* Baton Rouge: Louisiana State University Press, 1978.

Grider, Sylvia. "Memories That Never Were: Katherine Anne Porter and the Family Saga." In Machann and Clark, *Katherine Anne Porter and Texas,* 225–37.

Harrigan, Stephen. *A Natural State.* Austin: Texas Monthly Press, 1988.

Harris, Trudier. *Exorcizing Blackness: Historical and Literary Lynching and Burning Rituals.* Bloomington: Indiana University Press, 1984.

Hendrick, George. *Katherine Anne Porter.* 1965. Rev. ed., with Willene Hendrick. Boston: Twayne, 1988.

Hendrick, Willene. "Indian Creek: A Sketch from Memory." In Machann and Clark, *Katherine Anne Porter and Texas,* 3–12.

Herbst, Josephine. Letter to Katherine Anne Porter, September 1930. Beinecke Library, Yale University.

Hilt, Kathryn, and Ruth M. Alvarez. *Katherine Anne Porter: An Annotated Bibliography.* New York: Garland, 1990.

Holland, Richard. "Katherine Anne Porter and the University of Texas: A Map of Misunderstanding." In Busby and Heaberlin, *From Texas to the World and Back,* 78–96.

Humphrey, William. *Farther Off from Heaven.* New York: Knopf, 1977.

Ifill, Sherrilyn A. *On the Courthouse Lawn: Confronting the Legacy of Lynching in the Twenty-First Century.* Boston: Beacon Press, 2007.

Jameson, W. C., ed. *Notes from Texas: On Writing in the Lone Star State.* Fort Worth: Texas Christian University Press, 2008.

Jones, Anne Goodwyn. *Tomorrow Is Another Day: The Woman Writer in the South, 1859–1936.* Baton Rouge: Louisiana State University Press, 1981.

Jones, Jan L. *Renegades, Showmen, and Angels: A Theatrical History of Fort Worth from 1873–2001.* Fort Worth: Texas Christian University Press, 2006.

Kelton, Elmer. *Living and Writing in West Texas: Two Speeches.* Intro. Al Lowman. Abilene: Hardin-Simmons University Press, 1988.

Kennedy, David M. *Over Here: The First World War and American Society.* New York: Oxford University Press, 1980.

Lee, James Ward. *Adventures with a Texas Humanist.* Fort Worth: Texas Christian University Press, 2004.

———. "Porter and Dobie: The Marriage from Hell." In Busby and Heaberlin, *From Texas to the World and Back,* 66–77.

Lopez, Enrique Hank. *Conversations with Katherine Anne Porter: Refugee from Indian Creek.* Boston: Little, Brown, 1981.

Lytle, Andrew. Letter to Katherine Anne Porter, November 1930. University of Maryland, College Park.

Machann, Clinton, and William Bedford Clark, eds. *Katherine Anne Porter and Texas: An Uneasy Relationship.* College Station: Texas A&M Univ. Press, 1990.

McMurtry, Larry. "Ever a Bridegroom: Reflections on the Failure of Texas Literature." *Texas Observer,* October 23, 1981: 8–9.

———. "Southwestern Literature?" In *In a Narrow Grave: Essays on Texas,* 31–54. Austin: Encino, 1968.

Millington, Richard H. "Willa Cather's American Modernism." In *The Cambridge Companion to Willa Cather,* ed. Marilee Lindemann, 51–65. Cambridge: Cambridge University Press, 2005.

Montejano, David. "Old Roads, New Horizons: Texas History and the New World Order." In Zamora, Orozco, and Rocha, *Mexican Americans in Texas History,* 19–29.

Nance, William. *Katherine Anne Porter and the Art of Rejection.* Chapel Hill: University of North Carolina Press, 1964.

Nevels, Cynthia Skove. *Lynching to Belong: Claiming Whiteness through Racial Violence*. College Station: Texas A&M University Press, 2007.

Newton, Michael, and Judy Ann Newton. *Racial and Religious Violence in America: A Chronology*. New York: Garland, 1991.

Nunn, W. C. *Somervell: Story of a Texas County*. Fort Worth: Texas Christian University Press, 1975.

O'Connor, Flannery. *The Habit of Being: Letters*. Ed. Sally Fitzgerald. New York: Farrar, Straus, Giroux, 1979.

Pilkington, William T. *My Blood's Country: Studies in Southwestern Literature*. Fort Worth: Texas Christian University Press, 1973.

Porter, Harrison Boone. Letter to Mary Alice Jones, January 15, 1882. University of Maryland, College Park.

Porter, Katherine Anne. *The Collected Essays and Occasional Writings*. Boston: Houghton Mifflin, 1970.

———. *The Collected Stories*. 1965. Rpt. New York: Harcourt Brace Jovanovich, 1979.

———. Letter to J. Frank Dobie, October 3, 1956. Dobie Collection, University of Texas, Austin.

———. Letter to George Sessions Perry. Harry Ransom Humanities Research Center, University of Texas, Austin.

———. Letter to Harry Ransom, November 16, 1958. Center for American History, University of Texas, Austin.

———. Letters to Corp. Adams, Malcolm Cowley, Peggy Cowley, Mary Doherty, Donald Elder, Albert Erskine, Ford Madox Ford and Janice Biala, Caroline Gordon, William Goyen, Ann Heintze, Mary Alice Porter Hillendahl, William Humphrey, Erna Schlemmer Johns, Rita Johns, Matthew Josephson, Kathleen Millay, Jordan Pecile, Cora Posey, Harrison Boone Porter et al., Paul Porter, Eugene Pressly, Monroe Wheeler, Glenway Wescott. University of Maryland, College Park.

———. Letters to Delafield Day and Dorothy Day. Dorothy Day—Catholic Worker Collection, Marquette University.

———. Letters to Josephine Herbst. Beinecke Library, Yale University.

———. "Notes on the Texas I Remember." *Atlantic Monthly* 235 (March 1975): 102–6.

———. "Why [I] Selected 'Flowering Judas.'" 1942. In White Burnett, ed., *This Is My Best*. Reprint. *"Flowering Judas," Katherine Anne Porter*. Ed. Virginia Spencer Carr. New Brunswick, NJ: Rutgers University Press, 1993. 53–54.

Porter, Mary Alice Jones. Letters. University of Maryland, College Park.

Porter, Paul. "Remembering Aunt Katherine." In Machann and Clark, *Katherine Anne Porter and Texas*, 25–37.

Ransom, Harry. Letter to Katherine Anne Porter, November 7, 1958. Center for American History, University of Texas, Austin.

Robertson, Sarah. "Accessing Blood-Knowledge in Katherine Anne Porter's *The Old Order.*" *Mississippi Quarterly* 62, no. 1–2 (Winter–Spring 2009): 247–64.

Rocha, Rodolfo. "The Tejano Revolt of 1915." In Zamora, Orozco, and Rocha, *Mexican Americans in Texas History,* 103–19.

Rodenberger, Lou. "The Prodigal Daughter Comes Home." In Busby and Heaberlin, *From Texas to the World and Back,* 122–32.

Saldívar, Ramón. "The Borderlands of Culture: Americo Parades's *George Washington Gómez.*" In Zamora, Orozco, and Rocha, *Mexican Americans in Texas History,* 175–85.

Seidel, Kathryn Lee. *The Southern Belle in the American Novel.* Tampa: University of South Florida Press, 1985.

Stewart, Kenneth L., and Arnoldo De León. *Not Room Enough: Mexicans, Anglos, and Socio-economic Change in Texas, 1850–1900.* Albuquerque: University of New Mexico Press, 1993.

Stout, Janis P. "Estranging Texas: Porter and the Distance from Home." In Machann and Clarke, *Katherine Anne Porter and Texas,* 86–101.

———. *Katherine Anne Porter: A Sense of the Times.* Charlottesville: University Press of Virginia, 1995.

———. "'Practically Dead with Fine Rivalry': The Leaning Towers of Katherine Anne Porter and Glenway Wescott," *Studies in the Novel* 33 (Winter 2001): 444–58.

Strom, Ann Miller. *The Prairie City : A History of Kyle, Texas, 1880–1980.* Burnet, TX: Eakin Publications, 1981.

Tanner, James T. F. *The Texas Legacy of Katherine Anne Porter.* Denton: University of North Texas Press, 1990.

Texas Historical Association. *The Handbook of Texas.* http://www.tshaonline.org /handbook/online (accessed June 6, 2012).

Thompson, Jerry. *A Wild and Vivid Land: An Illustrated History of the South Texas Border.* Austin: Texas State Historical Association, 1997.

Thompson, Ralph. Review of J. Frank Dobie, *Apache Gold and Yaqui Silver. New York Times,* March 16, 1939, p. 28.

———. Review of Katherine Anne Porter, *Pale Horse, Pale Rider. New York Times,* March 30, 1939, p. 28.

Titus, Mary. *The Ambivalent Art of Katherine Anne Porter.* Athens: University of Georgia Press, 2005.

Trout, Steven. *On the Battlefield of Memory: The First World War and American Remembrance, 1919–1941.* Tuscaloosa: The University of Alabama Press, 2010.

Unrue, Darlene Harbour. *Katherine Anne Porter: The Life of an Artist.* Jackson: University Press of Mississippi, 2005.

———. "Katherine Anne Porter's Birthdays." In Busby and Heaberlin, *From Texas to the World and Back,* 38–53.

———. "A Newly Discovered Children's Story by Katherine Anne Porter: Foretelling the Mature Canon." *Mississippi Quarterly* 62, no. 102 (Winter–Spring 2009): 181–94.

———, ed. *"This Strange Old World" and Other Book Reviews by Katherine Anne Porter.* Athens: University of Georgia Press, 1991.

———. *Truth and Vision in Katherine Anne Porter's Fiction.* Athens: University of Georgia Press, 1985.

Vick, Frances Brannen. "Confessions of a Texas Publisher/Writer." In Jameson, *Notes from Texas,* 234–44.

Vliet, R. G. "On a Literature of the Southwest: An Address." *Texas Observer,* April 28, 1978, pp. 18–21.

Wade, Sally Dee. "'The Homeless One Home Again.'" In Machann and Clark, *Katherine Anne Porter and Texas,* 115–23.

———. "A Texas Bibliography of Katherine Anne Porter." In Machann and Clark *Katherine Anne Porter and Texas,* 124–82.

Walsh, Thomas F. "Deep Similarities in 'Noon Wine.'" *Mosaic* 9 (1975): 83–91.

———. *Katherine Anne Porter and Mexico: The Illusion of Eden.* Austin: University of Texas Press, 1992.

———. "The 'Noon Wine' Devils." *Georgia Review* 22 (1968): 90–96.

Walton, Edith H. Review of Katherine Anne Porter, *Pale Horse, Pale Rider. New York Times,* April 2, 1939, p. 95.

Warren, Robert Penn. "Irony with a Center, Katherine Anne Porter (1941–52)." In *Selected Essays of Robert Penn Warren.* New York: Random House, 1941.

———. Letter to Bill Wilkins, April 1, 1977. Beinecke Library, Yale University.

———. Letter to Katherine Anne Porter, January 12, 1972. University of Maryland, College Park.

Webb, Walter Prescott. *The Story of the Texas Rangers.* New York: Grosset and Dunlap, 1957.

Wescott, Glenway. *Continual Lessons: The Journals of Glenway Wescott, 1937–1955.* Ed. Robert Phelps with Jerry Rosco. New York: Farrar, Straus and Giroux, 1990.

———. *Images of Truth: Remembrances and Criticism.* New York: Harper and Row, 1962.

Young, Thomas Daniel, and John J. Hindle, eds. *The Republic of Letters in America: The Correspondence of John Peale Bishop and Allen Tate.* Lexington: University Press of Kentucky, 1981.

Zamora, Emilio, Cynthia Orozco, and Rodolfo Rocha, eds. *Mexican Americans in Texas History: Selected Essays.* Austin: Texas State Historical Association, 2000.

Index

Abels, Cyrilly, 133, 171
"Adventures of Hadji, The," 29
Agrarians, 42, 85, 86, 87, 131, 204
Alvarez, Ruth Moore "Beth," 35, 216n10, 219n6
Ames, Elizabeth, 101, 167
Anderson, Jane, 27, 216n12
"Anniversary in a Country Cemetery," 163, 206
Anzaldúa, Gloria, 4–5
Auden, W. H., 100
Austenfeld, Thomas, 219–20n5
ax murders: in Porter's works, 88, 93–94, 120–21; series of in Texas, 94, 121–22, 123–24

Bayley, Isabel, 52, 193, 216n6
Baym, Nina, 7, 181
Bedichek, Roy, 3
Best Maugard, Adolfo, 30, 32, 40
Bode, Winston, 13, 56–57, 173
Boni and Liveright, 43, 44
border-crossing, 5
borderlands, as metaphor, 4–5. See also Anzaldúa, Gloria; border-crossing; Texas: as borderland of South and West; Texas: as borderland with Mexico
Brace, Donald, 80, 83

Brinkmeyer, Robert, 71, 180, 195, 223n12
Brinnin, John Malcolm, 184
Brooks, Cleanth, 87, 180, 215 16n2
Brooks, Gwendolyn, 223n16
Brooks, Roger, 202, 205–7, 208, 225n1
Busby, Mark, 172, 202

Cárdenas, Lázaro, 50
Carillo Puerto, Felipe, 41, 201
Cather, Willa, 92, 93–94, 97, 136, 219n7, 221n15; 222n6
Century Magazine, 42
Charlot, Jean, 51
Cheney, Brainard, 87
Cheney, Frances, 87, 216n2
Chicago Tribune, 29
Christian Science Monitor, 30, 35, 51
"Circus, The," 65, 70, 71–73, 81, 171, 224–25n7
Cisneros, Sandra, 5
Ciuba, Gary, 57, 94, 112, 113–14, 119–20, 149, 220n10; 224–25n7
Civil War (American), xi, xv, 8, 10, 12, 18–19, 21, 22, 23–24, 26, 57, 58, 75, 86, 124, 130, 143, 220n10
Clifford, Craig, vi, 3, 6, 19
Collected Essays and Occasional Writings, 186
Collected Stories, 47, 65

corridos, 25
Covarrubias, Miguel, 41, 51
Cowley, Malcolm, 29, 42, 175, 222n3
Cowley, Peggy, 29, 37, 42, 51, 142
"Cracked Looking-Glass, The," 81, 183, 222n3
Crane, Hart, 47, 217n18
Crawford, Garfield, 39–40
Crawford, John and Becky, 44
Crawford, Kitty Barry, 17, 18, 27, 29, 39–40, 216n12
Crook, Elizabeth, 19, 22, 26, 214n15

Dallas Morning News, 29
Davis, Steven L., 166, 224n2 (chap. 9)
Day, Delafield, 42, 49
Day, Dorothy, 42, 46, 48–49
Days Before, The, 170
de Beauvoir, Simone, 178, 181
Debs, Eugene V., 38, 222n8
de la Selva, Salomón, 41, 51, 52
de Lizardi, José Fernández, 54, 56
Dell, Floyd, 29
DeMouy, Jane Krause, 62
Dobie, J. Frank, 3, 6–7, 164, 165–66, 175, 177, 203, 224n2 (chap. 9); as regionalist, 165–66
Doherty, Mary, 41, 54, 189, 217n1, 220n6 (chap. 6)
"Dora, the Dodo, and Utopia," 179
"Downward Path to Knowledge, The," 96
Durant, Kenneth, 20, 29, 38

Eisenstein, Sergei, 47–48
Elder, Donald, 53, 141, 143, 144, 178
El Heraldo de México, 34–35
Eliot, T. S., 166, 173, 200
Erskine, Albert, 25, 87, 100–101, 150, 151, 163, 167, 222n8
Europe, inter-war, 141–42, 144, 157, 211. *See also* Porter, Katherine Anne: Europe visited by
Evans, Ernestine, 29, 30

Evans, Rosalie Caden, 46
Everyland, 28–29

Faulkner, William, 3, 138, 152, 221n15
"Fiesta of Guadalupe, The," 35, 50, 215n3
"Fig Tree, The," 61, 65, 66, 67, 70, 77, 112, 218n6
Flanders, Jane, 107, 182
"Flowering Judas," 36, 44–46, 50, 81, 101, 177, 189
Flowering Judas, 81
Flowering Judas and Other Stories, 47, 80–81
Ford, Ford Madox, 55, 82
Friedan, Betty, 178, 181, 201
frontier, 3. *See also* Texas: frontier violence in
Frost, Robert, 219n4

Gamio, Manuel, 35, 36
Givner, Joan, 3, 12, 15, 17, 28, 42, 87, 89, 98, 130–31, 164, 165, 187, 206, 207, 218–19n4
Göhring, Hermann, 55, 217n2
Gold, Mike, 29
Gordon, Caroline, 37, 42, 47, 54, 86, 131–32, 193
Goyen, William, 1, 97, 101, 165, 170, 204, 209, 210, 225n2
Graham, Don, 3, 7, 10, 63–64, 98, 202, 203, 204
"Grave, The," 61, 65, 70, 73–75, 77, 111, 112, 221n15
Grider, Sylvia, 164
Guerrero, Xavier, 40, 41, 50
Gyroscope, 65

Haberman, Roberto, 35, 39
Haberman, Thorberg, 34, 35, 39
"Hacienda" (and *Hacienda*), 47–49, 50, 81
Hanna, Paul, 39
Harcourt, Brace, 44, 46, 80, 83, 143, 151–52, 166–67, 170

Harrigan, Stephen, 19, 202, 203–4
Harris, Trudier, 123, 124
Harrison, Barbara, 55, 81, 168
Harrison of Paris, 47, 55
"He," 43, 81, 131, 219n7
Hemingway, Ernest, 107, 146, 190
Hendrick, Willene, 202–3
Herbst, Josephine, 37, 42, 63, 81, 83, 84, 86, 132, 167, 170, 180, 223n13; betrayal of by Porter, 218n1, 224n3 (chap. 9)
Herrmann, John, 42, 81, 142
Hillendahl, Mary Alice Porter ("Baby," sister of KAP), 10, 11, 16, 82, 85, 194
Hinojosa, Rolando, 5
"Holiday," 177, 216n11
Holland, Richard, 172, 173, 223n1
Holloway, Gay Porter (sister of KAP), 10, 12, 14, 16, 90, 100, 163
Holloway, Mary Alice (niece of KAP), 16, 28, 42, 116
"House of My Own, A," 167, 185
Houston, Sam, 23
Howard Payne University, 202, 204–8
Humphrey, William, 1, 7, 165, 170

Ibañez, Blasco, 35
influenza epidemic of 1918–19, 27, 112, 144, 148–49, 161, 215n1 (chap. 1)
Itching Parrot, The, 54, 55, 56, 80
"It Is Hard to Stand in the Middle," 222n14

"Jilting of Granny Weatherall, The," 43, 81
Johns, Erna Schlemmer, 16, 156, 184, 211–12
Johns, Rita, 211
Johnson, Rhea, 177, 182
Jones, Anne Goodwin, 99
Jones, John and Caroline (maternal grandparents of KAP), 8
Josephson, Matthew, 44, 82, 180
Jovanovich, William, 151–52, 183

"Journey, The," 57–58, 65, 66–67, 119, 120, 130

Kahlo, Frida, 51
Katherine Anne Porter's French Song Book, 55
Kelton, Elmer, 26
Kimbrough, Hunter, 47–48
Koontz, John Henry, 14–15, 16, 17, 18, 38, 95, 102, 121, 155, 188, 194, 200, 209, 211, 216n11
Ku Klux Klan, 57, 127

Lane, Rose Wilder, 29
Lawrence, Seymour, 152, 171, 176, 177, 183, 184, 185, 186, 205
"Leaning Tower, The," 55, 143, 151, 157–60, 161–62, 167, 211, 222n3
"Leaving the Petate," 52
Lee, James, 6, 165–66
Long, Jane, 19, 214n11
Lopez, Henry (Hank), 3, 14, 16, 17, 28, 32, 75, 76, 187, 217n18, 217n2, 218n8, 221n9
lynching, 21, 24, 119–20, 122–30, 128, 134, 135, 137–38, 220n6 (chap. 7), 221n9, 221n14; and slavery, 123, 126
Lynes, George Platt, 56, 169
Lytle, Andrew, 86, 87, 131

Magazine of Mexico, The, 30, 35, 38
"Magic," 43, 81, 83
"Man in the Tree, The," xiii, 24, 83, 119, 127, 132, 133–40, 167, 211
Mansfield, Katherine, 96
"Many Redeemers," 81
Mardi Gras, 102
"María Concepción," 13, 40–41, 50, 81, 101
Marín, Guadalupe, 40, 51–52
Mather, Cotton, projected biography of, 43, 44, 46, 82, 133, 167
McCarthy, Cormac, 5, 213n8
McMurtry, Larry, xvi, 7–8, 24–25, 62

Méndez, Gen. Sidronio, 39
"Mexican Trinity, The," 36
Mexico, 21–23, 30–31, 41; politics in, 32, 34, 35, 38, 46, 47, 48, 50; visual arts in, 32, 34, 41, 50–51. *See also* Porter, Katherine Anne: Mexico important to; Porter, Katherine Anne: Mexico, periods of residence in
Millay, Edna St. Vincent, 29
Mitchell, Margaret, 3
Modotti, Tina, 51
Moore, Marianne, 154
Morones, Luis, 34, 35, 38, 39, 41
Ms. magazine, 178
My Chinese Marriage, 29, 35

Nance, William J., 117, 184
Nation, The, 39
"Negro Question, The," 139–40
Never-Ending Wrong, The, 43, 133, 212
New Republic, The, 42, 180
New York Call, 35
New York Herald Tribune, 42, 46
New York Times, 166, 184
Niven, William, 39, 40
"Noon Wine," 3, 14, 26, 80, 83, 87–89, 92–95, 120–21, 172
"'Noon Wine': The Sources," 3, 26, 33, 45, 50, 56, 57, 64, 75, 89–92, 94–95, 97, 142, 156, 173, 204, 221n15
"No Safe Harbour," 15, 143, 167, 170
"Notes on Teotihuacán," 36, 50
"Notes on the Texas I Remember," 10, 18, 58–59, 215n2 (chap. 2)

Obregón, Alvaro, 34, 36, 38, 39, 49–50; expulsion of Bolsheviks by, 39
O'Connor, Flannery, 100
"Old Mortality," 13, 56, 59, 61–62, 67, 69, 70, 75, 83, 84, 95, 101, 102–11, 112, 172, 182, 189–90
"Old Order, The," xiii, 33, 56, 61, 63, 65–75, 77, 81, 95, 101, 112, 142, 182, 218n8

Olivet Writers' Conference, 86, 100, 101
Olsen, Tillie, 180
"On Communism in Hollywood," 167–68
Orozco, José Clemente, 41, 51, 52
Outline of Mexican Popular Arts and Crafts, 40

"Pale Horse, Pale Rider," 28, 70, 80, 83, 84, 87, 101, 111–17, 143, 144–50, 161, 182, 184, 209
Pale Horse, Pale Rider, 100, 163, 166
Paredes, Americo, 25
Paris Review, 28, 63
Pecile, Jordan, 175, 183, 200
Perry, George Sessions, 43
Pilkington, Tom, 4, 5, 7–8, 18
Poe, Edgar Allan, 59, 70, 75–76
Populist Party, 37
Porter, Asbury Duval (paternal grandfather), 8, 12, 21, 24, 57
Porter, Catherine Ann Skaggs (paternal grandmother), 6, 8, 9, 10–12, *11*, 13–14, 21, 58–59, 60, 61–62; as storyteller, 12
Porter, Gay. *See* Holloway, Gay Porter (sister of KAP)
Porter, Harrison Boone (father), 2, 8–9, 10, 13, 25, 38, 57, 60, 61, 75, *84*, 86, 99, 104, 155, 167, 215n2 (chap. 2), 217n3, 218n8
Porter, Harrison Paul (originally Harry Ray; brother), 10, 14, 218n7
Porter, Katherine Anne, *11*, *56*, *151*, *168*, *169*, *174*; as actress, 14, 16, 39, 64; age of, 13, 182; ambitions of, 12–13, 62, 90; ambivalence of between South and West, 3–4, 5, 15, 57–58, 63; ambivalence of toward South, 8, 33, 64, 119, 138; ambivalence of toward Texas, xiii, xiv, 2, 30, 56, 64, 75, 86, 89, 163, 170, 202–3, 209, 212; anti-Semitism of, 131, 156; beauty of, 13, *15*, *17*, 56, 61, 75, 77, 98, 99–100, 107, 201, 206; bilingualism, lack of, 4–5, 55;

birthplace of, xi, 2, 12, 90, 173; border-crossing of, 5, 30, 32; on Catholicism, 36–37, 105; childhood of, xi, xiii, 3–4, 6, 7, 12, 14, 56, 59, 62, 65, 70, 75, 76, 83, 87, 96, 176; childhood home of, 10–11; and the Civil War, 18, 57, 75, 76, 130; communism and, 35, 37, 46, 49–50; Communist Party affiliation of, 35, 49, 54, 142, 216n2; death a fixation of, 9, 57, 60, 70, 73–74, 75, 76, 149, 188; death of mother of, 9, 12, 104, 111, 206, 207, 210; departures from Texas by, xi, 16, 18, 25, 27, 99, 162, 210, 215n2 (chap. 2); depression suffered by, 31, 54, 158, 167, 194; disaffection from Texas of, xii, xiii, 1, 2, 15–16, 18, 33, 90, 156, 162, 163, 166, 172, 202, 203, 210; Europe visited by, 54, 80, 82, 141, 142, 147, 171, 185; family of, 8–9, 11, 14, 33, 56, 57, 59–60, 70, 84, 85, 88–89, 102, 104, 113, 119 20, 132, 152, 170, 202, 204, 207; femininity of, 61, 107, 181; feminism of, 37, 39, 98, 107, 178–80, 200–201; Ford Foundation grant to, 17; Fulbright Fellowship awarded to, 171; gender and, xiii, 16, 29, 62, 64, 77, 98, 102, 107, 117, 176, 181, 193, 195, 200, 204; Germans disliked by, 54, 154, 156–57, 223n13; and Germany, 55; Guggenheim Fellowship awarded to, 47; history and, 19, 25, 131, 162, 211; homelessness felt by, 2, 82, 84, 163, 173, 185; homosexuality disliked by, 47, 81, 169, 195, 209, 225n8; house of her own wanted by, 2, 33, 49, 100, 163, 167, 169, 173, 183, 185–86, 204; husbands and lovers of, 15, 17, 18, 25, 28, 41, 42, 44, 46, 51, 62, 80, 87, 100, 101, 168, 170, 175, 182, 183, 200; illnesses and injuries of, 16, 27, 42, 46, 80, 95, 111, 127, 168, 170–71, 176, 186, 187, 205, 208, 212; Library of Congress appointment of, 168; marriages of, xi, 14–15, 16, 17, 18, 80, 82, 87, 95, 100–101, 151, 163, 164, 167, 195, 204; Mexico, importance to, 5, 30–31, 32, 39, 43, 44, 48–49, 193, 205; Mexico, periods of residence in, 31–32, 40, 42, 46, 47, 49, 142, 183; misrepresentations by, 12–13, 14, 18, 28, 32, 58, 60–63, 90–91, 95, 208, 217n18; moves and relocations by, 1, 14, 15, 16, 18, 28, 30, 31, 44, 55, 66, 87, 176, 186, 204; movie work of, 168 69; name of, xi, 9, 16; as newspaperwoman, 18, 26, 27, 28, 39, 99, 145; and the Oaxaca conspiracy, 39; as pacifist, 145, 150; in Paris, 66; politics of, 30, 32, 37, 38, 41, 142; pregnancies of, 41, 42; race and, xiii, 26, 53, 64, 77, 119, 130, 131, 132–33, 135, 137, 139–40, 156; reconciliation to Texas of, 1, 202, 205, 208; regionalism disparaged by, 3, 164–65, 166; religion of, 14, 15, 35–36, 37, 202; returns to Texas by, 18, 28, 39, 82, 83, 100, 111, 139, 163, 171, 202, 204, 206, 208; schooling of, 14, 19, 63, 213–14n10; sexuality of, 41, 42, 62, 81, 98, 101, 175; slavery and, 8, 56, 131–32; social class and, xv, 13, 61, 63, 87–88, 90, 95, 99, 131; as socialist, 145; as Southerner, xi, 3, 5, 8, 26, 47, 57, 76, 85, 211; as Texan, xii, 1, 3, 13, 33, 63, 85, 206; Texas disliked by, 2, 97, 204, 209–10, 212; Texas idealized by, xii, 2, 86, 97, 162, 204, 215n2 (chap. 2), 219n8; as Texas writer, xii, 1, 7–8, 202, 224n2 (chap. 9); on Twain, 176–77; and the University of Texas, 13, 171–75, 202; and violence, 18, 19, 31, 44, 46, 50, 56, 57, 89–90, 91, 94, 118, 119, 176, 188, 191–92, 204; war and, 143–44, 145, 147, 149, 150, 151; and the West, 5, 57, 151; West Texas visited by, 6, 13, 58; and the women's liberation movement, 178, 180, 183, 195, 198, 201

Porter, Katherine Anne, work of: Aunt
    Amy in, 59, 102–6, 108–9; and cari-
    cature, 32, 34, 51; children's stories,
    28–29; Cousin Eva in, 102–3, 107–
    10; family saga, 47, 55, 119–20, 134;
    Grandmother (Sophia Jane) in, 58,
    66, 67, 68, 71; Great-Aunt Eliza in,
    60–61, 68–69, 77, 104, 189; history
    in, 26; literary status of, 1, 13, 28, 30,
    138, 164, 166, 212; Maria in, 103–6,
    119, 134, 137; memory and, 33, 64, 66,
    74–76, 81, 83, 87, 89, 91, 102, 111, 152,
    189, 194; Mexico in, 30, 35–36, 38–39,
    40–41, 44–48, 50, 51–53; Miranda in,
    5, 60, 61, 62, 67–74, 78–79, 98, 103–6,
    107–17, 118, 134–135, 145–46, 188,
    189, 218n8, 220n6 (chap. 6), 221n15;
    Nannie in, xiii, 65, 66–67, 77–78, 130;
    novel, genre of, 33, 119, 153, 157; race
    in, 130–40; reviews, 35, 46, 130, 170,
    179; romantic love in, 105, 106, 111–
    17, 146, 161; sexes, conflict of, in, 179,
    187–88, 196–200, 201; style in, 44,
    121, 148; Texas in, 14, 33, 43, 44–45,
    56, 88, 102, 112–13, 146, 147, 149, 162,
    177, 188; Uncle Jimbilly in, xiii, 70–
    71, 91, 118–19, 130; violence in, 26,
    45, 57, 89, 91–92, 93, 120, 142, 156,
    190, 192, 196, 199–200. See also indi-
    vidual titles
Porter, Mary Alice ("Baby," sister of).
    See Hillendahl, Mary Alice Porter
    ("Baby," sister of KAP)
Porter, Mary Alice Jones (mother), 8–9,
    75, 76, 217n3, 218n8
Porter, Paul (nephew), 100, 152, 167, 169,
    172, 185, 187, 208, 212, 215n2 (chap.
    2), 219n3
Porter Holloway, Gay (sister). See Hollo-
    way, Gay Porter (sister of KAP)
"Portrait: Old South," 24, 57, 59, 62, 181
Pound, Ezra, 216n12, 222n4
Pressly, Eugene, 46, 54, 55, 56, 80, 81, 82,

83, 87, 100, 158, 142, 157, 158, 163,
    194, 220n7 (chap. 6)
Prettyman, E. Barrett, 185, 186–87,
    205, 208
"Promised Land," 83
"Pull Dick, Pull Devil," 75, 218n5

quilts and quilting, 65, 66, 67

race. See lynching; Porter, Katherine Anne:
    race and; Texas: racism in; white guilt
Ransom, Harry R., 172–73, 174
regionalism, 3, 166. See also South, the;
    Texas
Retinger, Joseph, 39, 40, 41, 51, 158,
    216n12
Rivera, Diego, 40, 41, 50, 51–52, 216n11
Rocky Mountain News, 27, 99
Rodenberger, Lou, 206, 207
"Rope," 43, 44, 81, 183, 187–88

Sacco and Vanzetti, 43, 133, 194
Sassoon, Siegfried, 222n7
Schlemmer Johns, Erna. See Johns, Erna
    Schlemmer
Seldes, Gilbert, 27
Shannon, Charles, 101, 168, 176
Ship of Fools, 15, 54, 55, 82, 83, 143, 156–
    57, 161, 171, 174, 176, 183–84, 187,
    193–201, 209, 210, 217n15, 223n12
Sinclair, Upton, 47
Siqueiros, David, 41, 50, 51
Skaggs, Harrison (great-uncle of KAP), 8
"Source, The," 66, 67
South, the: and race, 119, 122, 134, 137,
    221n14; and violence, 21, 57, 122–23,
    126, 137; literary status of, 3; mystique
    of, 7, 12, 19, 63–64, 112
Southern belle, 78, 98, 103–4, 106, 107,
    110, 112, 116–17, 182, 189
Southern Review, 87
Southern womanhood, 5, 7, 58, 59, 77, 99,
    101, 137, 181–82, 186, 190, 195

South Hill, 167, *168*, 169

"St. Augustine and the Bullfight," 50, 64, 188, 217n15

Stein, Gertrude, 141

Stephens, Wallace, 223n16

Stock, Ernest, 42, 43, 81, 100, 187, 188

"Strange Fruit" (by Abel Meeropol), 118, 136

Survey Graphic, 41

Taggard, Genevieve, 29–30, 42

Tanner, James, *8*, 63

Tate, Allen, 42, 47, 86, 87, 116, 131

Tejano Revolt, 25

Tejanos, 21, 22

Texans: pride in history of, 19

Texas: Anglos in, 20, 21, 23, 214n11, 214n13; ax murders in, 121–22, 123; as borderland of South and West, xii, 3–7, 56; as borderland with Mexico, 4; and Civil War, 6, 18, 24, 57; Czechs in, 6; farming economy in, 5, 6, 20; French in, 6, 20; frontier violence in, 2–3, 124; gender roles in, xii, xiii, 16, 99, 175, 181; geography of, xv, 1, 3–4; Germans in, 6, 37; history of, xii, xiii, 1, 2, 6, 8, 19, 22–23, 24, 93, 121, 123, 203, 214n13; lynchings in, 21, 24, 124–30, 138, 221n9; Mexican influence in, xii, 5, 30–31; Mexicans in, 21, 23, 24–25, 215n5; multiculturalism in, 6; mystique of, 19; Nueces Strip in, 22, 24, 25; proximity to Mexico of, xii; race in, xv, 6; racism in, xii, xiii, 19, 20, 21, 24, 57, 99, 120, 122, 132, 214n14; ranching economy in, 5, 6, 20, 31; slavery in, 20, 22, 23, 122–23, 214n16; Socialist Party in, 37–38; as southwestern, 3; Spanish in, 20; Spanish influence in, 5, 6, 7, 164; theater and concerts in, 96; violence in, xii, xiii, 2, 3, 15, 19–20, 21, 22, 23, 24, 25, 26, 57, 62, 91–92, 93, 94, 121–22, 123, 125, 126, 127, 129, 214n15

Texas Institute of Letters, 163, 164, 165, 166, 175, 202–3

Texas Observer, The, 3, 13, 56, 62, 173

Texas Quarterly, The, 174

Texas Rangers, 24–25, 132

Texas Revolution, 21–22, 26

"That Tree," 48, 52, 81

"Theft," 81, 183

Thompson Davis, Barbara, 28, 223n12

Thunder over Mexico, 47

Titus, Mary, 77, 113–14, 116–17, 186, 193, 194, 224n6 (chap. 10)

Twain, Mark, 176–77, 222n5

University of Michigan, 170–71

University of Texas, 13, 171–75, 202

University of Virginia, 152, 171, 175

Unrue, Darlene Harbour, 12, 15, 16, 17–18, 28, 29, 42, 66, 82, 117, 127, 157, 164, 187, 194, 206, 212, 215n3, 215n4, 217n3, 218–19n4, 219n9

Van Doren, Carl, 42, 82

Vasconcelos, José, 39, 51

Villa, Pancho, 38, 144

Virginia Quarterly Review, 47

"Virgin Violeta," 41, 42, 52

Vliet, R. G., 3, 4, 7, 213n6

violence: domestic, 15–16, 26, 92, 95, 187; masculine, 15–16, 26, 92, 120, 124, 135, 137, 138, 156, 176, 190, 196, 199; race and, 24, 124. *See also* lynching; Porter, Katherine Anne, work of: Texas in; Porter, Katherine Anne, work of: violence in; Texas: frontier violence in

Waco, 125, 127, 138

Walsh, Thomas F., 32, 35, 39, 47, 50, 71, 73, 75, 189–90, 215n1 (chap. 3), 216n4, 219n8, 220n3

war: effects of on language, 146, 147, 149, 222n9; effects of on civil rights, 145,

146, 167. *See also* Porter, Katherine
    Anne: war and
Warren, Robert Penn, 63, 87, 102, 121, 180
wars, U.S., 43–44, 145
Washington, Jesse, lynching of, 127,
    128, 138
Webb, Walter Prescott, 3, 24, 39
Wells-Barnett, Ida B., 128
Welty, Eudora, 100, 167
Wescott, Glenway, 81, 143, 150, 157, 168,
    176, 185, 188, 222n3; *The Pilgrim
    Hawk*, 160, 222n3
West, the, and freedom, 5, 7, 58, 62
westerns, 3
Weston, Edward, 51
Weston, Hattie, 190–91, 193
What Price Marriage, 42
Wheeler, Monroe, 55, 81, 87, 168
"Where Presidents Have No Friends," 36
white guilt, 120, 137, 140

"Why I Write about Mexico," 38
Wilder Lane, Rose. *See* Lane, Rose Wilder
Wilson, Edmund, 29
Winslow, Marcella Comés, 101, 168, 169,
    176, 182
"Witness, The," 66, 70–71, 118–19
women's liberation, 178, 180
"Wooden Umbrella, The," 222n4
World War I, 17, 27–28, 112, 113–14,
    141, 144, 147–48, 217n15; aftermath
    of, 157. *See also* influenza epidemic of
    1918–19
World War II, 82, 101, 141, 142, 150, 152,
    154, 159, 160, 164, 170

Yaddo, 101, 167, 184, 209
Yale Review, 89
"Ye shivering ones," 29

Zapata, Emiliano, 38